Illness in the Analyst

Illness in the Analyst

Implications for the Treatment Relationship

HARVEY J. SCHWARTZ, M.D.
ANN-LOUISE S. SILVER, M.D.
editors

Library of Congress Cataloging-in-Publication Data

Illness in the analyst : implications for the treatment relationship / Harvey J. Schwartz, Ann-Louise S. Silver, editors.
p. cm.
Includes bibliographical references.
ISBN 0-8236-2495-1
1. Psychotherapist and patient. 2. Psychoanalysts—Diseases—Psychological aspects. 3. Psychoanalysts—Death—Psychological aspects. I. Schwartz, Harvey J. II. Silver, Ann-Louise S.
[DNLM: 1. Disease—psychology. 2. Physician Impairment. 3. Physician-Patient Relations. 4. Psychoanalytic Therapy. WM 62 129]
RC480.8.I43 1990
616.89'14—dc20
DNLM/DLC
for Library of Congress 90-4463
CIP

Manufactured in the United States of America

In memory of Donald
In honor of Eric

H.J.S.

To my doctors–official and unofficial

A.-L. S.

I knew that I could not go on long with my peculiarly difficult work unless I was in completely sound physical health.

Sigmund Freud, *The Interpretation of Dreams* (1900, p. 231)

Contents

Acknowledgments

The following works are reprinted with permission:

Abend, S. (1982), Serious illness in the analyst: Countertransference considerations. *J. Amer. Psychoanal. Assn.*, 30:365–375.

DeWald, P. (1982), Serious illness in the analyst: Transference, countertransference, and reality responses. *J. Amer. Psychoanal. Assn.*, 30:347–363.

Housman, A. E. (1896), The chestnut casts his flambeaux. In: *The Collected Poems of A. E. Housman*, 1922. Copyright Holt, Rinehart and Winston.

Schwartz, H. (1987), Illness in the doctor: Implications for the psychoanalytic process. *J. Amer. Psychoanal. Assn.*, 35:657–692.

Silver, A.-L. (1982), Resuming the work with a life-threatening illness. *Contemp. Psychoanal.*, 18:314–326.

Contributors

Sander Abend, M.D.
Training and Supervising Analyst, New York Psychoanalytic Institute.

Jacob A. Arlow, M.D.
Emeritus Professor of Clinical Psychiatry, Albert Einstein College of Medicine, New York. Professor of Clinical Psychiatry, New York University College of Medicine. Training and Supervising Analyst, New York Psychoanalytic Institute and New York University Psychoanalytic Clinic. Faculty, Columbia Psychoanalytic Clinic.

Françoise Davoine, Ph.D.
Lecturer and Member, The Institute for the Advanced Study of Human Sciences. Member of the former Freudian School (Jacques Lacan, Director). Psychoanalyst, Psychiatric Hospital of Villejuif, France.

Paul A. Dewald, M.D.
Clinical Professor of Psychiatry, St. Louis School of Medicine. Training and Supervising Analyst, St. Louis Psychoanalytic Institute.

Stephen K. Firestein, M.D.
Associate Professor of Clinical Psychiatry, New York University School of Medicine. Training and Supervising Analyst, The Psychoanalytic Institute at New York University Medical Center.

Abraham Freedman, M.D.
Honorary Clinical Professor of Psychiatry and Human Behavior, Jefferson Medical College, Thomas Jefferson University, Philadelphia, Pennsylvania. Faculty, Institute of Philadelphia Association for Psychoanalysis.

David A. S. Garfield, M.D.
Codirector Residency Training Program and Associate Professor of Psychiatry and Behavioral Science, The Chicago Medical School, University of Health Sciences, Chicago, Illinois.

Richard Lasky, Ph.D.
Clinical Assistant Professor of Psychiatry, Columbia University College of Physicians and Surgeons, New York. Faculty and Member, Institute Board of Directors, Institute for Psychoanalytic Training and Research, New York.

Susan G. Lazar, M.D.
Associate Clinical Professor of Psychiatry, George Washington University School of Medicine, Washington, DC. Faculty, Washington Psychoanalytic Institute.

Amy Lichtblau Morrison, M.S.S.W.
Clinical Social Worker in private practice, Cambridge, Massachusetts.

Harvey J. Schwartz, M.D., F.A.P.A.
Director of Residency Training and Clinical Associate Professor of Psychiatry and Human Behavior, Jefferson Medical College, Thomas Jefferson University, Philadelphia, Pennsylvania. Candidate, Philadelphia Association for Psychoanalysis.

Ann-Louise Schlesinger Silver, M.D.
Staff Psychiatrist, Chestnut Lodge Hospital, Associate Clinical Professor of Psychiatry, Uniformed Services University of the Health Sciences, Bethesda, Maryland. Faculty, The Washington School of Psychiatry. Graduate, Washington Psychoanalytic Institute.

Thomas Wolman, M.D.
Clinical Assistant Professor of Psychiatry and Human Behavior, Jefferson Medical College, Thomas Jefferson University, Philadelphia, Pennsylvania. Faculty, Philadelphia Psychoanalytic Institute.

Normund Wong, M.D.
Clinical Professor of Psychiatry, University of California School of Medicine at San Francisco. Training and Supervising Analyst, San Francisco Postgraduate Institute for Psychoanalytic Psychotherapy and Psychoanalysis. Member, San Francisco Psychoanalytic Institute and Topeka Psychoanalytic Society.

Introduction

Illness tears at the fabric of our lives unexpectedly, unpredictably and permanently. We are inexorably altered by having been sick as danger and uncertainty inevitably reawaken the infantile assumption of talion. The fantasies stimulated by helplessness are always evocative of conflict and come to form a nodal point in our remembered history. Denial though contributes an essential ingredient to our retrospective vision. Conceptual tenets to the contrary, it feels best to forget having been sick.

As analysts, our narcissistic regressions are no less encompassing, masturbation guilt no less contaminating, and castration terrors no less intimidating than those of anyone else. Assumptions of magical causality are encapsulated within our fantasies of etiology, the analysis of which allows us to recognize the peculiar randomness of fate. Postillness, one is left with a sense of humility before nature that needs to be disentangled from its submissive look-alikes.

For the analyst recuperation demands the near impossible—sickness as manifest content. Illness induced survival instincts become a nidus for the more complex compromises of adult adaptation, requiring analysis even as we are weakened by the unfamiliarity of our new body ego. The return to clinical work provides the exterior structure within which we have the opportunity to encounter the inner ambiguity of what had previously seemed so brutally literal. The inevitable temptation of continued personal gratification in the treatment setting can, however, imbalance one's clinical stance, straining the constituents of one's neutrality and the resultant dimensions of one's analytic space.

Unlike any other human endeavor, the analytic requisite for unflinching honesty clashes with our quite reasonable need for a modicum of denial. In addition to this reflexive avoidance, personal meanings infiltrate our analytic presence causing a hesitancy about further public exposure. Intrapsychically, the action dimension of being ill leads to a projective augmentation of our fears of being critically scrutinized by our peers. Postillness fantasies over competency reverberate with the very real professional concerns over referrals, finances, and career advancement.

The invited contributors to this volume have in their own manner revealed to the reader a painful aspect of their lives. Personally and clinically each describes a particular angle of vision on what it means to work with it analytically. By applying the psychoanalytic paradigm to experiences that presumably transcend it, the authors demonstrate the dependability of the model's inclusiveness. Even in the face of misfortune, the vibrancy of the method can uncover, in both participants, forces of maturation.

The death of an analyst is a profound trauma in the life of the analysand. The often sudden loss of the person upon whom one's dearest fantasies have coalesced brutally brings to the fore all latent assumptions of predictability. This breech in the sustaining metaphor damages the integrity of the reassuring reality-fantasy barrier and seems frighteningly unpardonable. Confusingly though, the figure to be mourned is ambiguously veiled within the illusion of transference. Nature's provision of this unparalleled opportunity to study the nuances of transference as distinct from alliance has, however, rarely been taken advantage of. Neither those who reanalyze nor psychoanalytic institutes have devoted scholarly attention or policy guidelines to this matter in proportion with the frequency of its occurrence. The contributors to this volume on this subject have allowed us to observe matters which had been relegated to an affect filled silence, and in so doing have reminded us that we can speak about anything.

We have compiled this book with the intention of stimulating individual and collective attention to the understudied though common phenomenon of the ill and dying analyst. This topic is a rich source of subtle data on the very essence of what makes a relationship psychoanalytic. It is also an area requiring institutional consideration and recommendations for practice. We are deeply appreciative of the contributors who have written about their encounters with this experience. We are respectful of the many more who declined our invitation. We hope this work is of assistance to those who have been afflicted with illness and are engaged in the clinical challenges of psychoanalytic work.

H.J.S.

We hope this volume will serve two purposes. First, it may provide comfort and guidance to mental health professionals isolated by illness. Second, it may generate freer discussion of illness in professional settings. Additionally, this collection may spur organizations to review their current mechanisms for individual and group support of members when they become sick.

We are intrigued that it has taken the profession a century to acknowledge directly the specific effects of the morbidity and mortality of its practitioners. Our textbooks address the generic young and healthy reader who is in training and whose difficulties range from monetary concerns to the disruptions caused by vacations and relocations. As we become seasoned professionals, we learn through the life experiences of others and ourselves, to cope with our own calamities, or so it is assumed. But if we were to turn for guidance to our personal libraries, we might feel increasingly alone, seeing how completely the issue has been ignored.

Confronting one's own mortality does in fact happen for a uniquely "first time" whenever the calamity of illness strikes. One is robbed of one's prior healthy denial, one's underlying conviction that death will threaten only in the future. The potential imminent, permanent loss of one's being is something unique to each of us. It cannot be generalized nor formulated in advance. It has to do with self, not other. But it happens to every self "who ever was or is or will be living" (G. Stein, 1934).

The scars of illness optimally will mark the exploratory surgery of self-analysis in which we acknowledge our previous attitudes of contempt and pity for the sick. We then recognize how effectively we have on numerous occasions been able to forget these unfortunate beings and be done with them. In our sick state there is a universal desire to abandon this new patient who is our transformed self. Recuperation involves working psychically to forget the lesson of our actual mortality, and to regain "healthy denial." Winnicott's twelfth and final "rule" was: "The analyst survives."

When seriously ill, one is confronted with awesome uncertainty. One can feel that hope is gone, and if one's colleagues concur, the group together could take control of the sick one's destiny. We as analysts oppose in principle this stance in our work with our patients, interpreting it as identification with the aggressor. Would we wield professional death rather than acknowledge a shared uncertainty, as if requiring that the patient must always be the weaker one in the patient–analyst dyad? And is an ego grappling with its own mortality necessarily a weaker ego? Must the balance of ego strength always be tipped in favor of the analyst for the analysis to be a successful or valid one? Is it even possible to hide the fact of our personal battles for survival behind a veneer of analytic anonymity?

The complexity of these questions probably indicates why this topic has not heretofore received systematic exploration. Many potential contributors declined our invitation, with either direct statements or facial expressions indicating they viewed our offer as an attack, as if such publication were a sort of public professional suicide.

As the reader will discover, there is no obvious consensus that was privately in place and is now formalized in print. Instead, we find a vibrant discussion of various approaches, along with the rudimentary beginning of collection of data to fuel development of theory and technique in these painful situations.

This present volume is intended as an introduction to a massive and complex subject. A second volume dealing with specific illnesses and their ramifications would further our understanding of this topic. For example, how does chronic pain impact on the analyst, as in the lower back problems endemic in our profession? What are the implications of gradual impairment? What are the effects of debility, psychosomatic illnesses, or the gamut of mental illnesses? What might we learn from working analysts who are HIV positive? While we have touched on work with adult patients suffering a variety of mental illnesses, we need data on illness in the child or adolescent analyst or therapist. We are eager to hear from contributors, who may well wish to communicate anonymously. All of these topics have implications for each of us individually, for our institutes and societies, and for our profession in its totality.

References

Stein, G. (1934), *The Making of Americans*. New York: Harcourt, Brace & World, p. 123.

Winnicott, D. W. (1954), Metapsychological and clinical aspects of regression within the psycho-analytical set-up. In: *Through Paediatrics to Psycho-Analysis*. New York: Basic Books, 1975.

A.-L.S.

Part I

Personal Reflections

1

The Analytic Attitude in the Service of Denial

JACOB A. ARLOW, M.D.

It was 10:50 A.M. on May 20, 1977. From the window of my seventeenth floor office, I was looking out at the spring unfolding in Central Park below while talking to my wife on the telephone. It was my practice, if I had no pressing professional calls to make, to call my home, which is in the suburbs, and to chat with my wife for a few minutes. The subject of our conversation that morning was routine, casual, not at all fraught with any special significance. Suddenly I felt strange and I said to my wife, "I feel funny." The center of my field of vision was suffused by a silvery light, while at the periphery there was a vibrating, enclosing darkness and everything began to seem unreal.

I was dreaming—"I was very tired and I wanted to rest, so I decided to sleep on the carpet of the floor in my office. I thought, 'This is a strange place to sleep.' " and, as I had this thought, I began to wake up, realizing that I was on the floor, phone in hand, experiencing a waking dream. "A hypnopompic phenomenon," I observed to myself. What was most striking, however, was that I could recall the depth of unconsciousness I had experienced just prior to the dream. It was a feeling of the most profound peace, a deeper sleep or rest than I had ever known, so deep, so restful that it seemed not only pleasant but most appealing. "If this is death," I thought, "then I am not afraid of dying any more." I had felt no fear, only a sense of complete acceptance.

I got off the floor and put the receiver back on the hook. The phone began to ring immediately. It was my wife. During the time that I was unconscious she had functioned with astounding efficiency and effectiveness. She had made three telephone calls. The first was to my office partner who ordinarily would have been the nearest person at hand. On this particular day, unfortunately, he was practicing, as he often did, in the office in his home. It would take him at least half an hour to get to me. My wife then called my close friend and colleague, Dr. Irving Clyne, whose office was in the same building. She reached his answering service who told her that they were under strict orders never to interrupt during a session. "But this is an emergency," my wife replied. "It makes no difference," the telephone service responded. "He will not answer." My wife then called the building office, explained the situation, and asked that someone go to Dr. Clyne's office, knock at the door, and apprise him of the situation. In addition, in order to save time and bypass the regular elevators, which operated under automatic controls and could be delayed on intermediate floors, my wife urged that one of the service men in the building keep the service elevator at Dr. Clyne's floor and bring him to my office immediately.

When I answered the phone, I explained to her that I had passed out. "Lie down," my wife said, "help is on the way," and she told me what she had done. Judging by the fact that my wife was able to make three phone calls during the time that I was unconscious, I concluded that I must have been out at least a minute and a half, more likely, even much more.

But I could not lie down yet. While talking on the telephone, I was aware that my eleven o'clock patient had already arrived and was sitting in the waiting room. What would I say to her? I thought of the effect on the transference of telling her that I was ill, so I told her a half-truth, namely, that I had to cancel the session because of a "medical emergency." My patient was not deceived. She informed me later that she knew immediately that I was the medical emergency. I had not been aware of the appearance I presented. My face, she said, was pale, as if drained of all blood, and my hair was disheveled. In addition, I was not wearing my glasses. In fact, they had fallen off and were on the floor of the office. I recovered them only later. When she left the office, Dr. Clyne rushed by her from the back elevator. Her conclusions about the nature of the medical emergency were now confirmed. Her own father had suffered a cardiac arrest while talking on the telephone. Rather than leave, she decided to wait in front of the building to see if I would be taken away by ambulance. While waiting, she saw my next patient coming for his appointment and she told him that I would not be seeing him that day because I was ill. The two of them decided to wait together to learn of my fate.

Lying on the couch, I thought I might take a taxi to the hospital with which my physician is affiliated. This is in my hometown and would require a drive of an hour under favorable traffic conditions. When my friend arrived, I described to him what had taken place. I said I was not sure exactly what had happened, but I knew that what I had experienced was no ordinary fainting. While talking to him, I passed out two or three more times, regaining consciousness spontaneously. My friend, Irv Clyne, examined me briefly and called my physician, who recommended that I be taken to the nearest hospital. I gave Irv the name of a friend, an internist, who I thought was still practicing a block or two away, but a phone call revealed that he had left the area several years before. Now I began to lose consciousness every few minutes, but I felt no fear or apprehension. It never once occurred to me that I might not recover spontaneously. Instead I began to concentrate in an objective way on the details of the phenomena I was experiencing. I noted the sequence of events that took place with each attack. First was the intrusion of darkness into the peripheral field of vision. Following this initial disturbance, there would be an interval of four or five seconds before I lost consciousness. During that interval, I noticed that I began to feel numbness at the tip of my nose, the tip of my penis, and the tip of my toes, but not my ears or fingers. When I came to, Irv was massaging my chest. I told him that I had concluded that the difficulty must be circulatory because of the numbness I experienced at the extremities of the circulatory system. I also told him that I now knew that I had about four or five seconds between the appearance of the first symptom and the loss of consciousness.

Irv decided to take me to the nearest hospital, which was only a few minutes away. However, he would not call the police because they were unreliable and would take too long to come. In the meantime, he realized that he had to get down to his office to notify his patients not to wait for him and to cancel the rest of the day. He called a mutual friend who worked nearby to come and stay with me while he went to his office. While waiting for the friend to arrive, he arranged for an ambulance, notified the hospital that he was bringing me in, and called my wife to tell her of the arrangements.

After the decision had been made to take me to the hospital, it occurred to me that sometime during the past year I had dreamed that I had become ill in my office and had been taken to the emergency room of that hospital. I seemed to recall that, in the dream, the emergency room was suffused with a soft, pale green light. Also, in what seemed to be no time at all, the friend whom Irv had summoned appeared. Actually it must have taken at least ten to twelve minutes before she arrived.

During this time I was completely passive and compliant. I was quite content to be taken care of. I concluded that I must be suffering from something serious and I weighed the different possible causes for my condition. The facts seemed to point to some disturbance of circulation. However, I had no pain or discomfort. Could this be a silent coronary occlusion? Perhaps something was happening in my brain, an intermittent failure of circulation somewhere. In effect, I was doing a differential diagnosis on myself.

Things seemed to continue to happen quickly. In a very short time, the ambulance arrived. I was aware of gaps in my memory, of intermediate events forgotten. For example, I do not recall being put on the stretcher but I do remember being wheeled toward the elevator. An elderly woman neighbor, whom I had met many times in the hall, came out of her apartment and asked, "Can I do anything to help?" I thought it was ironic. I had seen her so many times and she always seemed so frail and helpless and now our circumstances were reversed; she was coming forward hoping to be of assistance to me. I have only a vague recollection of going down on the elevator or of passing through the crowd of people on the sidewalk in front of the building. Both my patients were there, but I did not see them.

My memory of events in the ambulance is vague, but I do recall being disoriented about the route the ambulance was taking. As I was being wheeled into the emergency entrance of the hospital, I saw my son Jon standing there. He lives in the city. I thought, "What a strange coincidence to run into him," and I said, "Hello, Jon. What are you doing here?" Almost immediately, however, the answer came to my mind. Obviously my wife had called him and alerted him to what was going on. I realized how disoriented I was.

Of the passage to the emergency room, I have no knowledge whatsoever. If I were pressed to describe even one detail of the physical characteristics of that room, it would be impossible for me to do so. I do recall Irv telling someone "... repeated periods of unconsciousness ... no pulse at all. ... " I also recall a few moments of minimal consciousness during which I was aware of overwhelming darkness, of a black cloud with brownish tones and of an irregular rift in the cloud, through which there appeared once again that pale green color of my dream. I felt perplexed and confused. "Where am I? What is happening?" I answered myself as one would respond to a child, "You are very sick, and these people are trying to help you."

After about fifteen minutes, I was fully awake again. I was being wheeled on a stretcher through the glassed-in passageway that led from the emergency room to the intensive care unit. Bright spring sunshine was streaming in through the windows, and I felt no sense of discomfort or illness whatsoever. If anything, I had a sense of enhanced well-being. I thought of my wife and how splendidly she had responded to the emergency. Now that I was well again, I felt guilty for having caused her so much anxiety.

Anxious she had been, indeed, and frightened! As she told me later, it had not been fifteen minutes that I was in the emergency room, but two-and-a-half hours. For two-and-a-half hours the doctors had struggled to get my heart beating again and to keep it going, while my wife sat in the waiting room. The information she gave me about the discrepancy of my time experience made me feel very good. "So it was two-and-a-half hours, not fifteen mintues," I told myself. "Because I was unconscious, my sense of time had been disrupted. The discontinuity of the experience of self had caused me to feel that time had been compressed." I was pleased to learn that my own experience was in keeping with certain theories that I had been developing for a number of years concerning the nature of the time experience and disturbances of the sense of time.

The subject had intrigued me from the very early days of my practice. A woman patient suffering from hallucinatory hysteria described how she had fallen into a daytime reverie while walking down one of the busiest shopping avenues in New York City. Totally engrossed in her visual daydreams, the patient had no sense of herself in relationship to her physical environment. Suddenly, when she stopped daydreaming, she was amazed to find that she had traversed six or seven of the busiest crossings in the City of New York. More than that, she had completely lost any notion of time having elapsed while she was so deeply engaged in her fantasy world. This experience set me thinking about what components enter into the sense of time, and I began to observe closely distortions of the time experience my patients reported. One of the hypotheses that I developed was that the sense of duration and of the passage of time was in large measure determined by the memory of discrete moments of self-awareness, coalesced in retrospect, abstracted and conceptualized into the notion of a continuing entity, the self, existing in time. Now, indeed, from what my wife reported to me, I had an additional observation that I could use to buttress my theory, an observation from my own experience. Not for a moment did I contemplate how close to death I had been.

The cardiac intensive care unit was a new experience for me. The unit seemed to be a regular medical ward, refurbished by the addition of technological equipment unknown forty years earlier, when I was a medical resident. Comfortably set in a hospital bed, I felt a little foolish to be in the ward, feeling so well in the presence of so many people who were really sick. From time to time, I turned around to examine the monitor behind me, but it was difficult for me to maneuver because my left arm was tied down to a board attached to the bed in order to keep the infusion needle from slipping. Besides, after a while, the regularity of the electrocardiograph configurations became repetitious and boring.

But I was not bored for long. At the far end of the ward was a very sick old man gasping for breath. Suddenly a bell sounded, the nurse rushed to him, doctors and orderlies appeared with an ominous looking metal cart, weighted down with electrical equipment. From behind the drawn curtains came the sounds of thumping on the chest and the thwack-thwack explosion of the defibrillator. One could almost see the convulsive heaving of the patient's chest. There was a frantic call for bicarbonate, for adrenaline, and then silence. Before long, a draped body was wheeled away. I thought of my own days as house officer on medicine and how practice had changed with time.

A few hours later, as the nurse in charge was passing by the foot of my bed, I began to experience the premonitory symptoms indicating that I would soon become unconscious. I called out to the nurse. Exactly what I said was not clear. It was either, "Nurse, I'm about to pass out," or "Nurse, I am going under."

It was a strange and annoying dream. Why were eight men jumping up and down on my chest? When I opened my eyes, I was surrounded by a group of people—four, five, I was not sure. They were backing off from my body with obvious relief. "We had a tough time bringing you around," one of the doctors said. My thoughts turned to what I had said to the nurse. It seemed to me that "I'm about to pass out" was quite appropriate but to say, "Nurse, I'm about to go under" seemed strange. It occurred to me that this could be the English translation of the Yiddish expression used in my childhood for fainting or losing consciousness. If so, I interpreted to myself, this would appear to be a form of regression, perhaps a childish, anxiety-laden appeal to the protective mother.

A short time later, a member of the visiting staff explained to me that, in view of the repeated episodes of cardiac arrest and the difficulty in resuscitating me, I should have a temporary pacemaker installed immediately. It was clear to me why a pacemaker was necessary, but why a temporary one? Apparently, on a late Friday afternoon of a beautiful spring weekend, it would have been difficult to contact the surgeon. I agreed to follow the doctor's advice and signed the necessary papers.

Now I was concerned. How long had I been unconscious? Had my brain been deprived of oxygen? Perhaps I had already been damaged. As I was being wheeled toward the operating room, I began to think of how I could test myself to see whether my mental functioning had been impaired in any way. I decided to test my memory. What was the longest poem I knew by heart? Could I repeat it now to myself? I thought of one of my favorite poems, "The Chestnut Casts its Flambeaux" by A. E. Housman. It consists of twenty-eight lines, long enough to qualify for the test. I first came upon the poem when I was seventeen years old but have thought of it many times since. I ran through the poem and stumbled on the second line, but that did not perturb me. For a long time, I had not been sure of that second line. This was nothing new. The rest of the poem came readily to memory and I felt greatly relieved. When I passed my wife in the hall, I waved her a cheery "hello."*

The insertion of the temporary pacemaker I found a very

*The poem is reproduced in its entirety at the end of this chapter (see p. 25, this volume).

interesting experience. It required an incision into the femoral vein, which was done under local anesthesia and I felt nothing whatsoever. The catheter was to be inserted into the femoral vein and pass through the inferior vena cava, into the right auricle and thence to the ventricle. The pacemaker apparatus itself was a cumbersome affair. It must have weighed six pounds and its dimensions seemed to be six by four inches by four inches. I was fully awake and alert throughout the procedure. I do not believe I had been given a sedative. I was in a semireclining position, placed so that I, like the surgeon, could watch the progress of the catheter upwards inside my body on a nearby fluorescent screen. The doctor was calm, efficient, even casual. He explained the procedure as he went along. All of this I found most fascinating, and I watched the screen as if I were observing someone else's operation.

"Now we are passing the point where the renal vein enters. One can almost see the outlines of the renal artery," the doctor said. Straining at the fluorescent screen, I felt I could make out the faint trace of a line of increased opacity.

"When we get to the auricle," the doctor said, "you'll notice how the catheter makes a slight turn and goes a bit downward." And indeed it did. At this point, he stopped and explained to me that the catheter had to be passed into the ventricle during the phase of diastole, because then the valves were open and would permit passage of the catheter. I felt grateful for the explanation, because I was wondering why he had stopped his maneuvering at that point, whether the procedure had been completed. He tried once without success; then he waited a bit and tried again, but there was no change. Finally, on the third try, there was no doubt that he had penetrated the barrier. Even though the distance covered was small, it seemed as if the catheter had lurched forward to find its appropriate nidus in the ventricle.

"Well done," I said approvingly and with enthusiasm. Throughout the operation, I had been engrossed in what was going on. This was a new and interesting procedure. I had never seen it before, and the doctor seemed to have exercised his skill in an exemplary fashion. Not for a moment had it occurred to me that something could go wrong. I had experienced the entire procedure as if it were happening to someone else, to some other person, whose inner workings I had been observing on the fluorescent screen in the darkened room.

Back in bed, however, my mood changed. Perhaps it was the cumbersome box between my legs that made all movement difficult and kept reminding me that I was being treated for something very serious. I could no longer deny that I was a patient suffering from a heart condition. But what was the condition? Was the danger really over now that I had an electronic ally working within me? Whatever the process that caused the cardiac arrest, could it be evolving into something that would ultimately prove fatal? It seemed to me that having the reassuring presence of the pacemaker permitted me finally to stop denying the gravity of my condition. I could die and I had to face it. That night I received a sedative and was able to enjoy a restful night's sleep.

Shortly afterwards, when I saw my wife, I asked her to bring me my tape recorder and my address book. She brought them the following day, and that evening, after lights were out and my fellow patients were asleep, I leaned close to my tape recorder and dictated summaries on each of my patients. These summaries were to be used for making referrals should I die. I had by no means, however, accepted the possibility, because I continued to use the code initials for my patients rather than mentioning their names, a practice I employ to conceal the identity of my patients from my secretary. On a second cassette, I identified each patient with the proper code letters, together with an address and telephone number. This second cassette was to be held at home and given to whatever colleague would be making the necessary referrals.

Having discharged these obligations, I turned over, hoping to get another good night's sleep, but it did not turn out that way. All night I found myself engaged in anxious, obsessional thinking, not about myself, not at all, but about my wife. How would she fare financially after I was gone? Would it be more advantageous if I died at this time or at that time, if I did x, y or z? None of this made any sense or had any realistic bearing on the problems that would have to be faced. Try as I would to reason with myself, these senseless thoughts kept intruding upon my mind. This was the first and the only time throughout the entire experience that I felt anxiety. Toward morning I fell asleep and, when I awoke, I felt well again, completely at ease.

Four days later, a permanent pacemaker was implanted in my chest. This time I was not conscious at all during the operation, and I felt no pain or discomfort afterwards. Once out of the intensive care unit, I reverted to my previous mode of behavior. When asked about my illness, I would say, "It's just a slight matter of the electrical conductivity of my heart. The pacemaker takes care of that. No problem at all."

I dictated a description of the events of my illness and placed the notes in my files. I had no occasion to refer to the notes until recently, when I received the invitation to make a contribution to this volume on illness in the analyst. On rereading my description of what took place some eleven years earlier, I was struck by how strong was my need to deny the gravity of my illness and how this tendency was buttressed by my adopting at the time an "analytic" attitude of participant observer in relation to my own experience.

The process of denial set in instantly and automatically. I had responded immediately to a correct but threatening insight into my condition. I had, in fact, almost died, but I told myself, "If this is what dying is like, I no longer have reason to fear death." This bit of reassuring denial I was to repeat many times in the days that followed, when I described to friends what had happened to me. Both immediately after the experience and in its retelling, I could luxuriate in the memory of a profound and peaceful nothingness, but only after I was comfortably aware that I was still alive.

The dream I had on the floor of my office served the same purpose. In it I denied the reality of what had happened. I had not fainted and lost consciousness—quite the opposite. I told myself in the dream that I had been in control, that I had been tired and decided to take a nap. In the dream, it did occur to me, however, that the floor of my office was hardly an appropriate place to sleep. But the defensive function of the dream, so transparent in retrospect, did not occur to me at the time. Instead I adopted a quasi-analytic attitude that continued the process of denial. "A hypnopompic dream," I observed, as if I were awaking from a normal sleep instead of from a bout of unconsciousness that had brought me close to death.

I was behaving as if I were the participant observer in an analytic situation, only in this case I was also my own patient. I was interested in observing the alterations in the levels of consciousness and my awareness of its physiological concomitants. The progress of the catheter through my venous system intrigued me and I also could improvise on the spot a rough but fairly reliable test of whether my memory had been impaired.

If, indeed, I was acting as my own analyst, I certainly was not a good one. Countertransference is a serious detriment to any self-analysis. I was quite blind to how pervasive the mechanism of denial was. I failed to appreciate the periodic enhancement of a sense of well-being which sometimes bordered on euphoria, nor did I recognize the inappropriateness of certain courses of action I had recommended to myself, as, for example, the idea of taking a taxi back home to my internist's hospital. In addition, I was thoroughly convinced at that time that I had indeed dreamt sometime before of being cared for at the emergency room of the hospital to which I was going to be taken. Only recently, rereading my notes, did I begin to doubt the plausibility of that event. Now it seems much more likely that the thought functioned as a sort of *déjà révé*, depicting me as already in the more secure surroundings of the hospital, where I could be taken care of. It seems most likely that it was a dream that I had while emerging from one of the periods of cardiac arrest.

But by far the most ludicrous, almost laughable, form of denial was my response to the information my wife gave me to the effect that I had been in the emergency room not fifteen minutes, but two-and-a-half hours, before my cardiac function was restored to the level where the doctors felt it safe to have me brought to the intensive care unit. What should have been horrifying information I treated as gratifying confirmation of my theory that the sense of time is experienced as compressed as a result of interruption in conscious awareness of the self. What I thought was a rather clever exercise in self-analysis was actually a defensive distortion of my own experience.

Even under ordinary circumstances, if indeed there are such, self-analysis represents a problematic enterprise. Critical reflections on one's own self require a relatively stable affective atmosphere. In times of crisis, denial, intellectualization, or extreme objectivity may contribute to calm in the face of danger, but they hardly serve the goal of insight. It would seem, on the basis of my own experience of this illness, that one should be extremely conservative concerning what can be expected from self-analysis. Even the impulse to conduct self-analysis may serve any of a number of conflictual elements in the mind. In the specific example that I am describing here, clearly defense against anxiety was paramount but, to be sure, in this and in other experiences, many additional elements of conflict may contribute to how self-analysis is effectuated. In any event, with the pacemaker inserted within my chest, I gained sufficient ease not only to take appropriate steps to discharge my realistic responsibilities but also, after a night of anxious rumination, I could put aside my fears and continue to function with a sense of equanimity equal to that which I experienced before my illness.

How life-threatening illness in the analyst may affect patients constitutes a serious issue of technique. Silver (chapter 8) has reviewed much of the literature on this question. Keeping in mind the effect upon the transference, the analyst has to decide how, what, and when to tell the patient of his illness. To be sure, most of the time the circumstances surrounding the onset of the illness and the nature of the condition constitute the major determinants for the technical approach adopted. No one method is suitable for every situation or for each patient. Abend (chapter 5), Dewald (chapter 4), Schwartz (chapter 6), Silver (chapter 8) have all reported how they managed the situation during their illnesses. There is one aspect of this problem in technique to which I would like to direct attention. What the analyst tells his patients is determined by conscious, but also by unconscious motives, motives reflecting defensive and instinctual needs. The information the patient gets may serve a wish for the patient to be kind to the analyst, to feel sorry for him, to feel remorse or admiration. Illness in the analyst may become an opportunity for the evocation and expression of countertransference tendencies, but what the analyst tells his patient may also express his own defensive need to deny the gravity of his condition.

For example, when I told my patient that I could not see her because of a medical emergency, I was really trying to create a mental set that could lead to the conclusion that not I, but somebody else, was ill. This, indeed, was a prognosticator of the defensive stance that I was to assume during much of the ensuing illness. To be calm and self-possessed in the face of grave illness may indeed serve to reassure the patient. However, adopting such a brave stance may serve to enlist the patient as a witness to the analyst's omnipotence and immortality, deeply felt illusions now crumbling in the face of mortal danger. When confronted with his own mortality, the analyst may try at least to buttress the illusion of his omnipotence in the patient's mind. Even for the so-called well-analyzed person, the illusion of immortality is hard to surrender.

Much has been written in recent years concerning what has come to be known as the "near death" experience. Some authors describe the "near death" experience in terms of consciousness of an experiential apprehension of death. Judging from my own admittedly single and isolated brush with mortality, it would seem that the nature of the "near death" experience is related to the awareness of how close one had been to dying without actually dying, together with the defensive responses to the knowledge of the close escape. It is in that sense that the emergence to consciousness from the experience of cardiac arrest may be described as a hypnopompic phenomenon, in this instance not related to the emergence from ordinary sleep, but a mental reflection, taking the form of a dream, on the danger of having almost died.

What is striking about the "near death" experience that I have reported is the fact that the feeling of blissful peace, of a gentle serenity, almost to be longed for, occurred only with the very first attack of unconsciousness. I had no such feeling with any of the subsequent attacks of cardiac arrest. I am in no position to judge whether the first bout of unconsciousness was any longer than the subsequent ones. Certainly, during the two-and-a-half-hour period in the emergency room of the hospital, I must have experienced a depth and time period of unconsciousness at least comparable to the initial attack. Yet I have no recollection of any sense of appealing peacefulness during that period. In fact, the only recollection that I do have is one of confusion and anxiety. "Where am I? What is happening to me? I am very sick and these people are trying to help me." Once I had reassuringly regained consciousness, I had an enhanced sense of the beauty of life, of being alive, as I appreciated the splendor of the spring sunshine streaming through the windows of the corridor, surely a symbol of life renewed.

These observations would seem to strengthen my opinion that the "near death" experience is a form of hypnopompic phenomenon, the result, expressed in dreamlike fashion, of the awareness of a sudden, drastic confrontation with mortality, defensively warded off by the idea: "If this is death, it's not bad at all. I'm not afraid of it. I could really enjoy it." Other accounts of the "near death" experience would seem to illustrate how this defensive maneuver may be embellished and elaborated by evoking, and depicting as visually fulfilled, cherished wishes of reassurance or erotic gratification. Such wishes of the past may have been conscious or unconscious.

Which elements of the individual's previous psychic life will permeate the manifest nature of the "near death" experience will depend, it seems to me, on the nature of the individual's childhood conflicts and the manner in which he was able to achieve effective compromise formations concerning those conflicts. Greenson (1971) reported a dramatic example in which a patient, drowning in gasoline during aerial combat in World War II, recalled or dreamt bits of a song in a language he did not recognize, but which turned out to be lines from a lullaby sung to the patient by a nurse in a long-forgotten language of his childhood. It should come as no surprise that some patients report the "near death" experience in terms of an erotic embrace with an all-powerful father figure or in terms of a reassuring sensation of protection in the arms of an all-embracing mother. In "The Theme of the Three Caskets," Freud (1913) described visions of death in terms of being taken into the arms of the eternal mother figure. Abraham (1912) described certain elaborate bedtime ceremonials of a young woman as articulating a fantasy of a nightly encounter with the father in the form of death, the lover. There is a long tradition in poetry and art that articulates the erotization of death. In this tradition, art and mythopoesis contribute defensive creations serving to deny the ignominy of death.

References

Abraham, K. (1912), A complicated ceremonial found in neurotic women. In: *Selected Papers on Psychoanalysis*. London: Hogarth Press, 1942.

Freud, S. (1913), The theme of the three caskets. *Standard Edition*, 12:291–302. London: Hogarth Press, 1958.

Greenson, R. (1971), A dream while drowning. In: *Separation—Individuation*, ed. J. McDevitt & C. Settlage. New York: International Universities Press, pp. 377–384.

A. E. Housman
The Chestnut Casts His Flambeaux

The chestnut casts his flambeaux, and the flowers
Stream from the hawthorn on the wind away,
The doors clap to, the pane is blind with showers.
Pass me the can, lad; there's an end of May.

There's one spoilt spring to scant our mortal lot,
One season ruined of our little store.
May will be fine next year as like as not:
Oh, aye, but then we shall be twenty-four.

We for a certainty are not the first
Have sat in taverns while the tempest hurled
Their hopeful plans to emptiness, and cursed
Whatever brute and blackguard made the world.

It is in truth iniquity on high
To cheat our sentenced souls of aught they crave,
And mar the merriment as you and I
Fare on our long fool's errand to the grave.

Iniquity it is; but pass the can.
My lad, no pair of kings our mothers bore;
Our only portion is the estate of man:
We want the moon, but we shall get no more.

If here today the cloud of thunder lours
Tomorrow it will hie on far behests;
The flesh will grieve on other bones than ours
Soon, and the soul will mourn in other breasts.

The troubles of our proud and angry dust
Are from eternity, and shall not fail.
Bear them we can, and if we can we must.
Shoulder the sky, my lad, and drink your ale.

2

Acute Illness in the Analyst

NORMUND WONG, M.D.

In December 1983 I underwent an esophagoscopy (endoscopic examination of the esophagus) and pneumatic bag dilatation for achalasia (hypomotility or disturbance of esophageal motility and a premalignant lesion of the esophagus) and became one of the 2 percent of individuals whose esophagus and stomach rupture during the procedure (Payne and Donoghue, 1970). This unexpected and acute treatment complication required extensive surgery and medical care. Consequently, I had the opportunity to observe my reactions, do some self-analysis, and experience as a patient the procedures and healing processes I had participated in more than twenty-five years ago as a student and as a house officer on the medical and thoracic surgery services. In this paper I will examine the multiple meanings of my illness and the reactions stimulated within myself and my patients. As Dewald (chapter 4) has done, I will discuss the role of countertransference in response to acute illness in the analyst and its impact upon one's environment and the treatment setting and the patients.

Because of the thorough discussion of the rather scant literature regarding the clinical meanings of illness in the analyst reported by other authors in this book, I shall not engage in the customary literature review.

The Illness

For several years I had experienced transient difficulty swallowing and had periodic dysphagia, but had put off consulting a specialist until one night when I was awakened suddenly by a violent coughing spell, having aspirated some food I had eaten several hours before going to bed. I finally accepted the seriousness of the condition, saw my internist the following morning, and was immediately referred to a gastroenterologist for an endoscopy. My mind reeled with numerous possibilities including cancer and I prepared myself for the worst. Prior to this dramatic event, I was like the many doctors observed by Marzuk (1987) who feel immune to the very illnesses they treat and are masters at denying illness in themselves. Thus, they often ignore themselves the very warnings they give to patients about the danger signals of illness.

I was relieved to learn that I had primary achalasia and not cancer and was offered the choice of two therapeutic approaches. The first was a noninvasive procedure that could be performed by my gastroenterologist, who would dilate the distal third of the esophagus by rupturing the lower sphincter to relieve the persistent cardiospasm that hindered food from entering the stomach, and then use medication as necessary to promote esophageal motility and to control any gastric reflux. The second option was an operation that would incise the muscle layers of the distal esophagus and require a thoracotomy. Harboring a distaste for surgery, and following the recommendation of my gastroenterologist, I opted for the noninvasive pneumatic dilatation procedure because it would only require an overnight stay in the hospital. I was informed that rupture of the esophagus was possible, but unlikely, and that a thoracic surgeon could be requested to be on call, although it was not essential.

Before the procedure, I believed (as do most patients and physicians in particular) that adverse reactions and complications occurred only in very debilitated or ill patients or only in the hands of poorly trained and inexperienced practitioners. My gastroenterologist had been highly recommended to me by the most respected and senior internist at our hospital. As a physically active and a reasonably fit person, I used denial, relying on my sense of omnipotence, and gave my consent for the procedure. I dismissed the procedure as a minor undertaking. In fact, it was only at the persistent urging of a friend that I permitted someone to accompany me to the hospital and that I selected a surgeon in the event surgery became necessary.

These two precautions turned out to be lifesaving. In retrospect, I also agree with Marzuk (1987) that when a physician treats a physician patient, the latter may wind up giving very "uninformed" consent to procedures and treatments when the treating physician errs on the side of providing too little information for fear of insulting his colleague. The physician patient frequently colludes in this arrangement, possibly due to embarrassment about not appearing up to date on medical knowledge and may seem more knowledgeable than he actually is.

The Catastrophic Event

Experiencing only mild anxiety, I entered the hospital during a lull in the holiday season, planning to stay just one night. Fully expecting to return to the office by the second day, I did not notify my patients, supervisees, or my administrative staff of anything unusual. Little did I know that Murphy's law ("Anything that can possibly go wrong will") may be especially true when the patient is a doctor.

According to the operative record, the endoscopy and esophageal dilatation were carried out in routine manner and, aside from a chart notation that "the patient was having some discomfort during this portion of the procedure," nothing unusual was observed. Later in my hospitalization, however, the gastroenterologist shared with me his belief that the intravenous anesthesia (50 mg meperidine hydrochloride and 12.5 mg diazepam) had sedated me so heavily that I could not respond immediately to the irritating presence of the blood and air from my esophagus (which had been perforated during dilatation) that seeped into my mediastinum, pleural cavity, and gastrointestinal tract.

After the customary recovery period in the postoperative care unit, I was moved to my hospital room, where I suddenly awakened. Although my vital signs had remained stable, I experienced intense abdominal and chest pain, a viselike grip in my chest, and had difficulty breathing. The pain and respiratory distress were so severe and so obvious that the floor nurse, summoned immediately into the room by my friend, called a Code Blue (hospital acute distress alarm) over the hospital paging system. As I lay in bed, I heard the code calling out my room number; a crowd of somber-faced people quickly filled the room, bringing with them carts loaded with cardiopulmonary resuscitation equipment. A sense of panic overwhelmed me. Instantaneously, the thought flashed into my mind, "Oh, no! This can't be happening to me!" I tried to speak but no words came out as I struggled for air. I vomited bright red blood, everything faded, and I mercifully lapsed into unconsciousness. Within an hour of the Code Blue alarm, I was in the operating room undergoing a thoracotomy (surgical incision of the wall of the chest). The surgeons found an anterolateral rent approximately 8 to 10 cm in length extending from above the gastroesophageal junction into the stomach. The blood loss was extensive totaling 1800 ml. The diaphragm was incised and a Thal fundic patch repair was performed using the fundus of the stomach to close the laceration in the esophagus.

Because esophageal perforation is associated with a high mortality and morbidity, prompt recognition and treatment are essential when perforation or rupture occurs. I was extremely fortunate to be in the hospital and treated under sterile conditions as mortalities of 10 to 30 percent occur with the usual surgical interventions in cases of thoracic esophageal perforations (Payne and Ellis, 1979).

When I awoke five hours later in the intensive care unit, I was aware of being connected to a mechanical respirator with its periodic clicking, of monitors beeping, and of numerous tubes protruding from my chest, arms—and seemingly every orifice. My left side was bandaged and felt completely numb. Although groggy and struggling to regain my orientation, I sensed that I had survived a catastrophic event. I did not recall being told but I knew that I had undergone extensive surgery—and I was in acute pain. Along with the discomfort caused by the surgery, the blood and corrosive contents of my stomach caused searing pain. Because of the danger of mediastinitis (inflammation of the tissues and organs separating the lungs) and shock, I remained hooked up to monitors in the intensive care unit for seventy-two hours.

The Loss of Connection with My Former World

Once over the initial sense of exhilaration that I had survived, I began to take stock of myself, focusing primarily on my body. The world and my body as I had known it just twenty-four hours before no longer seemed familiar. In the intensive care unit, I had lost all sense of time because there was no clock on the wall, the lights were on twenty-four hours a day, and I slept most of the time.

I slowly came out of my total narcissistic withdrawal and gradually reinstated my self-boundaries through selfobjects—loved ones and friends who came to my bedside. Each time I heard a familiar voice, saw the face of a friend or relative, or was physically touched, I was reminded of my body boundaries and a sense of myself. Otherwise, I slept, remained immobile, and did not resist the mechanical respirator which breathed for me. Though mentally alert and retaining voluntary control of my muscles (I was not receiving any curarelike drugs during this time), I was simply in too much pain and exhausted to breathe for myself. I normally have a very sensitive gag reflex, but the presence of the endotracheal tube and even the frequent tracheal suctioning did not bother me, so immersed and self-preoccupied was I.

My bowel and bladder functions appeared beyond my control, for I had an indwelling Foley catheter in place and a temperature probe in my rectum. I received parenteral nourishment through an indwelling subclavian vein catheter, intravenous fluids and antibiotics through my veins, and medications through my nasal gastric tube. I compared my situation to that of a premature newborn who was totally dependent upon the external environment for survival.

Because of my intense pain and episodic shivering from the combination of psychogenic shock and loss of body heat, I was given intravenous chlorpromazine and morphine on demand. With an endotracheal tube in place, I could only communicate through facial expressions and limited hand motions as I was fearful that I might dislodge the arterial and venous lines in both arms. I did not mind being immobile, for physical movement intensified the chest pain, and I was unduly wary of disturbing the two huge drainage tubes dangling from my thorax. I continued to decathect the outside world and remained extremely focused on my body, conserving my energy and reserves. I visualized myself huddled into a small ball and speculated on the meaning of immobility for catatonic schizophrenic patients, drawing a parallel to my own narcissistic withdrawal from the environment. I did not think about my patients or my work; no one else in the world but me seemed to matter.

Each hour, blood samples were drawn bringing additional pain; the nursing staff and my doctors cajoled me to breathe on my own and to cough. Although rationally aware that I should cough and breathe deeply to avoid atelectasis (incomplete expansion and collapse of the lungs) and pneumonia, I stubbornly and passively resisted in order to avoid further pain, choosing to ignore the intrusions from the outside. I was simply too tired and in too much pain to care.

The Loss of Omnipotence and Control Over Myself and the World

During the first three to four days, I felt totally at the mercy of the hospital staff members and my physicians. My electrolyte imbalance had been corrected within twenty-four hours, and I began to resist the mechanical respirator. Initially, when I was taken off the respirator, however, I had trouble breathing and had to be reconnected. Once, in a fit of exasperation, I scribbled a note to a startled nurse telling her I felt like a balloon being inflated and deflated at the machine's will. Yet because of the pain, I could not marshal sufficient strength or determination to breathe effectively on my own. At first, the respiratory therapists worked with me every four to six hours. After forty-eight hours, however, I was off the respirator and back on my own, although I required continuous oxygen. Once off the respirator, my sense of control and omnipotence began to reemerge.

The friendly smiles and patience of the hospital staff members were greatly appreciated, and I concocted jokes and engaged in macabre humor about my plight. The extensive use of denial was apparent during this phase of my recovery. I never consciously entertained the thought that another adverse complication might occur, although I was told that my liver function tests were grossly abnormal. After forty-eight to seventy-two hours, I moved rapidly from almost total narcissistic withdrawal from my surroundings to a state of denial and hypomania. I became focused on the pleasure of small gains such as getting off the respirator and breathing on my own, removing the rectal thermometer, and no longer needing my Foley catheter. At least I was in control of my basic bodily functions and relieved not to be totally dependent—a state unusual for an analyst. In *Anatomy of an Illness*, Cousins (1979) points out the elements that played an important role in his own recovery from serious illness: "a well-developed will to live . . . [and] laughter" (p. 125). Although not suffering from terminal or chronic severe illness, I resorted to the same adaptive devices I used when I was well, and they were even more important now.

I luxuriated in the belief that I had regained control over my body and my world. Yet every morning the intensive care nurse to whom I had become attached, much as a child clings to its mother, rolled me about in the bed like a rag doll as she changed the bed linens and bathed me as she would a small child. I found myself greatly dependent upon her, grateful for her attention and care, but felt sheepish because I was so weak and infantilized.

Altogether, I was only in the intensive care unit for four days, but I underwent vast physical and emotional changes during that time. I was aware that as I began to libidinize my body and its functions, I also recathected objects in the environment. I felt myself sexually aroused by the nurses, no longer perceiving them as mother figures but as attractive young women. Surprisingly, I experienced little concern about food because I experienced no hunger. In fact, I dreaded having to ingest my first meal, reviewing in my mind the anatomy involved in my surgery and feeling apprehensive about the potentially paralytic ileus and pain I might encounter.

With the removal of the endotracheal tube, I was able to speak but was surprised at the quavering and weakness of my voice. My fever had subsided, but I continued to receive intravenous antibiotics every four hours. I was amazed that I could so sensitively taste the antibiotics as they were injected into my blood stream. I was intrigued by the complex calculations required to regulate the antibiotic plasma levels, and was annoyed by the endless venipunctures. I was literally seeing my veins shrivel up from the irritating intravenous medicines and numerous needle sticks; even years after this hospitalization I no longer can see veins in my forearms. With each passing day the numbness in my body began to abate.

I was moved to a regular hospital room on the fifth day where I remained for the next ten days before I was discharged. Although weak and easily fatigued, I marveled at the return of my body sensations and my motoric activity, limited as they were.

The systematic removal of mechanical life-support devices and tubes from my body brought forth a sense of pleasure; each change was an event to celebrate. The nasal gastric tube with its suction machine was removed five days after surgery, and it became one less irritant to stimulate complaints. I gained great satisfaction from being able to breathe freely through my nose and to move my head about, but I was keenly aware of my subclavian vein catheter with its ever-present threat of tearing loose or becoming blocked or infected. Now I was more mobile and able to sit up for brief periods of time; still, I despaired over my resting pulse rate of 110 (compared to my normal 48), for I was anemic and additional blood transfusions were not recommended because of the potential for hepatitis or a transfusion reaction (AIDS was not recognized at this time). I was impatient with my unaccustomed shortness of breath, lightheadedness, pain, and weakness.

The Loss of Competence and Complete Reasoning

Each day brought forth appreciable gains in my endurance and strength. I was surprised that I possessed such a positive attitude and remained in excellent spirits. In my hypomaniclike state, I discussed my work schedule with my staff by telephone and in person and reassured them that I would be back in my office in two weeks ready to see patients, and that I would be able to attend two previously scheduled out-of-town meetings. I reviewed the office work that needed to be done as a department head, and my staff, colleagues, and friends were sensible enough not to argue with me. Everything seemed to be going well, and I believed I would soon be back on the job, despite the advice of colleagues who had undergone major surgery and who warned me to anticipate a recuperative period of six months to a year before I would feel completely well again. I would prove them wrong! My stream of mental activity and work pace were definitely out of synch with my body rhythms and the healing process.

I marveled at how I seemed to be thriving and recovering without having taken any solid food or nourishment by mouth for almost a week. True, modern medicine had concocted an almost complete liquid diet (which entered my body through parenteral infusion pumps) to supply vital nutrients and amino acids necessary for tissue repair. Little did I appreciate that during the week I lost fifteen pounds. My narcissistic state and grandiosity were shattered when I ate my first meal and the feared intestinal colic appeared. I developed a transient dumping syndrome (nausea, weakness, sweating, palpitation, and varying degrees of syncope often with diarrhea and a sensation of warmth after the ingestion of food by patients who have had a partial gastrectomy or removal of the stomach). After eating, I became lightheaded and nauseated, perspired profusely, and had immediate diarrhea. The combination of narcotic analgesics and intravenous medications such as cimetidine exerted their toll on me, and I experienced momentary memory lapses and mild confusion, even forgetting the names of close friends who came to visit me.

I struggled to remain rational and oriented in my waking hours, but my state of confusion and fragmentation were revealed in my sleep through disturbing dreams. As an analyst who prides himself on the study of dreams, I was dismayed at the primitive representations in my productions. They were disconnected, chaotic, and difficult to recall when awake. It was as though I were in a delirious state as I dreamt. I was reminded of dreams I had as a child when I lay ill with a high fever and as an adult when I was in the prodromal phase of a viral illness. I experienced few dreams in the intensive care unit, probably because of the heavy and frequent sedation, but as I began to recuperate slowly, I voluntarily requested a decrease in my pain medications and began to recall dreams that appeared nightly.

In almost every dream there were symbolic representations of my body, and I was flooded with associations to earlier physical injuries. As a youngster playing football, I had been upended once and was unable to breathe for what appeared to be an eternity. Then twenty years ago, while skiing I tumbled downhill striking the left side of my chest on a ski pole, producing excruciating, although short-lived pain. Ten years ago, I fell against the corner of a table, badly contusing the left side of my chest: and I had a left-sided thoracotomy. Fragments of all these incidents reappeared in my dreams, usually triggered by the chest pain that awakened me periodically throughout the night as the analgesics wore off.

A week-and-a-half postoperatively, the drainage tubes were removed from my chest and with them went another suction machine. Appalled by the length of the two tubes (eight to ten inches long) that had been inserted into my chest, I thanked the surgeon for not informing me of their size before removing them at my bedside. With the bandage removed I could assess the extent of my thoracic incision; I was amazed at the three-inch-wide, black, swollen area where my ribs had been spread by a rib retractor to permit the surgeon access to my stomach and esophagus. No ribs had been removed, but the sixth intercostal space had been expanded at least five inches, which accounted for the numbness, swelling, and discomfort in my chest. I freely discussed my wound with visitors, availing myself of the opportunity for catharsis and abreaction.

The removal of the chest tubes brought forth changes in the content of my dreams. That night and the following two nights, I dreamed of war movies and visualized scenes from television showing mutilated bodies and victims of gunshot wounds. I was keenly aware of the two holes left in my chest wall after the removal of the dime-sized drainage tubes. My dreams were attempts to master and work through the sudden and unexpected trauma.

The combination of narcotizing analgesics and Tagamet (cimetidine) continued to trouble me. On several occasions, I was aware of illusions and even visual hallucinations. As it was the holiday season, I playfully interpreted them as Walt Disney characters to reassure myself. My reality testing was sufficiently intact for me to be aware of what was happening and I promptly asked my physicians to change my medications.

In large part, my returning sense of competence and reasoning necessitated an understanding and reconstruction of events of the previous two weeks, and I found myself speculating about what had happened and what was being done. To fill in the amnestic periods and to regain a sense of continuity, I now actively questioned my physicians, the hospital staff, and my colleagues who came to visit me. Although trained at a time when no patient was allowed to examine his chart, I decided to assert my rights as a present-day patient and to become an active participant in my own care. I asked to see my medical chart and was permitted to study carefully what had ensued during my illness and treatment. My sense of uncertainty and apprehension were considerably resolved when I no longer needed to speculate on events and future directions regarding my care. To my pleasant surprise, my physicians and nurses were gracious and responsive to my suggestions.

The results were mutually beneficial and rewarding. For example, in order to decrease the amount of analgesics I was taking, I suggested that diazepam or a similar medication be used and that the dose of narcotic analgesic be reduced. Thus, I was given a combination of Phenergan (promethazine hydrochloride) and Talwin (pentazocine lactate) and promptly fell asleep in the midst of a conversation with a friend despite vigorous attempts to stay awake. Although lethargic and drowsy, I continued to experience pain, so I asked the physician to stop the combination of medications. Soporifics did little for pain and only created frustration and aggravation.

All the confusion did not reside within me. Because I had three attending physicians writing orders, the treatment situation tended to get confused. My gastroenterologist thought that I should not take any medications in pill form and that I should be on a liquid diet. But my thoracic surgeon ordered a regular diet for me, unaware of his colleague's orders. My abdominal surgeon treated me for an upper respiratory tract infection during the course of my hospitalization and ordered that all medications be taken orally. My thoracic surgeon wanted me to exercise the muscles on my left side as soon as possible, whereas the abdominal surgeon cautioned me against exercising until I was well into the sixth week of the recuperative process. And so it went.

Despite the good intentions of many well wishers and visitors who came to support me, at times they could be too draining and intrusive. I was still ill at ease and even dissociated myself from the rapid turn of events. After repetitiously relating my plight humorously and intellectually to some friends who were visiting me for the first time, I became aware that I was in too good a humor and that I was too isolated from my feelings. In the solitude of my room one early morning ten days after the catastrophic event, I suddenly began to cry. I accepted how close I had come to death and was in touch with my feelings of emotional pain and suffering which I had stoically suppressed. Casting aside my denial, I acknowledged my mixed feelings of dependency, disappointment, and anger at my gastroenterologist at the outcome of a seemingly benign procedure gone awry.

All along my colleagues and even my treating physicians had expressed their shock and regrets over an unfortunate event; only I, resorting to glib rationalizations, had chosen to ignore the seriousness of the situation. As I immersed myself in self-analysis, my disturbing dreams diminished and became more organized. I sensed a feeling of great relief and a toning down of my buoyant enthusiasm, making more realistic plans for a period of recuperation and returning to work.

Return to Work

Because I was fully salaried by my institution, my decision to return to work was not strongly motivated by economic factors. Instead, I was aware of administrative commitments made in advance where my presence was essential, emotional satisfaction from work that reaffirmed my professional identity, the needs of my residents, supervisees, and patients, and neurotically driven pressures.

Before my illness, I had been away on a sabbatical of three months and in a sense was fortunate because I had few patients in treatment at this time. But receiving a sabbatical from a private psychiatric hospital was a rare and privileged event, stirring up great envy and resentment among some of the staff. They had shouldered many of my responsibilities in my absence and once again had to bear the burden of my work when I was acutely stricken. Two of my analytic patients, who were borderline, again faced a harmful interruption of their treatment. My supervisees and administrative assistants experienced mixed feelings about my unexpected absence. Thus, not only was I struggling with a sense of physical debilitation and the fatigue from my illness, but I had to deal with my own guilt and anger over my obligations and the realistic demands made upon me.

Priorities had to be set as to how I would ration my working hours. A month after my acute illness, I was still too fatigued to return to a full work day at the office, but I felt internal pressures to perform reasonable duties. Thus, for two weeks I compromised by having my key staff come to my home in the late mornings and afternoons to discuss matters which required immediate attention and handling. My supervisees were informed that they could telephone me for consultation if any critical events were occurring with their patients and they needed my assistance. I decided not to come to the office to see my patients until I had been out of the hospital for six weeks. I canceled one out-of-town meeting, but fulfilled my obligations to be present for another.

Resuming Patient Care

Until I was able to return to work full time, I had to be selective about which patients to see. Following my surgery, my secretary informed all my patients that I was ill and that they would be notified as soon as possible, but no definite date was given. Two weeks after my illness, she called them again to tell them I was still unavailable but would most likely call within a two-week period. When I began seeing patients again, appointments were scheduled a week in advance for those individuals I felt were most affected by my absence. The "healthiest" patients would be worked into the schedule as I resumed a full clinical practice. I was able to see my residents and supervisees and to carry out my administrative duties, although on a reduced scale.

The nature and intensity of the responses to my absence

varied considerably from patient to patient. An analytic patient, a nurse in the institution where I was hospitalized, acknowledged that she knew about my illness from her medical colleagues, but she refrained from mentioning my sickness for many sessions. When asked about her avoidance of the subject, she admitted that she was apprehensive about broaching what she felt to be a dangerous topic.

She had become sexually involved with her previous therapist, who referred her to me for analysis. During the analysis, she continued to be intimate with him and obeyed his prohibition about not discussing their relationship. Not until a year into the analysis did she reveal their sexual relationship, and only when he was discharged for being involved with another patient. Also, as a young child she had been sexually abused by her father and was warned not to reveal the affair to anyone. When he subsequently suffered a heart attack, she felt she had caused it.

The patient labored under the belief that her erotized feelings were bad and destructive and anyone intimately associated with her would be hurt or destroyed. Furthermore, she was not to talk openly about any of these feelings. Prior to my illness, she was developing an intense, erotized transference toward me. Upon my return she was no longer able to discuss her positive feelings. It took her several months before she could admit her shock upon learning of my hospitalization and deal with her fantasies that a disaster would occur whenever she became involved with a forbidden love object, whether in fact or in fantasy.

Another patient with a severe narcissistic disorder had been informed that I was ill but no further details were given. A widow whose husband had died of heart disease, she initially offered polite condolences about my illness, but by the third session she had brushed aside any genuine feelings of concern and was well into thoughts of revenge because I had greatly inconvenienced her. She stated she was only staying in the city, which she hated, for the sake of her analysis, and my unavailability had delayed her plans about moving away. My abrupt interruption of her treatment in some ways paralleled the situation with her husband, when he died unexpectedly after a heated argument with her. In the sessions prior to my illness, she was in the midst of a negative transference. She had been unable to deal with her guilt that her anger had contributed to her husband's death and now was defending against her unconscious guilt for having contributed to my illness by getting angry and blaming me.

An older patient whom I had seen in supportive psychotherapy reacted intensely to the changes in my physical appearance. She noticed my weight loss and fatigued expression and voiced great concern and anxiety. She had a bad association to hospitals. While in therapy with me many years ago, she underwent surgery and had a horrible experience with her surgeon. I found it necessary to see her several times in the hospital because of her agitated state and she very much appreciated my presence. Her husband, toward whom she harbored ambivalent feelings, had died suddenly while undergoing diagnostic procedures in the hospital. Many of her conflicts with men and authority figures were linked to her father, whom she idolized but who abandoned her when she was five. She demanded to know the details of my illness and whether I would require further hospitalization in the future. The abruptness of my illness and my going into the hospital stimulated her fantasies and associations of painful losses in the past.

A very disturbed borderline patient interpreted my changed physical appearance as a confirmation that her "badness" had injured me just as it had driven her friends away. She was intensely uncomfortable with intimacy, and fearing rejection, engaged in outrageous acts to terminate developing relationships. She was fearful she had repeated this pattern with me.

Most patients were reluctant at first to express their anger at being abandoned. In their associations frequent references were made to my fragility and anxiety was expressed that their anger might physically injure me. I would not be able to tolerate their intense feelings of anger in my weakened state. There was concern about my well-being and whether I would need to go back into the hospital and again abandon them. Some patients reacted intensely when their telephone would ring wondering if my secretary were calling to inform them I would not be available because of a recurrence of my illness.

The gamut of emotions experienced by my patients about my illness ranged from genuine concern and anxiety for my well-being to marked indifference; from complete repression of anger to open rage about being abandoned and vulnerable; and from guilt to the projection of blame. Each patient reacted to my illness in a highly unique and personal way.

Like Dewald (chapter 4), I adopted a policy of giving factual information about my illness depending on my assessment of each case. Those in analysis received little to no explanation, depending on the stage of treatment, the nature of the transference, and their fantasies or misconceptions as revealed over the span of several sessions. My patients in supportive psychotherapy were given a brief explanation and a fuller response to their questions. Even in these instances, I paid close attention to transference implications and attempted to minimize the distortions. Supervisees and residents who had visited me in the hospital were provided with a full accounting of my illness if they asked.

Countertransference

My countertransference reactions varied with different individuals. My responses ranged from feelings of guilt and concern for disrupting the care and welfare of a few patients, especially those just engaging in treatment, to feelings of anger and resentment for starting back too soon, feeling fatigued and lacking a keen clinical edge. Being on medication for gastroesophageal reflux slowed my mental processes until my body and mind could adjust to the adverse side effects of the drugs. Sitting in my normally comfortable analytic chair hour after hour left me stiff and in pain because of my sore side and still tender scars. Sometimes the residua from my illness preoccupied me and interfered with my free associations to the patient's productions and wreaked havoc with my evenly hovering attention. It took me several months before I regained the clinical acuity that had existed prior to my illness. For a time I consciously became less active and was more cautious in making interventions.

In addition to the masochistic elements driven by my feelings of guilt in the countertransference, I was on guard against satisfying narcissistic and exhibitionistic urges when explaining my absence to some patients. Seeing patients fulfilled a sense of meaning and professional identity for me. While I sometimes felt guilty toward patients who expressed their anger and pain about being abandoned by me, at other times I was aware of neurotic feelings of resentment when my sacrifice for coming back so soon was unappreciated. Yet most patients were able to regain their therapeutic momentum despite the realistic interference with the therapeutic frame. Even when I made clumsy and inarticulate interventions or errors, in retrospect, I found my patients to be generally forgiving.

I was sensitive to the impositions on colleagues who had covered for me. For the first time, I took notice of the vigor and energy of my supervisees and residents and compared myself to them with some envy. And unlike Silver's experience that the holding environment of her stable institution proved to be positive and nuturing, I was exposed to an environment filled with strife and turmoil (see chapter 7). For me the environment was unhealthy. Ironically, two of the people who greatly influenced the atmosphere of the department were ill with cancer and subsequently died of their primary illness or a related cause.

How I came to write this paper bears some explanation. Prior to my illness I had organized and chaired a conference on the interface between medicine and psychiatry and was in the process of editing the proceedings. What was obviously lacking was the perspective of the patient. I was about to assign this task to a colleague when I became a patient. It seemed natural that I assume the assignment. Thus, even when I was in the intensive care unit I was making mental observations and doing my research. Obviously, I was also engaging in denial and intellectualization to deal with my anxiety. And like Silver (chapter 7), I was aware of feelings of confusion within myself. I found it helpful to compare my recollection of the events with the detailed nursing notes and entries of the attending physicians in the medical chart.

Like Abend (chapter 5), I was initially reluctant to write this paper feeling that what I observed or underwent must have been experienced by many others and I could offer little new or important to the field. I was also acutely aware of exposing so much of myself to professional scrutiny and possibly suffering a blow to my analytic ideal. But because I must continue to live with the residua from my illness and face the eventuality of more surgery, I have found it helpful to reexamine and try to understand and analyze those traumatic moments of my life. I have had to acknowledge the aftermath of the illness upon my work. Finally, with the writing of this paper, I hope to focus further attention on an important and much neglected area with which all analysts must come to grips one day.

REFERENCES

Cousins, N. (1979), *Anatomy of an Illness as Perceived by the Patient: Reflections on Healing and Regeneration.* New York: W. W. Norton.

Marzuk, P. M. (1987), Sounding board: When the patient is a physician. *New Eng. J. Med.*, 317:1409–1411.

Payne, W. S., & Donoghue, F. E. (1970), Surgical treatment of achalasia. *Mod. Treat.*, 7:1229–1240.

——— Ellis, F. H., Jr. (1979), Esophagus and diaphragmatic hernias. In: *Principles of Surgery*, Vol. 2, 3rd ed., ed. S. I. Schwartz, G. T. Shires, F. C. Spencer, & E. H. Storer. New York: McGraw-Hill, pp. 1081–1125.

3

Delusion as a Way of Knowledge

FRANÇOISE DAVOINE, Ph.D.

Some years ago, when I was in supervision with Gisela Pankow, a German psychoanalyst treating psychotic patients in Paris, she told me: "You know, there is no such thing as professional secrecy when psychosis is involved." I always kept this statement in mind, struck by the strong impression it made, and forgot the explanations she gave me.

This paradox touches a delicate aspect of psychoanalytical ethics and has overtones of scandal attached to it. Everybody would be shocked if therapists were allowed to betray their patients' trust by gossiping about the last session. On the other hand, Gaetano Benedetti (1980) states that, as far as psychosis is concerned,

> the possibility for the therapist of living some perceptions of his patients as an act of creation of a common reality is the actual basis of the therapeutical process. But this process is not completed without the experience of sharing with peers when we communicate it to colleagues or discuss it in our writings; through this common creation, we perceive a new dimension of reality which in our three-dimensional world does not exist [p. 167].

As I understand these two experienced therapists, the paradox is resolved if we reconsider the concept of *privacy* in the frame of psychotic transference. Instead of debating about how much of a case should be hidden or distorted in order to be unrecognizable, I would emphasize how much of the *analyst's* private life must become a public thing, in order to be used in the working through of the psychosis.

In keeping with the topic of this book, I choose the particular case of a threatening illness in the analyst's life, as the private item paradoxically explored by her patient's delusion, as an example of how to begin the reestablishment of a sharing situation. This social experience of sharing, of which the Finish analyst Martti Siirala (1983) speaks, is emphasized also by Otto Will (1965), who focuses on a whole social field beyond the two-person situation implied in our usual case descriptions. In this respect, the "public" handling of the analyst's secret, in a critical moment of transference, becomes a way of creating a social link that has been broken by social catastrophes.

A vignette will explore this creation of a new social link through the patient's delusional response to the analyst's illness. This fragment of analysis will be considered in detail in the second part of this text. Thanks to the use of a foreign language, and a distant publication, I will allow myself some freedom in mentioning the uncanny coincidences that transgress the boundaries of privacy, which I usually overlook or forget when speaking in my own language. I am encouraged to do so by Martin Cooperman's remark, about how ridiculous we look in symposia, when we describe tiny details of psychotic transference and personal communications, while others present impressive results via statistical tables. But these details are the only cognitive items worth sharing if we are to pursue the knowledge that those psychotic or borderline patients are trying to share with us.

For my part, I ask the reader to view this story through the thinking of three theoreticians, none of whom is easy to understand: Harry Stack Sullivan, Ludwig Wittgenstein, and Jacques Lacan, each of whom has been influential in developing the items of this paper. All of these men have concerned themselves with the boundaries of language, and each in his own way has elaborated effective tools to tackle the anomalies that appear at these limits.

From Sullivan (1927), a psychiatrist, I follow the emphasis on social maladjustments, when he considers schizophrenia as a set of techniques to deal with "societal relations; relations of the individual to one, two, or many other people" (p. 164).

From the philosopher Wittgenstein (1953), I use the concept of "language-game," especially when he develops it in relation to abnormal situations involving "the abrogation of the normal language-game with the expression of a sensation" (§ 288).

From the French psychoanalyst Lacan (1966), I take the concept of "the Réel." This refers to the realm of unnamed and unimaginable things, and is summarized by Lacan in enigmatic formulas: "the Réel is the impossible; that which has been foreclosed from the symbolic order (the realm of speech, including the speech of the unconscious), comes back in the 'Réel' " (p. 388).

These notions will become clear through the dynamics of the story itself. Indeed, the patient whom I will quote now complained about an experience he could not put into words, after his recent delusional episode, from which he recovered being as he said, incapable. I met him in the state hospital where I work every week, in the suburbs of Paris. My function there is "psychotherapist," being neither a medical doctor, nor a psychologist. The medical director, Edmond Sanquer, M.D., a psychiatrist working also as a psychoanalyst in private practice, insisted on having lay-psychoanalysts on his staff.

Case Example

That morning, the medical director was interviewing Charles, a man in his forties who was emerging from an acute psychotic episode. He was a lawyer, had been married, and was now separated; his adolescent son was living with his wife. It was his first time in the ward, where he had arrived the previous week, alone, in an extreme state of agitation and disorganization, deeply anxious and probably hallucinating. Some years earlier, he had been advised to see E. Sanquer after a severely depressive episode. A psychoanalysis had even been suggested as well. But he had not followed this advice and had been treated instead with psychotropic medications. He had been diagnosed as schizophrenic. During his summer holidays, some months earlier, he had been delusional and was hospitalized in a state hospital in northern France, from which he had been discharged heavily medicated.

Despite his prior history, Charles described himself as an alcoholic. "I love medications," he said, "it is excellent with a few glasses of wine."

When I entered the room where the medical doctor had called for me, Charles was trying to suggest this diagnosis to the boss, which the latter was resisting.

"If you want to find out what is happening to you, you should talk to this lady," said the medical director.

It was agreed that the patient would be discharged in a week or two, on condition that he would undertake analytically oriented psychotherapy. Since he lived not very far from my office in Paris, he would come to see me there.

The first time I saw him was in the hospital right after the interview. His name sounded familiar to me, but why it should be familiar didn't register. He started to give a clear account of the facts, with an undeniable aptitude for analysis. His mother, a very old lady, was visiting him in Paris for the first time in the almost twenty years he had lived there. She came from a remote village in the mountains to see the marks of her son's social achievement. He did not know why, but this time she had become more and more manic and talkative.

This change in her behavior had happened before, most notably after the death of his father when he was eleven. His father was an artisan in the village. Their economic situation had become so precarious and frightening at his death that there was talk of sending the patient to an orphanage. He actually went there for some months during his mother's manic episode. She was diagnosed as manic-depressive, and he learned to expect trouble when she started buying luxury articles, ones she would never have even dreamed about when sound of mind.

Recently, in Paris, she had been feeling intensely guilty, and wanted to go to church for confession every day. He could do nothing about it, and had even gotten into bed with her at night, trying to soothe her. He does not remember the details, but this act had thrown him into total confusion.

"You see," he said half jokingly, "I did not know I would meet you, but I have already explored the oedipal possibilities."

I ignored this remark, and asked him if it was her first trip to Paris.

"Not quite. She had lived in Paris before my birth, before her marriage with my father. She was then a widow, having lost both her first husband and her first baby. I don't know how. She would not talk about it. After her husband's death, she had to earn her living and came to Paris to work in a café. The owner was her cousin. I have seen photos from that period. One of them is of a baby . . .

"The dead baby?"

"No, this cousin's son, older than me. A queer thing happened about this photo, which stayed on a shelf at home. When I was a child, I used to say 'that's me,' showing this picture. When contradicted, I burst into tantrums which lasted for hours."

"And why do you insist on being called an alcoholic?"

"Because of my mother. Although she is almost blind, she can smell wine from quite a distance. You can never fool her."

At that time, I did not realize the connection between his pseudodiagnosis, his mother's guilt, and the café in Paris. I discovered it much later through transference. To work in a café, a public place, for a woman at that time, meant somehow to be a public woman.

As usual, all the clues of his disturbance were revealed in this first interview. His history was knitted in the same pattern as a Sullivanian childhood: unsaid tragedies, unknown territories, and cultural maladjustment can make a youngster brilliant and lonely, one who does not belong. This was especially true at the time of his arrival in Paris to study. At first, the estrangement was so great that he fled back to the country. He returned the following year to take and pass his exams, and later on, he found a job that enhanced his self-respect. He had lived in Paris ever since, but he never adjusted to the social life of the city, and spent all his free time going back home.

There were two spaces not communicating with each other, exactly as they had not communicated already for his mother. At the limit of those two social spaces, he used, as a child, to burst out into "tantrums." Temper tantrums, in Sullivan's conception (1927), "outbreaks of rage behavior, represent not repressed material which makes its presence painfully felt in the dream-work, but material freely elaborated in the growing sentiment of self which renders the submission of the child to necessary and unnecessary adjustive demands, an intolerable insult to self-esteem" (p. 163).

During his tantrums, he asserted that his self was this baby, a witness to his mother's life, during those years cut out of history. The negation of his right to witness the very part of his mother's unspeakable adventure was an intolerable insult to his self-esteem. Unwittingly, he did not want to adjust to the necessary and unnecessary tall stories he was told. After her second marriage, and her longing for a second pregnancy, 'and here he was' she had become extremely religious, and virtuous.

He told himself he was a "pseudopod" of his mother. Her marriage had not been a love-match, and her only passion was for her son, replacing the dead baby, revenging her difficult years, and even more so after her second husband's death. He felt linked to her by a symbiotic bond, feeling depressed each time she became manic, or in good shape. But I prefer to stress here the cognitive use of those tantrums, and later on of his delusion, as a way to knowledge, of exploring this field where "le Réel" is at stake, in between two deaths, just after the crash of her family, and just before a possible social death. To find a place in society, to reestablish herself, his mother had

had to expell the truth about her former life after her first widowhood. She would never talk about it.

Françoise Dolto, a French child analyst, who recently died, used to say the same thing in another way. She compared disturbed children to sleepwalkers trespassing on the forbidden dreams of their parents. I like this image depicting those children walking without knowing, right through the "no-entry" signals of their parents and demonstrating publicly the poorly kept secrets. The patient theorized about what happened to him in the same way:

"When I start a delusion, I am like an actor in a scenario I do not know, saying by heart a part I have never learned. Cameras are focused on me."

I responded: "We will work together to find it, or to write it if it does not exist."

In spite of that reassuring answer, I did not know by then that I would have to play a part in that scenario, not knowing this part but saying it by heart. This scenario was at the junction in between two spaces and two times which were not accustomed to communicating with one another.

The link between the two spaces happened to be spun in my very office the day he first entered it. He looked extremely tense, and sat in front of me, staring far beyond me. Wondering if he were hallucinating something, I quite illogically looked backward, in the direction of his gaze.

"What are you looking at?"

"Do you know the name of these two wooden objects which are on the shelf behind you?"

These objects are six inches long, pointed, with black and white thread wound around one end. I had found them in my grandmother's wardrobe, after her death in a small town located in the same province as Charles' home. So I answered:

"I suppose they are sewing kits for women in the country, to take out when they worked in the fields."

"Not at all. They are sewing kits for soldiers during the First World War. If you pull on the little round handle, you will find a metal perforating punch. They are called 'cousettes.' I have one at home. It belonged to my father."

Suiting the action to the word, he seized one of these "cousettes," and showed me the hidden metal punch.

So from the first minute, he had taught me a new name. At the same time, I realized that those objects which I believed to be my private property, by heritage, had been at a time the collective property of the French Army. This reversal illustrates a mechanism that will repeat itself one year later, in more chaotic circumstances.

Before I come to that episode, let us finish the account of this particular session. Instead of speaking about his present anxiety, we let the thread of the discourse follow its own path speaking about history. He began to relax and to tell me his family's saga.

Starting with World War I, when his father had been gassed, we continued with the story of his father's childhood. His father's mother had been a young country girl serving as a maid in the house of a distinguished citizen in the chief town of the province. When he got her into trouble, she had to leave, bringing with her a picture of this man so as to be able to show the child his father later on. She knew there was no hope of his giving his respected name away by acknowledging the child. She managed to raise the baby somewhere, pretending he was her brother. When she married, her husband believed this. Learning the truth, he gave his name to the child. He was the only child they raised.

He continued in my office by telling me of the shock he received, the day of his father's burial, when he asked his mother why she had not invited his grandfather.

"You have to know the truth now," she said. "Your grandfather is not your grandfather."

She had always disliked him when he lived with them. From that time on, Charles almost lost track of the old man of whom he was fond.

"But where did he live?" I asked.

"In G., a small town of the province, one hundred kilometers from our place."

Hearing that name, I was startled. This town was my grandmother's town, familiar to me, because I had spent the early years of my childhood there. At once, I saw the cemetery: my grandmother used to go there every week, following the custom, to tend the flowers on her family graves. Meanwhile, I would play, hopping among the stones of this pretty country graveyard. Now, I was sure, Charles' family name appeared carved on a grave nearby those of my grandmother's family.

"Where is he buried?"

"In the cemetery of this town. His whole family is from that place."

Of course I remembered, having met some people with this name. I did not tell him about this coincidence.

Then came time to end the session. After his departure, I wondered about the unlikely intersection of our two trajectories in Paris, which had made possible a link between two incommunicable spaces. This town G. is in a region of the country that is dying.

The economic death of his hometown was of great concern to him. And we had no difficulty during the following year creating a language-game, so easy for me to use, for I had learned to speak in it. Charles was very reluctant about psychoanalysis. His wife, who had been previously in analysis, had pushed him to see an analyst before they were separated. He resented it as a humiliation. Our meeting had been made possible only several years after, when he had been driven into a state of emergency. So, when he came, he would usually stay silent, except for one or two polite sentences.

I spoke to him in an informal fashion, with the blend of sarcasm, understatement, provocative directness and aggressive humor, which is the style of talk in this area where we both came from. Even now, it is difficult for me to describe it, for I certainly had never talked like that in Paris to anybody, and certainly not to any patient of mine. While talking, and having him forget he was in a foreign country in the middle of Paris, I discovered why it took so long for me to be able to talk in Paris in front of an audience. It was not a matter of patois, which neither he nor I could speak. Talking patois at school had been forbidden by law for several generations. My mother had lost her mother's accent: she considered such an accent to be a shameful stigma. His syntax was perfect, surely better than mine. It was a matter of something much more undefinable: a matter of style, of tone, of voice, in fact the common language-game in this native territory.

Close to a border, the area had been periodically devastated. For centuries, the inhabitants had been accustomed to having their towns burned, their dreams broken, their traditions jeopardized, their hopes destroyed. No wonder in that context that a current educational principle for the children had become: "Don't read! Work!" This was in case books making them feel, imagine, remember: feeling and imagining open the door for remembering and suffering. When she had been forced to leave this town, my grandmother, lighting a bonfire in the garden, had burned all her photos and souvenirs, to prevent them from falling into the hands of foreigners who could not even give them a name.

The first year, he improved very quickly. Some of his oddities, such as a plain way of living, an absence of cultural recreation, a disgust for parties, could be related to the way of life in his home region. He hated city manners, and we could mock the Parisians, so ridiculous out of their context. At that time, I half hoped that this "cultural analysis," as they call it in textbooks, would be sufficient. What happened next demonstrated I was half wrong. The craziness found this new space created in between us and safe enough for it to enter. But still, even during the most despairing year, which followed this one, I had a cast-iron belief that whatever happened, we would carry the adventure through. Today, several years after these events took place, it looks as if we succeeded.

Summer holidays where approaching. I was exhausted. In June, I had cancelled several social evenings, attributing this negligence to my now revived rural origins. I had planned a journey to China in July with my family, and told Charles we would resume our work in August. At last, off we flew. We stayed two nights in Bangkok, and jumped in the hotel swimming pool. Then, lying down, right afterwards, I discovered a large bump on my belly. Quite amazed not to have noticed it before, I told my husband. We decided to go on, did not say anything to the children, and I planned to see a physician, one month later, in Paris.

One month later, the surgeon diagnosed a huge ovarian cyst, and decided to operate right away. At the same time, I had received a letter from a psychiatric hospital in a neighboring European country, saying Charles was a patient. He had been found by the police, in town, delusional and hallucinating, had stayed in the hospital a fortnight, and received such and such treatment. He was discharged by the end of July.

Very quickly more news arrived. He had been seen wearing dark glasses entirely painted in black, driving crazily on the boulevard, preferably on the left side, entering no entry streets. More than that, the rumor said that at his work in a venerable institution, he had made a complete mess, spilling kilos of sugar in the most confidential files, smacking his superiors in the face with an undisguised felicity. And then his trail had been lost.

But I had to take care of myself first. I wrote him a note saying I had to be operated upon, and would see him again when possible. He answered very quickly, remembering his mother's real or fancied miscarriages, and bid me good luck. So I went to the hospital, wondering if this was a real or fancied miscarriage of his analysis. I went out with the diagnosis of "borderline." Cancerous cells had been found, but the situation was not clear enough to start any kind of therapeutic procedure. I was to be under close supervision for some months, through periodic visits to the Curie Center in Paris.

Then Charles came for his first session after those events. I greeted him with the words:

"So we were both in a hospital. And here we are, looking as if we had to survive."

He asserted right away: "Your operation was in the belly."

"Yes it was. How did you guess?"

"Before your departure I knew it."

What kind of knowledge was that? Telepathy? Had he *looked into my soul?* Was it a mere chance of guess?

He then told me how anxious he had been in June, seeing

I was deteriorating without noticing it, before his very eyes. He had not said anything for fear of scaring me and making things worse. Then he added: "You were acting like a robot, only moved by duty."

Shamefully, I had to acknowledge that none of this psychical as well as physical distress had reached my awareness. He had seen me behaving like a country woman right in the middle of Paris. Huge tumors removed from country women who had worked in the fields until the last moment were commonplace in country folklore.

Actually, I was not very proud of being witnessed in my private world. Moreover, he had spread all over a negative therapeutic reaction, a relapse into sickness, a failure of his therapy, a "defeating process" as defined by M. Cooperman (1983); he had even exported all that mess to a foreign country.

On his side, he felt more and more ashamed too, to an extent which reached insensibility, unfelt despair. At first, his anxiety had exploded right after my departure, as if he had been liberated, free to make public the reality I was hiding from myself. Doing that, he had felt in great shape. Unfortunately, he did not remember all of his deeds and that worried him more and more. Acting out of his mind and out of my privacy had made a huge wound in his self-esteem, which enlarged itself to the point where he said he was no longer anybody. He claimed at times he was a collective being, certainly not a somebody.

For the time being, he recalled what had happened. Here I was in June, with an unnamed, even unfelt impending disaster. So he had to do all the work producing this phenomenon on the public stage, demonstrating that something was hidden, calling for its inscription in the collective institution of language. In order to get in touch with this Réel, he had "to assume the abrogation of the normal language-game with the expression of a sensation." (Wittgenstein, 1953, § 288). He had had to trespass all its laws, ruling a series of dual necessary oppositions, separating for instance:

—the *I* (am the analyst) from the *you* (are the patient)

—the *my* (body), from the *his* (body)
—the *inside* (my private life) from the *outside* (my public life)
—the *subject* of the verb (I feel) from its *object* (my pains)
—the *no* (-entry) to the *yes* (-entry)

The new language-game he was exploring ostensibly had functioned according to different rules. These are explored by Wittgenstein as well, and give us some tools when "the tool of the words is broken." Let us quote some of Wittgenstein's clues (1953) relevant to this new language-game.

First the scenery. "I can perhaps, even imagine (though it is not easy) that each of the people whom I see in the street is in frightful pain, but is artfully concealing it" (§ 391). I was artfully concealing to myself that I was in pain.

Or a little more strange: "Can't I imagine that the people around me are automata, lack consciousness, even though they behave in the same way as usual? If I imagine it now—alone in my room—I see people with fixed looks (as in a trance) going about their business—the idea is perhaps a little uncanny (§ 420). He saw me acting like a robot.

—Then the performance. "Perhaps I look at one and think: 'It must be difficult to laugh when one is in such pain,' and much else of the same kind. I as it were play a part, act as if the others were in pain" (§ 391). To face this uncanny situation, he undoubtedly acted as if I were in pain, prohibited from speaking, and feeling. The title of the play could be "Witches." His delusion was: he was surrounded by sorcerers, performing witchcraft against him. He was isolated, the only one to know the truth, standing on the only uncontaminated place. He had to save the world from these destructive powers. For that exorcism, he had used sugar, supposed to be good against that evil, burned most of his souvenirs in an auto-da-fé, and had almost sacrificed his dog, persuaded that it was a devilish creature.

Many interpretations can certainly be developed from the content of this fecund moment, according to different theories. But according to his own theory, for me he was only playing a part, acting and speaking as if a secret danger had to be controlled, for instance a life threatening illness. However, says Wittgenstein (1953), "the subject of pain is the person who gives it expression" (§ 302): so I, who was in pain, but could not articulate it, nor even feel it, was not the subject of the pain; he was.

Therefore it was possible to conceive a language-game in which he was the subject of my pain, giving it expression. This expression was of a monster in my belly. Through this channel, knowledge through delusion became possible.

During my vacations, he had hallucinated a scene from *Rosemary's Baby*. "I had seen in front of me, clear as I see you now, the cradle in which the monster lies coming from Mia Farrow's belly. Then I knew I had to leave Paris, cross the border, in order to *hide Hyde*." (The pun was in English although he had always disliked the native tongue of Dr. Jekyll.) "On my way, I stopped at my birthplace, grabbed and destroyed my mother's glasses, went to the graveyard where my father's mother is buried, and continued on my trail. I knew I was seeing this day-nightmare through her spectacles."

Again we have to ask: What kind of knowledge is it? This knowledge does not consist of looking into the other's soul, brain, or parapsyche. This knowledge had been acquired through an indirect way, here figured by the other's glasses. Even if his mother had tried to hide trials from him, he had often seized her spectacles to see the world as she was seeing it. It was an infernal and unbearable world, from which she had tried to protect him and herself. "You know, one day she threw the fairy tales I was reading in the fire, saying they were creatures of the devil."

This remark almost put me on the wrong track. It would have been easier, and much more exotic, to fancy primitive beliefs in his faraway country, with an anthropological concern for native conceptions, fascinating though limited in their intellectual faculties. "Medieval beliefs, in the middle of the French country." What a scoop! I was too tired yet to get excited by this picture, and too affected by the miserable part which I had played in this superproduction.

For sure, hiding from him a threatening event in my belly, I had hit against the space where his grandmother had escaped, hiding her unnamed and then falsely named baby. This was the same space where his mother had escaped in her turn, hiding her dead baby: Paris, the town of corruption, of vice, temptation, for unprotected women, unmarried mothers, or young widows without any money, without any social status. Whose belly was it which I called mine, to bear so many impending untellable stories? Whose body was mine for him to guess its suffering? Let us quote Wittgenstein again.

> Is this body my body?
>
> Is this sensation, my sensation? (§ 411).
>
> When I open the front-door in the morning I always doubt whether an abyss does not yawn behind it, and I make sure about it before I go through the door (§ 84).

This chair sometimes is there and sometimes disappears.

What am I to say now? (§ 80).

These questions are raised in Wittgenstein's *Philosophical Investigations* (1953) when he decides to explore the borders of language, the ones where comprehension gets its bumps. Of course, those questions, perhaps silly in everyday life, sound relevant when someone wakes out of a nightmare, according to Sullivan's *Schizophrenic Onset* (1927). Wittgenstein's answer (1953) is: "It is what human beings *say* that is true and false; and they *agree* in the language they use" (§ 241).

If Charles' delusion spoke the truth, we had to discover the language in which it was possible to agree. I discovered with him what this agreement meant. The questions above were exactly the ones which bothered him day after day, or at least twice a week when we regularly had sessions together. We were in low spirits; past the first salvo, we were alive. I was waiting for the verdict of cancer, he was guessing the verdict of craziness in every tacit glance from charitable colleagues.

"Are you sure it is not midnight?" he asked anxiously when our appointment was at two o'clock P.M.

"Of course not, look at my watch."

"But who knows, your watch is perhaps wrong. When I talk with my computer, who knows if the other, inside, is not trying to fool me?"

"What?"

"Besides, policemen and firemen I saw in the street are there to protect me, but I am a potential terrorist. I could take you as a hostage. I have nothing to lose."

"Of course, after having told secrets, and acted them out, you have nothing more to lose."

It was no use trying to dissuade him with stupid rational remarks, for he was the most cartesian philosopher I have ever met, practicing the methodic doubt exactly. He was like this "man who walks alone in darkness," in Descartes' *Discourse of the Method* (1637), and who, in the middle of the seventeenth century, discovered the conditions for the writing of science. Charles had been fooled like Descartes by mixing up nightmares and reality, and disturbed by the lack of boundaries between them (if we are to follow Baillet's testimony, [1691], Descartes' contemporary biographer, about a crazy night preceding the writing of this text). So both had had to start all over again building rationality. The only issue stands in a language upon which people can agree.

"You may doubt about what you want," I said one day. "But you cannot doubt that your observation was perfectly right in my case. You had guessed my illness all right."

He had been the clinician, and obliged to be delusional to say the truth. But only through a shared language, built during the previous year, could we agree now about the necessity to put into language things which had remained unnamed.

Now, it is possible to understand his metaphor of the broken glasses. With schizophrenic techniques, he had acted in a nonmetaphoric way. Wittgenstein (1935–36) tells us about a similar situation:

> Let us consider this case: someone says:
> I can't understand it, I see everything blue today and vice versa.
> We answer:
> It must look queer.
> He says that it does and, e.g. goes on to say how cold the glowing coal looks and how warm the clear (blue) sky. . . .
> On the other hand: someone tells us today that yesterday he always saw everything red blue, and so on. We say:
> But you called the glowing coal red, you know, and the sky blue.
> That was because I also changed the names.
> But didn't it feel quite queer?
> —No, it seemed all perfectly natural [p. 24].

Be it queer or perfectly natural, the answer to this logical aporetic statement is given here by Wittgenstein through the parable of the spectacles.

> I teach a child the names of colors . . . not by pointing to a sample. . . . Instead, I have various spectacles each of which, when I look through it, makes me see the white paper in a different color. These spectacles are also distinguished by their outside appearance. . . . Now everyone can guess the method of teaching the child the names of the colors in an indirect way: so that, I led the child to correlate the word red with something which I didn't see, but hoped the child would see if he looked through such and such glasses [Wittgenstein, 1935–36 p. 27].

Remember that we have to answer the enigma: How did Charles happen to know and see things that I did not see? The bump on the belly was there, obviously for some days or some weeks, and had not popped like a mushroom during the night. A kind of thing relevant to Wittgenstein's question: "*Can't I say something to nobody, neither to anybody else nor to myself?*" (p. 45).

In order to answer, and to name that queer thing, Charles used an indirect way of knowledge, between his mother or myself. He used her spectacles, through which he had learned to name in a so-called "private-language" the impressions he had received from her vision of an unspeakable truth. Through these spectacles, he had learned a language-game, in which the impressions of weariness had to be related to unnamed creatures inside the women's womb, related to evil powers which his mother's devotion tried permanently to ward off. But one cannot permanently prevent the Réel from being named, once it has hit against our speaking world.

To conclude this vignette, I want to stress that this knowledge in which the delusion consists is a description of an impression, a "sense datum" in Wittgenstein's formulation, received as prints of things which the other cannot say to anybody else, not even to himself. This description, whatever is the medium and the matter, is necessarily addressed to an other, and can never be considered as a secret or private language. And these prints are carried through bodily impressions in various ways. But for sure, as Wittgenstein says, "What we call a description of my sense datum of what's seen, independent of what is the case in the physical world, is still a description *for the other person*" (p. 57).

A little story will illustrate the importance of these last words "for the other person," which are so simple to understand and so difficult to realize. When a delusional patient addresses the Pope, the President, the crowd, or the universe, for instance, it is extremely difficult to realize that he addresses the person who is sitting in front of him, be it a psychotherapist or somebody else. This story is taken from everyday life and from one of these childhood tantrums which can happen to everybody.

Let us go back to the journey in China which went quietly, except for a brief episode. In a Chinese town, we decided to visit the zoo. In the zoo, a space was entirely closed by a tent; I did not understand the Chinese characters, and we paid the cent in order to get in. Once inside, it was too late to withdraw. It was an exhibition of genetic monsters, in pictures and in jars. Siamese twins, hermaphrodites, everything that you can or cannot imagine. Looking calm, cool and collected, I took a scientific tone of detached objectivity, to explain to the children that such things exist, and there was nothing to be scared of.

The following night, the older child, who was ten years old, could not sleep; then his anxiety rose to the point that he could not avoid visualizing those monsters. I tried to tell a tale, sing a song as in the good old days. The effect of my reaction was only to increase his anguish. I even tried to remember the old American movie *Freaks*, in order to tell how monsters could be nice and more human than normal humans. But this humanism had no effect. On the contrary, now he was screaming, risen from his bed, seeing the monsters right in the middle of the room.

At last, I said very quickly: "You know, you are scared, but I am the one who ought to be scared: for I discovered an abnormal bump in my belly the other day. I will take care of it when we come back to Paris and show it to a physician. Be sure that I will do all I can to be cured."

"Oh!" he said. "So I looked for something to be scared of."

And, as it was very late, he fell asleep immediately.

There are many grand tombs in China, and visiting them, the children were joking about the monumental one they would build for me. Instead of flowers, they would pour on it some "water of life" (eau-de-vie, in French), which means liquor made from fermented fruits, and served in the old days in cafés. They had also found a language-game to imagine and to name something that I could not say even to myself.

So, here I am, writing this story, with no more disasters impending in Charles' and his analyst's lives. Indeed, this fragment of an analysis focused a "foreclusion" from the symbolic chain, something impossible to speak and to imagine, which occurred in between the analyst's unperceived illness, and her patient's unacknowledged perception. His delusion appeared in that context, as an exploration of the Réel, and a successful attempt to put it into pictures and speech, prefiguring the possibility for other unspeakable and unimaginable parts of his ancestors' history, to be part of, inscribed into, the text of his history. The analyst's illness was a way of entering this particular field, where the psychotic transference attempts to formulate and inscribe the impossible. Benedetti calls it an "area di morte," and Lacan "the field in between two deaths" (1986).

Why this focus on naming and language? The stake of psychosis is precisely the "formulation" (Sullivan, 1950, p. 201) of catastrophes, which have been expelled from the shared experience of speech, if psychosis is not to be considered as a defective process. In order to reestablish a symbolic network around such a clash of all laws, psychotic specific techniques are developed by the patients, inquiring about, exploring, surveying the devastated territories. At the same time, their negative and destructive behavior tends to destroy the catastrophic and monstrous thing, in order to get it named and at last repressed, that is to say forgettable. Otherwise ghosts arise all over the place, as in a novel by Faulkner, sucking the life out of the survivors.

What do I mean by catastrophes? The reader, especially if he deals with the day-to-day despairing work in a psychiatric hospital, would perhaps suspect these still abstract considerations of some grandiosity. Actually, catastrophes in the social link can be massive as an earthquake, a war, a civil war, a genocide, as much as they can be microscopic, in the case of a treason, a betrayal, an abjuration. But the scale does not matter. Tiny disavowals can affect by degrees "all my relatives," including earth and sky, the Northern American Indians say during their ceremonies.

Among other Northern American medicine men, Harry Stack Sullivan recommended in the 1920s, the twosome laboratory as an exploration of social processes, especially when cultural maladjustments or social cataclysms occur as points of disaster for adolescents, when they have to face new relationships. Helen Swick Perry (1982), in her illuminating book *Psychiatrist of America,* tells us about those unformulated tragedies, experienced by Sullivan's family itself on an extended period of time. Sullivan (1925) says in that case: "The child, having come to an exceedingly primitive but inherently coherent world representation, is not left for long in this happy state. By their behavior, especially speech, the parents convey to the child a wealth of cognitive items in the structure of which is much that is indemonstrable and false" (p. 93).

In his late productions, Sullivan's theoretical approach (1950) is surprisingly close to Lacan's formulations. In a much debated conference, with an almost Lacanian title, "The illusion of Personal Individuality," the whole emphasis is on language,

> [A]nd the knot, nexus, where things get together and are snarled up or tangled. . . . It is probably true that we can experience almost anything for an indefinite length of time; and if we do not fortunately run it through the process, which we call formulating, we don't really know what we are doing,—although we may get more and more clever at eluding unpleasantness, and so on—and we certainly can't tell our children about it. . . . The coming of "I" (different from "me"), as a term, is a great stuff [p. 201].

When things stay unformulated, expelled or foreclosed from the language between people, these things then seem to belong to the *private life* of the subject, totally out of the grasp of any kind of therapeutic approach. This apparent *privacy* of a disorganized or delusional world has often been alleged to demonstrate its inaccessibility to transference. The question remains of how much is still a language in the most withdrawn silence or incomprehensible delusion.

Sullivan (1946) tackles this issue during his lectures at Chestnut Lodge (talking about his dog, who was present).

> That there are particular human lives, each with a unique career line, I no more deny than do I the fact that I am a particular person who has a particular dog. . . . I act in two modes—my public mode and in the private mode in which I feel my inviolable isolation from my fellows. So doubtless does my dog . . . he doubtless acts much more frequently in the private mode than could I think I do, and I

doubtless act much less frequently in the private mode than it is easy to think that I do. The immutably private in my dog and in me escapes and will always escape the methods of science, however absorbing I may once have found the latter. . . . [but] I seek here to stress the central fact that the true or absolute individuality of a person is always beyond scientific grasp and invariably much less significant in the person's living than he has been taught to believe [p. xii].

This declaration should appeal to Vicky Hearne (1986). The author of *Adam's Task Calling Animals by Name* is a genuine psychotherapist. As an animal trainer using Wittgenstein's philosophy, she would probably agree with her favorite author's provocative saying (1936): "The 'private experience' is a degenerate construction of our grammar (comparable in a sense to tautology and contradiction). And this grammatical monster now fools us when we wish to do away with it; it seems as though we denied the existence of an experience. What would it mean to deny the existence of pain?!" (p. 65).

This grammatical monster is exactly what fools us when we consider a patient's delusion as his property, well-protected behind the defenses of his mental process. Whether we like it or not, "some pictures force a particular use on us" (1953, § 140), and we cannot help considering the "mental illness" as a "mental process" pertaining if not to brain damage, at least to some perturbation in the inner, deepest archaic levels of this psychic apparatus, which we tend to locate more or less inside the head. As a consequence, the patient's disorganized world seems to us his own possession, which stays out of our reach, unless medicine tries to attack the cause of the disease in the core of molecules, or in the profound layers of his psyche.

In that respect, it would be a shame if we did not follow Wittgenstein's advice to get out of the impasses created by such an expression of privacy. When psychosis is at work, this grammatical monstrosity indeed acts like a spell. It has the power to transform the so-called mentally ill into some monstrous creatures, flying periodically into tempers, filled with secret phantasms, becoming more and more alien and potentially dangerous.

Now, Wittgenstein (1953) was a very practical man. He never leaves us hopeless, but shows the solution right in the middle of the problem. His aim, at least in his second philosophy, is "to shew the fly the way out of the fly-bottle" (§ 309). To describe the way out of this fly-bottle Wittgenstein sketches out a little scenario.

> Think of the tools in a tool-box [§ 11].
>
> Now suppose the tool with the name "N" is broken. Not knowing this, A gives B the sign "N". Has this sign meaning or not?
>
> What is B to do when he is given it? We have not settled anything about this. One might ask:
>
> What will he do?
>
> Well, perhaps he will stand there at a loss, or shew A the pieces. Here one might say:
>
> "N" has become meaningless and this expression would mean that the sign "N" no longer had a use in our language-game. "N" might also become meaningless because, for whatever reason, the tool was given another name and the sign "N" no longer used in the language-game.
>
> But we could also imagine a convention whereby B has to shake his head in reply if A gives him the sign belonging to a tool that is broken.
>
> In this way, the command "N" might be said to be given a place into the language-game even when the tool no longer exists, and the sign "N" to have meaning even when its bearer ceases to exist [§ 41].

I have quoted this passage extensively because it outlines in a dramatic way the paradigm supported by the story I just told and perhaps also the history of Wittgenstein's own life. A recent biography issued by Brian McGuinness (1988) confirmed this intuition, pertaining to the number of broken names which occurred in his family. The book starts with the renaming of the Jew as a Napoleonic law, in Austria, at the beginning of the last century. This fact is followed by the baptism of Wittgenstein's ancestors at an unknown date. After describing the overwhelming though unexpected social achievement of Ludwig's father in the next generation, the biographer enumerates, as in a Greek tragedy, the fate of Ludwig's three elder brothers who comitted suicide one after the other. Wittgenstein himself was haunted by suicide and repeatedly compares philosophy with a therapy in the course of his *Investigations*.

Psychosis also is an investigation of the situations where the tool of names has been broken. And the psychotic transference is a therapeutic process to fix this breakdown of the symbolic network. The private breakdown in the analyst's health may stand for this shake of the head. It offers not only a comprehension or empathy for the other sick person, but a way to enter this space in between two deaths, full of suspense and emergency, a new way of looking at things (§ 401), opening the door for the invention of a new language-game, a new way of speaking (§ 400), relevant with the situation which once broke the tool of the names.

References

Baillet, (1691), *La vie de Monsieur Descartes*. Paris: Hortemels.

Benedetti, G. (1980), *Alienazione e personazione nella psicoterapia della malattia mentale*. Turin: Einaudi.

Cooperman, M. (1983), Some observations regarding psychoanalytic psychotherapy in a hospital setting. *Psychiatric Hosp.*, 14:21–28.

Descartes, R. (1637), *Discours de la méthode*. Paris: Gallimard.

——— (1691), Extrait de la biographie de Descartes par Baillet. In: *Olympiques*. Paris: Garnier Fréres.

Hearne, V. (1986), *Adam's Task Calling Animals by Name*. New York: Alfred A. Knopf.

Lacan, J. (1966), *Ecrits*. Paris: Editions du Seuil.
——— (1986), *L'éthique de la psychanalyse*. Paris: Editions du Seuil.
McGuinness, B. (1988), *Wittgenstein: A Life*. London: Duckworth.
Perry, H. S. (1982), *Psychiatrist of America*. Cambridge, MA: Harvard University Press.
Siirala, M. (1983), *From Transfer to Transference*. Helsinki: Therapeia Foundation.
Sullivan, H. S. (1925), Peculiarity of thought in schizophrenia. In: *Schizophrenia as a Human Process*. New York: Norton, 1974.
——— (1927), Criteria of malignancy in schizophrenia. In: *Schizophrenia as a Human Process*. New York: Norton, 1974.
——— (1946), *Conceptions of Modern Psychiatry*. New York: Norton, 1940.
——— (1950), The illusion of personal individuality. In: *The Fusion of Psychiatry and Social Science*. New York: Norton, 1970.
Will, O. (1965), Beginning of psychotherapeutic experience. In: *Modern Psychotherapeutic Practice*, ed. A. Burton. Palo Alto, CA: Science & Behavior Books.
Wittgenstein, L. (1935–36), *Notes for Lectures on 'Private Experience' and 'Sense Data.'* Trans-Europ-Repress. Printed and edited in France.
——— (1953), *Philosophical Investigations*. Oxford: Basil Blackwell.

Part II

Clinical Implications

4

Serious Illness in the Analyst: Transference, Countertransference, and Reality Responses—And Further Reflections

PAUL A. DEWALD, M.D.

After a week of diffuse pain I awoke one morning with a large swelling of the parotid gland. I personally canceled my morning appointments and arranged a consultation with an otolaryngologist. His diagnosis was acute parotitis and I was hospitalized with the recommendation that a day or two of intravenous broad-spectrum antibiotic therapy would alleviate the condition. Thus began a progressively more serious and at times life-threatening illness that eventually included meningoencephalitis as well as a thrombosis of the cavernous sinus, and required a six-week hospitalization followed by a one-month convalescence at home. One of the longer-term residuals was an oculomotor palsy with severe diplopia.

In this paper I intend to use the experience of my illness as a stimulus to consider the multiple meanings and reactions such an event stimulates in both patients and analyst. And I particularly intend to consider the issue of the countertransferences of the analyst in situations where he or she faces serious or life-threatening illness. A search of the literature reveals very few references to this topic, suggesting that the anxiety and conflict it arouses is generally handled by avoidance and denial.

Literature Review

Little (1967) described the impact of his countertransference response on the analysis of one of his patients following a myocardial infarction. His essentially positive evaluation of his countertransference-inspired delay in dealing with the trauma was not shared by six discussants of his paper. Chermin (1976) described some of his reactions to an unexpected illness from pneumonia, including his previously unconscious omnipotent fantasies, his sense of guilt at abandoning his patients, and the anger, depression, and personal isolation experienced during convalescence.[1] Eissler (1977) discussed the effect of the analyst's aging on the practice of psychoanalysis, indicating that it might be a negative one. He raised the possibility of the death of the analyst during treatment, with the recommendation that this be discussed in advance between the older analyst and the patient. Michaels and Schoenberg (1966) discussed the issue of a retirement policy for training analysts, with only brief mention of disability by illness which would be "assessed individually" by a committee. Burton (1978), in a questionaire regarding attitudes toward death, which included a group of psychoanalysts as subjects, concluded that "everyone defends against death," including the psychoanalyst.

Informal discussion with colleagues regarding arrangement for the care of patients and records in the event of death or serious disabling illness revealed that none had made such plans. This further suggests that denial of such a possibility is not uncommon among psychoanalysts.

[1]Engel (1975) described in detail his reactions to a myocardial infarction, but the thrust of his presentation was on how that event reverberated with significant object losses in his own life, and there was no mention of its effects on his work with patients.

The Illness

My own denial was manifest in the way in which I arranged to have my patients notified of my illness. I asked my secretary to call and inform them I was ill in the hospital but hoped to be back to work the following week. At the end of the first week, when it became obvious that I would not be going back to work, I asked her to again call each patient with the message that I was still in the hospital but hoped to be back at work the following week. This procedure had been rationalized by me as *protecting the patients* from undue anxiety associated with learning I was seriously ill, and only the increasing seriousness of my illness made it manifestly impossible to maintain the denial. At that point the message to the patients was that I would be away from my practice indefinitely and would contact them when I was ready to return.

As my illness deepened, my previous sense of responsibility and concern for the welfare of my patients, questions about how they would manage this interruption, and planning which of them might require referral to an interim therapist began to fade. Even my concerns about the loss of income, coupled with the medical expenses, began to fade as the regression deepened and I became increasingly self-centered and preoccupied.

One important issue is the question of how much factual information to provide for the patients while the illness is acute. In terms of the future of the therapy, the more extensive the reality information the patient is given, the less free and uncontaminated are the transference distortions likely to be. Detailed reality information may interfere with the subsequent evolution, analysis, and working through of the patient's unconscious fantasies and affective reactions to the illness. On the other hand, to leave the patient without factual information when there are no analytic sessions in which the transference implications can be brought to conscious awareness and ultimately analyzed may overburden the patient's adaptive capacity. To give extensive factual information may unnecessarily allay anxiety and the occurrence of transference fantasies if the illness turns out to be relatively benign. But to provide detailed factual information may further activate and intensify frightening fantasies if (as in my case) the illness becomes increasingly life-threatening.

Information as well as misinformation regarding my illness, its causes, its current status, and its treatment was already widely disseminated. This was further complicated by the fact that, at the onset, I did not immediately know the extent and severity of the illness, and at the height of my illness decisions were made and communicated to the patients by people other than myself who would not be in a position to know or anticipate the transference repercussions. What the patient hears and retains from the information provided is significantly influenced by transference factors. But not knowing precisely what was said to the patients complicates the analyst's task when treatment is resumed.

As the patients found out about the severity of my illness and where I was hospitalized, some of them sent cards, flowers, or other signs of interest, concern, and sympathy. One patient, for example, wrote several lengthy letters offering suggestions and advice in regard to the medical treatment of infectious disease. Several others came to my hospital room in an effort to see me, and others asked questions of my friends and colleagues regarding my condition.

The countertransference issues stimulated by these behaviors revolved around the question of the reversal of roles, and the way in which such gestures should be acknowledged, and by whom. During the height of my illness my wife acknowledged the various cards and gifts. Since she had not personally experienced the therapeutic process and the nature and meanings of transference reactions, the feelings expressed in these ways by the patients became a source of some conflict and misunderstanding for her, thus indirectly increasing the countertransference implications for me. Such acknowledgment to the patients, either by her or by me following my recovery, had an unavoidable impact on the ultimate therapeutic process and its transference–countertransference interactions when the treatment was resumed. But to remain abstinent and not acknowledge the patient's gestures would also have affected the therapeutic process.

Of my entire caseload (seven patients in analysis and ten patients in psychotherapy) only two patients indicated a need for an interim therapist to support them through the period of separation. This was arranged by a colleague. The other patients indicated a wish and capacity to wait until I would return. However, following the resumption of treatment, it became clear that a number of them had been troubled by fantasies that I might never return, or that I would return to a reduced practice, and they would be the ones eliminated from my active load.

Convalescence

Following my recovery from the life-threatening portions of my illness, the deeper implications of the denial and the narcissistic fantasies it concealed became obvious to me. There had been long intervals in my illness when I was semicomatose and for which there was and still is an amnesia. The realization during the recovery phase that this had occurred to me and that I had been helpless to do anything about it forced upon me the recognition that I had previously considered myself invulnerable to illness or disability. I had anticipated that I would always be effective as a therapist, and would practice indefinitely with no possibility of chronic illness, disability, or early forced retirement. My own personal and professional life planning had been significantly determined by such denial.

With convalescence there occurred a reversal of the regression and a return of concern regarding the patients and their welfare, which had been absent during the height of the illness. Gradually, I became increasingly restless and eager to return to the work I found gratifying. I also needed to reestablish my self-esteem, to prove myself competent, intact. These pressures had to be tempered by the recognition that I was not yet ready for this. The result was a compromise through partial resumption of professional activities— answering accumulated mail, reading professional literature, preparing bills, and so on.

With regard to billing, I elected to wait until after I had resumed practice and had personal therapeutic contact with patients who owed me money before actually presenting them with bills. Although the lack of income for several months had depleted my finances, I did not want the patients' first contact from me to be an impersonal demand for money.

The decision when to return to work was made in the face of a variety of conflicting forces. Personal motives and the emotional satisfactions derived from work made me want to return as soon as feasible. The genuine needs of the patients, some of which were communicated by letter or telephone, served to encourage resumption of practice. There were economic pressures. Then there were more neurotically determined pressures—fears of being professionally displaced, losing patients who could no longer wait to resume treatment, and the need to reassure myself that my professional skills had remained intact through the illness (derivatives of deeper castration fears activated by the experience of physical defect and dysfunction).

Simultaneously, however, there were the recommendations from family, friends, and others to prolong the convalescence and possibly take a vacation. This raised problems of affording a vacation in the face of the financial drain of the illness, as well as guilt at the prospect of taking even more time away from practice. There were also the regressive pleasures and satisfactions of the invalid status and the justified avoidance of responsibility, in contrast to whatever degree of conflict or discomfort I experienced in that passive and dependent status, and the multiple defensive or adaptive resolutions my professional role provides.

Return to Practice

Following such an illness and convalescence, one ordinarily would return to practice gradually, beginning on a part-time basis and slowly increasing one's work load toward resumption of full-time activity. This introduced the problem of which patients to see first. When several patients know one another (as with a training analyst) this problem becomes even more complex. The patient may feel that being "chosen" is confirmation of the severity of his illness (if the fantasy is that the analyst is beginning with the sickest patients), or of the analyst's countertransference (if the fantasy is that the analyst is beginning with his favorite patients and leaving the ones he does not like for later).

In this instance I began work by seeing candidates for their psychoanalytic supervision, and by seeing patients who were in weekly or biweekly psychotherapy, thus minimizing the initial work load, and interspersing appointments with rest periods. Subsequently, when I began work with my psychoanalytic patients, I did so by first seeing the three patients who knew one another well, leaving the others to resume more gradually over the following few weeks.

Upon returning to treatment, the patients described a range of correct information, pure fantasies, misconceptions, factual distortions, and exaggerations regarding my illness. This varied from one patient who had indirect access to my hospital records to patients who knew only that I was hospitalized. The oculomotor palsy required that I wear a patch over one eye. This visible sign of continuing disability served as a further stimulus for a variety of fantasies and potential transference implications. Following initial exploration of these reactions, I was confronted with the question of how much information to provide the patients about my illness and eye dysfunction.

In general, the amount of factual information I gave to patients varied with my assessment of each case. Patients being seen for supportive or superficial psychotherapy received the most immediate and detailed information and answers to their questions. This was in keeping with the overall therapeutic strategy of minimizing the conscious awareness of transference distortions, fantasies, and responses in such cases.

Two patients who were in the beginning phase of treatment and had not yet developed a regressive transference neurosis received moderate factual data and explanation following brief transference exploration. For them it was not yet possible in the early postillness period to explore the deeper implications and fantasies connected with the events. And it was my judgment that at that time in the therapeutic relationship for me to be evasive, secretive, or manipulative about the facts of the illness would have interfered with establishment of the therapeutic situation.

Those patients in the middle phase of analysis received the least factual information and the greatest encouragement to expose and explore the transference-inspired distortions and reactions to the event.

Two patients who were in the termination phase of analysis were able to resume the analytic work and to explore their fantasies about the illness without needing factual information from me.

With the return even to part-time practice one must deal with a number of personal issues. Not only is there a heightened susceptibility to fatigue, but there is difficulty in returning to an optimal analytic posture and stance of free-floating and evenly hovering attention. Instead, there persists a degree of self-absorption and continuing preoccupation with the residues of the illness, thus interfering with the optimal levels of attention and clinical skill.

Immediate Transference–Countertransference Responses

The return to work may also entail a kind of sacrifice and heightened effort, for which the analyst may expect appreciation and approval by the patients. However, patients may or may not recognize this; they may not only be unappreciative, but may express hostile, aggressive, disappointed, or depressive feelings regarding the separation and what they experienced as sudden abandonment.

The analyst may also harbor exhibitionistic or masochistic fantasies stimulated by his suffering. These may lead to feelings that the patients now owe him more, and should make up for the pain and suffering the analyst has undergone. In addition, the analyst may be aware of a continuing partial disability, or at least may have questions and some anxiety about his capacity to function at an optimal level, particularly if the illness has temporarily impaired some of the functions necessary for effective analytic work. This is likely to be heightened by the occurrence of any parapraxes, inarticulateness, memory distortions, or other technical difficulties.

At the same time, the return to the role of therapist with a sense of being wanted and needed by the patients may provide a gratification for the analyst. Resuming the previous professional identity and role may serve to help reestablish a positive self-image. But there may also occur an overidentification with the powerful physician of the recent illness, taking care of the relatively needful patient which the analyst was a short time previously.

The major technical issue is the question of how extensively can and should the patient be encouraged or helped to describe and deal with the multiple conscious and unconscious reactions to the analyst's illness, both during the time of the separation and when the analysis is being resumed. The meanings which the analyst's illness has vary widely from patient to patient. They depend simultaneously on transferences from earlier life experiences and fantasies, the duration and progress of the analysis prior to the illness, the nature of the patient's neurotic disturbances, previous transference fantasies which may be confirmed or contradicted by the occurrence of illness in the analyst, as well as the nontransference components of the patient–analyst relationship, and how much factual information the patient had about the illness.

For example, one patient who had set a natural termination date prior to my illness spontaneously described the capacity to separate transference from reality responses, and to feel a sense of concern for me while simultaneously finding herself capable of healthy integrated living. Her responses confirmed for both of us the appropriateness of termination. To have interpreted her responses as defensive against strong unconscious affects would have been an expression of countertransference needs. At the opposite extreme was a patient early in treatment who resumed analysis with no mention whatsoever of the separation, essentially picking up where he had left off prior to my illness. After several sessions, this was called to his attention, at which point he could begin to elaborate some of his conscious fantasies regarding my possibly dying, as well as mild feelings of disappointment and anger that just as he had begun to make progress I had become ill. The deeper meanings of the situation remained repressed in the immediate postillness phase. Many months later, after the analytic situation had developed further and the transference had deepened, he was able to express some of his specific transference fantasies relating to the eye patch.

The analyst may have various countertransference responses to interpreting the patient's resistances against discussing the illness and its affective meanings. The analyst must recognize the possible temptation to use such technical interventions to fulfill the sense of having been missed, the recognition of the analyst's importance to the patient, the use of the patient to express the analyst's unresolved anxieties, or for exhibitionistic or masochistic gratification. At the same time, for the analyst such material in the patient's associations may reactivate a variety of difficult or painful memories, guilt for the patient's pain and symptoms during the separation, difficulty tolerating the patient's anger and aggression, as well as doubts about the extent of his own recovery of the capacity to function analytically.

For example, one patient requested that the first returning session be conducted face to face (the request was not granted). Her motivation turned out to be the wish to better check me out and see whether or not I was capable of functioning effectively, and thus to offset her own anticipations of me as still being sick, weak, and possibly hampered in my analytic skills. The reverberation with my own questions in regard to the same issues was significant. Another patient felt that because of the effects of my illness I would no longer be able to tolerate the intensity of her aggression, which was stimulated in response to the illness and the sense of abandonment it entailed.

A patient whose father had frequently traveled for prolonged periods during her childhood had adopted a defensive attitude of conscious indifference toward such separations. She responded to my illness in much the same defensive way, verbalizing "realistically appropriate" concerns but maintaining repression and denial of affects relating to the deeper aspects of our relationship.

A woman whose father had suffered a minor stroke when she was twelve years old complained that "things seem different here ever since you got sick, and I have to handle you carefully. All the time I'm talking about you I keep thinking about my father, and how unpredictable he became, and we had to handle him with kid gloves, and let things go with him because he was sick." Even though the transference elements are obvious in this situation, the analyst must still consider and identify how much of what the patient feels may be an accurate perception of change resulting from the illness.

One of my psychotherapy patients arrived for her scheduled appointment two days after I was hospitalized, found the door locked, and reported that when she called my office the person answering the phone told her she did not know anything of my whereabouts. Because she was being seen only once per month, she was not repeatedly contacted by my secretary, and she reported that she found out I was ill only indirectly. The trauma of the separation thus seemed to have been unnecessarily compounded. However, transference elements in this situation arose from the fact that the patient's father developed a severe chronic illness when she was ten years old, and the family sought to keep his medical condition a secret from her. She would repeatedly return from school during adolescence to find her father unexpectedly hospitalized; he finally died when the patient was sixteen. In this instance we were never able clearly to distinguish the reality events of my illness from the transference distortions and repetitions.

Long-Term Transference and Countertransference Reactions

The analyst must remain sensitive to the likelihood that reactions to the illness are not limited to the period immediately after resuming practice, and that working through may require repeated return to these issues and responses. For several patients the major effects had been worked through in the one or two months after my return, and the analysis or psychotherapy proceeded as it had before my illness.

Several other patients with multiple and rigid defenses against manifest dependency or affective therapeutic involvement continued to use the fact of the illness to rationalize their avoidance of transference experience and interaction. They repeatedly expressed in fantasy the anticipation of a recurrence of my illness. Any telephone call, parapraxis, cancelation of a session, or other departure by me from strict therapeutic routine activated fantasies that revolved around the possibility of my again being ill. Working through of these defenses is a process that cannot be rushed and delays the resumption of a full analytic experience. Sustained analytic attention to this constellation, however, permits the eventual exposure of specific transference fantasies that underlie such characteristic defenses. For example, one patient fantasied that his oedipal wishes had produced my illness. For another patient the fact that I became ill meant I was human, not godlike, and therefore could not be trusted or depended upon.

Several patients with significant conflict over aggression were unable, in the early phases of my recovery, to express directly any of the angry resentment activated by their sense of abandonment and involving wishes to retaliate. As these patients increasingly recognized that I had fully recovered and was back to my premorbid level of functioning, it became possible for them to experience and express the rage and wishes for revenge directly in the transference. It was as if they needed the reassurance that I was strong enough to tolerate their aggression and that it would not again make me ill before they were able to face and begin to work through some of these affects.

A patient who began analysis four months after my return to full-time practice came across an Institute Newsletter that referred to a financial contribution to the Institute in honor of my recovery. The patient was immediately alerted to my having been significantly ill. She experienced concerns as to the nature of the illness, whether or not it would be chronic, all of which tended to delay entrance into a therapeutically appropriate transference relationship and experience. I answered the patient's question regarding my illness directly and factually, and encouraged her to tell me her fantasies and elaborations of responses to this information. From time to time, references to the illness emerge in the patient's associations, but these can now more readily be interpreted directly in the context of their transference meanings.

For most of the patients still in treatment, the approach of the one-year anniversary of my illness reactivated or intensified feelings and associative material indicating a continuing conflict about the event. This was true even for those patients who had apparently worked through their reactions to it. The reactions varied from brief and mild rememberings of the affects experienced at the time, to a sustained upsurge of resistive withdrawal and renewed use of the event to "justify" chronic defenses against transference regression.

As my recovery progressed and my concerns about my capacities were allayed by self-observation of return of analytic and other functions, the countertransference anxiety and inhibitions about dealing with the material connected with my illness subsided. It became increasingly possible objectively to observe the analytic process and phenomenology surrounding the illness and its long-term effects from a position of relative analytic composure with minimal continuing countertransference inhibition. This in turn helped make it possible for the patients to deal more directly with its impact.

DISCUSSION

Serious illness in the analyst probably occurs more often than we tend to acknowledge. Although this paper is based mainly on my personal experience, I have also observed the effects of such illness in patients previously in treatment with analysts who became ill; in patients who heard about another analyst's illness and responded with multiple fantasies; in colleagues who became ill; and in students in supervision.

I would guess that many analysts harbor a fantasy that their own personal analysis has "immunized" them against some of the diseases that afflict others. Although I have no statistics, experience demonstrates that analysts can and do have serious and life-threatening illnesses and accidents. The thrust of this presentation is that such an event will inevitably stimulate transference responses in the patients and personal as well as countertransference responses in the analyst.

The intensified countertransference problems arise from the fact that in such a situation there are greater than usual emotional pressures and intrapsychic responses. In addition there are reality factors and changes which are perceived, or are at least perceptible, by the patient. These include the reality experience of the separation and its impact and the changes in the analyst's external appearance and behavior resulting from the illness. In my case the continuing presence of the eye patch led to extensive associated reactions in all the patients, but more subtle changes, such as weight loss and a surgical scar near one eye, were perceived and reacted to only by some of my patients. Other subtle changes in behavior, attitude, or functioning may at times be more difficult to recognize immediately, and may thus exert a less easily identifiable impact on the analyst's judgment or therapeutic skill.

When something realistic in the analyst's behavior stimulates difficult or painful responses in the patient, countertransference reactions tend to be more intense and defensive; it becomes more difficult to sort out and differentiate the patient's transference-dominated perceptions and reactions from those in which sensitive and subtle reality perceptions play a significant role.

The therapeutic problem lies in the need adequately to explore the full gamut of patients' responses, affects, and associations to the illness, and to do this in the face of countertransference temptations either defensively to promote premature closure and evasion of more threatening affects, or to use the experience for exhibitionistic, masochistic, narcissistic, or other neurotic satisfactions.

To the extent that such responses in both participants remain unacknowledged or unanalyzed, important resistances and counterresistances to deeper analytic work will persist. Whereas there may be some patients for whom such unanalyzed elements would have only minor or transient effects, the more common result will be a significant disruption of the optimal analytic process. And for some patients the failure to analyze reactions to the illness has resulted in an analytic stalemate or in significant acting out of the conflict.

The nature of the onset of the analyst's illness is probably another significant factor in the total reactions of both the patient and the analyst. If the interruption is for an already recognized condition and for planned medical treatment, the analyst can personally inform the patient and begin to analyze the reactions in advance of the occurrence. When the onset is sudden and unexpected, the analyst may not be available to help the patient analyze and cope with reactions stimulated by that event. Even notification of the patient may be carried out by someone other than the analyst, which in turn allows for a variety of slip-ups, misinformation, or misinterpretations by the patient.

A related issue is the question of permanent or progressive disability which might seriously interfere with the capacity effectively to conduct psychoanalytic treatment. Were the analyst to suffer a chronic illness, or one likely to recur, or to have significant residual defects or deficits, it is my anticipation that resolving the transference and countertransference problems described above would be considerably more difficult, and the effects on the therapy considerably more intense and prolonged.

Given the reactions mentioned above, the tendency of the analyst to deny such disability would very likely be high, and would interfere with judgment as to what is best for the patient or how to proceed technically. Having observed such a situation in a colleague, I can recognize that this type of occurrence raises serious reality and ethical problems, not only for the analyst, but also for those colleagues who recognize the disability, and must face the difficult question of whether to intervene.

There is need to recognize that issues of serious illness in the analyst may become a significant problem for all of us.

Summary

Serious illness in the analyst has a disruptive effect on the therapeutic process. Transference and countertransference responses are highly idiosyncratic and variable, but must be dealt with effectively when the therapeutic process is resumed. Some effects are relatively brief and immediate; others become manifest only after a significant delay. This paper uses the experience of such an illness to call attention to this topic which has been relatively ignored in the psychoanalytic literature.

References

Burton, A. (1978), Attitudes toward death of scientific authorities on death. *Psychoanal. Rev.*, 65:415–432.

Chermin, P. (1976), Illness in a therapist—Loss of omnipotence. *Arch. Gen. Psychiat.*, 33:1327–1328.

Eissler, K. R. (1977), On the possible effects of aging on the practice of psychoanalysis. *Psychoanal. Quart.*, 46:182–183.

Engel, G. L. (1975), The death of a twin: Mourning and anniversary reactions. Fragments of 10 years of self-analysis. *Internat. J. Psycho-Anal.*, 56:23–40.

Little, R. B. (1967), Transference, countertransference and survival reactions following an analyst's heart attack. *Psychoanal. Forum*, 2:107–126.

Michaels, J. J., & Schoenberg, M. L. (1966), Some considerations for a retirement policy for training analysts. *Psychoanal. Quart.*, 35:199–216.

Further Reflections

Presentation of my original paper on "Serious Illness in the Analyst" at the December 1980 meetings of the American Psychoanalytic Association evoked a response analogous to the myth of the Emperor's New Clothes.

There was considerable active discussion at the time of the original presentation. A decision was made to organize and develop a series of discussion groups on this topic at the meetings of the American Psychoanalytic Association. Six workshops were held during the next three years.

Additionally I received a variety of mail and telephone communications from people around the country expressing interest in the topic and describing personal experiences with illness which they had been hesitant to discuss previously. It was as if once the blinders of denial had been removed a number of individuals previously isolated and unable to verbalize their concerns now felt free to begin to approach a topic previously considered "taboo."

Initially the workshops met without a fixed agenda and the participants engaged in a type of catharsis and group process of listening, mutual support, and acceptance in regard to the many issues raised by illness experiences. Workshop members, some for the first time, expressed their own feelings about their illnesses and the reactions of isolation, anxiety, and difficulty in understanding or knowing how to handle the situation with regard to their patients. There were concerns about themselves and their own health, feelings of guilt and shame for illness, fears that in not feeling completely well they were exploiting their patients. They had doubts about their own personal and professional futures, concerns about how they would be perceived by their colleagues and how this would affect patterns of referral, and reflecting the whole issue of professional and economic survival.

Many of those individuals attending the workshops and participating in these discussions had experienced some of the problems relating to illness in the analyst at first hand. Some had experienced the issues from the position of the analyst who was ill and others had experienced the problem from the position of a patient of the analyst whom they knew to be ill. This knowledge evoked intense conflict regarding how to cope with the additional stress upon their psychoanalytic experience, and in the case of candidates, upon their careers.

Initially, the group served a function as a listening body allowing for catharsis, and acceptance by other individuals personally involved in illness experience. As such it served a useful but limited function and few systematic efforts were made to collate or coordinate the clinical experiences or to extrapolate from them the principles of how to cope with situations of illness in the analyst.

Subsequently an attempt was made to plan the workshop around a specific clinical problem in which the presenter would have been, in one way or another, involved in the issues of the effect of illness in the analyst upon the psychoanalytic situation and process. In those meetings the discussion became more focused and more specifically oriented both toward the techniques which different individuals used to try to deal with such situations, and also to try to delineate some of the characteristic problems which such situations produced.

Descriptions of the methods by which the analyst dealt with the issues relating to his or her illness varied widely, and no general consensus was ever established by the workshop group. Some individuals tried to maintain a relative anonymity and abstinence in regard to providing their analysands with factual information in regard to the nature or prognosis of the illness. At the other extreme were a number of analysts who, during the course of both the acute illness and the subsequent recuperative phase, kept their patients repetitively informed. Where possible these analysts themselves made calls to the patients, describing the current situation and setting, explaining the nature of the medical procedures being conducted, and providing detailed and factual information in regard to current status and future anticipations.

No general consensus emerged among workshop participants as to whether there were specific advantages in one or the other form of management of these situations. In most instances, upon resumption of analysis patients were acutely aware of the analyst's changed appearance, behavior, vigor, or other signs of disability and illness. One of the crucial variables appears to have been whether the illness would, in all likelihood, be chronic and/or potentially recurrent or whether it was a "one-shot" affair with minimal expectation of recurrence or return of symptoms or disability. The latter seemed more readily tolerable to patients who experienced less conflict than was the case when the illness might readily be recurrent and chronic.

For the group which had experienced the situation from the position of being the analysand in treatment with an ill analyst, issues were raised in regard to the conflicts they felt upon recognition of the analyst's disability and difficulty in optimal function. There was a realization that the analyst was limited and ineffectual in some aspects of his analytic functions and a wish that a more regular analytic process could be undertaken with an analyst more fully competent and capable. At the same time, however, these individuals recognized how hard the analyst was trying and what a struggle it was for him or her to maintain even the level of function that was occurring at the time. There was a recognition that they, as one of a few analysands, might be significantly crucial in maintaining the analyst's professional viability and income, as well as feelings of intense guilt that to terminate and transfer to another analyst would be an act of disloyalty. Additionally, they felt that to bring up and focus upon the analyst's illness would be cruel and sadistic, particularly since the analyst was already weakened and in all likelihood already aware of his own limitations and disability. The paradigm was as if roles were reversed and the analysand became the responsible caretaker of his analyst, analogous to the adult child caring for a weakened, ill, or aging parent who was no longer capable of effective and optimal function.

One of the most difficult situations was that of observing one's analyst in the throes of a gradual aging process without acute or specific illness, but manifesting progressive dementia and inability to function. Several instances were described in which the analysand essentially waited and supported the increasingly incompetent analyst, anticipating the analyst's death or ultimate retirement, but meanwhile spending as much as three or four years in a nonproductive and inappropriate situation.

In some cases the analyst was clearly failing and progressively ill but had not mentioned it or allowed his health to be addressed as part of the analysis, and continued to try to function. Eventually, shortly before death, these analysts abruptly left their practice. The analysands experienced bitter disappointment that they had been unable appropriately to say goodbye to their analysts, analogous to the anticipated death in other human relationships where opportunities for an appropriate farewell are provided. These individuals felt cheated and unhappy at not having had the opportunity to acknowledge *with* the analyst their gratitude, their personal feelings, their concern, and their sense of sadness and loss at the analyst's illness and death.

Several workshop participants described their perception of themselves in their analytic function and the conflicting emotional state of experiencing their disability, recognizing their altered appearance and yet attempting, as much as possible, to continue to attend to the welfare of their patients. They described this as a situation of far from optimal analytic neutrality and free floating attention to the experience of their patients, and recognized how much their own symptomatology and the exacerbations and remissions of their conditions had impacted upon the analytic process. Almost all felt a sense of guilt and shame at being at less than optimal levels of function and, at the same time, all felt a sense of responsibility that they continue to function for the welfare of their patients as best they could.

Several analysts described experiences with cancer, and particularly with the problems of radiation or chemotherapy, over a prolonged time frame following the return to analytic work. For example, the scheduling of chemotherapy so that it would be given on a Friday afternoon in hopes that the major side effects and somatic distress would occur during the weekend so that the analyst would begin to feel somewhat better by the time Monday began the new work week. Hair loss, skin color, weight loss, and other physical changes were a constant reminder to both participants of the analyst's disability.

Another analyst described having undergone a mild bleeding leak from a berry aneurysm at the base of the brain some years earlier. Recovery from the initial episode had been complete but there was constant awareness that another episode could occur suddenly and at any moment. This "Sword of Damocles" hung over everything he did. There was recognition of his need to monitor his own emotional state and consciously acknowledge his own concern. He recognized that if there was a significant interval in which he was not having anxiety dreams in regard to the possibility of a cerebral hemorrhage, that his anxiety was mounting and that it would be necessary for him specifically to focus his self-analytic experience upon the possibilities of a rupture of the aneurysm.

Several individuals with chronic heart disease described a somewhat similar pattern, with the potential for a recurrent episode of disabling angina or a myocardial infarction constantly present. They recognized the increase in physical and emotional fatigue that accompanied their analytic work and interfered with their optimal analytic posture. At the same time there was a sense of obligation to the patients in their care and to the continuation of those treatment processes already begun, with the recognition that although not at full effectiveness the initiation of a transfer to another analyst would be difficult for their patients as well as for themselves and their professional futures. At the same time, however, there was recognition that having a chronic illness was deleterious to the continuation of the analytic work and that in some respects they felt they were being dishonest and cheating their patients in regard to what the patient had a right to expect from an analyst.

Another difficult problem was a situation in which the analyst had a chronic depressive disturbance, known and recognized by friends or colleagues, but not known to his patients (at least in a consciously identifiable fashion) and not acknowledged by the analyst to the point that he obtained personal analysis or therapy. The analyst made a significant suicide attempt which was interrupted and treated and he returned to his practice within several weeks of his abrupt departure. A friend and colleague knew of the events and was aware that the analyst was not at full function, that his patients were not receiving appropriate care, and that his general reputation among colleagues and friends was suffering. At the same time there was a sense of personal loyalty to the analyst, and a wish to protect his privacy through maintenance of confidentiality in regard to the nature and extent of the illness. Additionally, there were feelings of personal friendship as well as anxiety and concern at the prospect of disrupting the colleague's practice, both for the sake of the analyst and also for the analysands. Additionally, some of the analysands were in training, and efforts to enlist the awareness and help of the responsible members of the Institute and Education Committee were met with denial, hostility, and an inability effectively to grapple with the implications of the situation, both for the welfare of the training analyst, and also the welfare of the candidates. Attempts to encourage the analyst in question to acknowledge his disability and interrupt his professional work met with denial and refusal to take action. The colleague in question experienced intense conflict and guilt in what appeared to be an insoluble situation.

After some period of time the analyst again attempted and this time completed the suicide, thereby bringing the crisis to a full and undeniable awareness for everyone involved. At that point several of the analysands felt betrayed that they had not known earlier of the nature and extent of the disability; and finally the Institute could no longer avoid conscious recognition of its failure effectively to intervene and protect the interests both of the training analyst and of the analysands in his care. However, plans to anticipate and act in the event of similar occurrences in the future either by individual analysts or by the institute hierarchy were not effectively established.

The overall conclusion from the six workshops was that illness in one form or another among analysts is not uncommon; that it is frequently subject to denial and other forms of defense both by the analyst and also by analysands, as well as by colleagues and friends; and that each situation has multiple specific variables. There are such things as the duration and extent of the disability, the nature of its impact (whether on the analyst's general health, or upon specific function as an analyst). There is a question of whether it is readily observable to others or is observable primarily by the analyst himself. Is the condition recurrent or chronic, or is it a single, nonrecurrent episode? All these issues have a major impact upon the effects of the illness. Such additional things as the economic situation of the analyst, his social support system, and the point in his career when the illness occurs will also impact upon the response of the analyst and the patients he is treating.

A major factor determining the response of the analysand to the analyst's illness is the nature of the specific transferences experienced by each patient. These conscious and unconscious transference meanings account for the wide variety of responses experienced and expressed by patients to the shared stimulus of the analyst's illness and observed changes.

Additionally, there are issues raised for colleagues who are aware of the disability and its extent, and questions of responsibility to the analysands from others either in the professional community or, in the case of candidates, of the institute.

From the point of view of psychoanalytic technique, there were wide variations in terms of how to cope with the various problems raised by an analyst's illness. No consensus among workshop participants was established since widely differing methods of handling the situation seemed to be equally successful or unsuccessful in terms of the final outcome both for the analyst and for the analysands.

There was general agreement that it is a highly complex situation with multiple conflicting issues and responses, and that for the present each case must be resolved on its own merits, using the best of individual ad hoc judgment. The main conclusion, however, was that the patterns of denial so prominent among analysts in regard to their own vulnerabilities or in regard to the effects of illness should be acknowledged and that various efforts should be made to see to it that whatever conflicts or disabilities occur not be ignored by any of the people involved in such situations (the analyst, the analysand, the institute, and the analyst's professional friends and colleagues).

5

Serious Illness in the Analyst: Countertransference Considerations

SANDER M. ABEND, M.D.

Some years ago I had an illness that necessitated interruption of my practice for a number of weeks. There was a substantial interval between the establishment of the diagnosis and the actual institution of treatment, during which I was able to continue working, so there was ample opportunity for me to consult with colleagues about how best to handle the situation with my patients. As Dewald (chapter 4) points out, the literature offers next to nothing of use on the subject, a fact which in itself requires explanation. I made notes on my patients' reactions to what I told them in anticipation of the break in our work together, and then again after its resumption. However, without much critical self-examination, I subsequently decided that what I had observed was not worth reporting. When the opportunity arose to discuss Dewald's excellent and courageous study, which focuses on his own as well as his patients' reactions, I was stimulated to reconsider my material and the reasons for having put it aside.

It is my intention to raise certain questions about the technical management of these situations when they arise, and about the role of countertransference reactions in influencing technical decisions. I shall also attempt to demonstrate that some of those countertransference factors may play an underestimated role in contributing to analysts' evident difficulty in studying and reporting on the problem.

For the sake of clarity, it will be necessary for me to make a few comments on the subject of countertransference in general, and on the so-called reality relationship between analyst and patient. As important and interesting as both topics are, I have no intention to treat either extensively, nor even to attempt to present arguments for my views. I merely wish to avoid possible misunderstandings and to provide an accurate framework for the discussion of the specific issues related to illness in the analyst with which this paper is concerned.

The term *transference* should be understood to denote all the influences of unconscious mental forces—that is to say, the wishes, fears, and defenses of infantile origin, and the complex compromises to which they give rise—on the analysand's relationship to the analyst, as it is perceived, remembered, wished for, and enacted. These vary at different times, ranging from being silent and undetected to becoming so blatantly manifest as to totally dominate the clinical picture, and hence command the full attention of analyst and patient. Regardless of the apparent intensity, or clinical significance of the moment, transference forces are ubiquitous, since they are manifestations of a fundamental and omnipresent feature of human mental activity. Our term for them derives from Freud's initial grasp of the essential feature that they originate in the individual's childhood experiences and relationships.

My view of countertransference is that it is a full counterpart of this broad understanding of transference. It includes the impact of the analyst's unconscious mental life—all of the residua of childhood instinctual conflicts—on his or her analytic activity with each patient. Once again this should be thought of as a ubiquitous factor that affects the analyst's work at all times. In optimal circumstances, its interference is minimal, negligible, or easily corrected with the aid of our habitual self-scrutiny. More limited definitions of countertransference as denoting only those unconscious reactions stimulated by the patients' material are less useful, I think, since they suggest a fundamental distinction that is misleading. When they are of significance in the analytic situation, countertransference forces mobilized by events in the analyst's life have the same nature, composition, and effects as those stimulated by the patient. They are detectable, and hence correctable, only by the same means—self-analytic activity.

The reality relationship between analyst and analysand presumably refers to those features of their contact reflective of their mutual status as adults engaged in a specific activity—psychoanalysis—which has certain agreed-upon goals and features of conduct. Many aspects of their interactions with one another can of course be designated as derived from this adult dimension of their relationship, but analysts vary greatly in the way they think about this undeniable fact, and in how their views influence technique. My own position is that for all practical purposes the reality relationship is always experienced by the analysand (and the analyst, too, of course, though we hope to a lesser degree) as inextricably intertwined with its unconscious reverberations and meanings. It is to these latter that the analyst's attention should always be directed. Here I differ, in degree at least, with Dewald (chapter 4) and many other colleagues as well. In my opinion optimal analytic technique is more likely to suffer from an analyst's explicit focus, in conjunction with the analysand, on the reality relationship than it will by the analyst's insistence on attending to its unconscious meanings instead.

From the foregoing it can readily be seen that I would seriously question the validity of certain distinctions. For example, it has been suggested that some emotional reactions stirred up in the analyst by major events, such as life-threatening illness, ought not to be regarded as countertransference, but as a sort of "normal" emotional turmoil. These are certainly normal in the sense of being usual, or unsurprising in the circumstances. However, the nature of the upheaval produced by such events will be specific for each individual, largely on the basis of its unconscious significance. In their composition and in their potential effect on analyzing capacity, these reactions are in no way distinguishable from other responses we unequivocally consider to be countertransference manifestations. In that sense, "normality" could only express a retrospective judgment that some reactions did not (in more-or-less ideal situations) adversely hamper analytic functioning.

Likewise, it is artificial to attempt to separate analysands' "realistic" perceptions, thoughts, worries, and judgments about the analyst and the analytic situation from unconsciously determined transference reactions. This is not to deny that there are real events which have an impact on the analytic situation, or that analysands, as well as analysts, possess the capacity to perceive and think about things realistically. I mean merely to emphasize that what is "real" for every patient is what that patient observes, feels, thinks, wishes, fears, wonders about, and decides by means of the operations of a mental apparatus of which the *unconscious* component is invariably a significant part, just as is true for every analyst. While we surely attempt to keep reality factors in mind in our work, they should never be exempt from the general rule of paying attention to the unconscious component.[1]

Dewald (chapter 4) has summarized the very scanty literature applicable to the topic of the emotional consequences of the analyst's illness on analytic work. He has also documented quite convincingly the important role of denial and its potentially injurious effect on practice. His descriptions of the narcissistic concerns, the fears of vulnerability and of loss of capacities, the financial worries, and the guilt about enforced neglect of patients' needs when we are ill are all familiar to me and, I am certain, to others who have had similar experiences. I agree, too, with his observations about the effect of illness-induced regression on the relatively mature functions and capacities essential for the adequate performance of our workaday tasks as analysts.

My own experience was more favorable than Dewald's in

[1]For a more complete exposition of this point of view see Brenner (1976, especially pp. 29–33, 119–130). See also Stein (1981) for an excellent clinical demonstration of the value of this approach to analytic technique.

that I was able to handle personally all communications to my patients before and after my illness. However, my observations on analytic patients who had had other experiences with analysts who became ill or died has convinced me that, as Dewald has stated, a knowledge of what was actually told patients, by whom, and under what circumstances is helpful in understanding and analyzing their responses to such events.

The countertransference issues of the postillness phase are especially important. I am aware of the desire to return to work in order to restore one's confidence and self-esteem through competent activity, and of the uncomfortable resonances patients' expressions of doubts and fears regarding the analyst's intactness may arouse. A subtle reluctance to surrender the "legitimized" gratifications of illness and convalescence, that is, enforced passivity, helplessness, and dependency, may influence an analyst to delay his return to work. More likely, however, reaction formations against these regressive gratifications may encourage taking on work burdens somewhat sooner than is medically or psychologically desirable. Finally, I agree that the technical handling of patients' responses after analysis has been resumed provides a field for the expression of the analyst's wishes to be reassured that he was missed, needed, and appreciated, and for the gratification of exhibitionistic and masochistic preoccupations as well.

My observations are also completely in accord with those of Dewald on an essential point with important implications for technique. He amply documents that the meaning of the interruption, of the analyst's illness, and of any observable alteration which persists, is different for each patient. It is responded to by every analysand according to his unconscious disposition, which is another way of saying according to the state of the transference. As I have indicated, where I may differ with Dewald and others is with regard to the question of whether there are other factors, in addition to the transference meanings, which need to be taken into account by the analyst in handling the situation with patients. I fully agree with Dewald that, "The therapeutic problem lies in the need adequately to explore the full gamut of patients' responses, affects, and associations to the illness, and to do this in the face of countertransference temptations either defensively to promote premature closure and evasion of more threatening affects, or to use the experience for exhibitionistic, masochistic, narcissistic or other neurotic satisfactions" (see chap. 4, this vol., p. 89). As a general statement, this is a prescription with which few analysts would quibble, but precisely how is one best to pursue this worthwhile aim? Dewald has modestly refrained from recommendations; instead, he told what he did, which was to vary his approach to suit the needs of each of his patients, according to his best clinical judgment. The crux of the matter rests in how much factual information should be provided. It is my contention that the chief significance of the powerful countertransference elements mobilized by the analyst's experience of serious illness is their tendency to influence analytic technique. This means, among other things, that the very clinical judgment relied upon to assess the specific needs of patients (with respect to how well they can maintain analytic productivity in the absence of factual information) is exactly what is under pressure from the countertransference; at no other time is the analyst's judgment about this technical problem *less* likely to be objective and reliable. Countertransference reactions are liable to affect the analyst's perception, understanding, capacity for instinctual control, and judgment in subtle or sometimes not so subtle ways, and therefore may well color his opinion of his patients' needs and capabilities.

In the years since my own experience with illness I have discussed this technical problem with many able colleagues, some with formidable analytic experience and highly respected clinical and theoretical judgment. Each was interested in talking about the subject and had given it thought. Many acknowledged some uncertainty or dissatisfaction with their management of these situations. Almost to a man, they had arrived at something equivalent to Dewald's solution; that is, providing some factual information, varied in timing and dosage according to their assessment of each patient's needs. There apparently exists a sort of commonsense consensus as to management, yet the impression of malaise about it and the paucity of reported observations, not to mention thoughtful studies in the literature, support my view that countertransference issues which are particularly difficult to examine play a role greater than hitherto suspected in determining both the technical handling and the reluctance to write about such events.

The essential argument to be considered asserts that while too much factual information may inhibit the range of expression of patients' reactions, and thereby constitute an interference with analyzing fully, too little information may, for some patients at least, prove too burdensome, thus serving to limit the analysis of transference fantasies. It seems advisable to consider the potential countertransference motives for modifying the principle of abstinence in such situations. We are in general committed to the technical precept that it is the *patient's* thoughts, feelings, and fantasies that matter—nothing else; and our uniform clinical experience confirms that each patient reacts to the analyst's illness in unique and personal ways. What is the beneficial effect of revealing anything more informative than the fact of interruption and the scheduling of the resumption of sessions? What is the basis for deciding that specific information relieves unbearable anxiety? If we tell some patients something in advance (when possible) it must be on the grounds that prior assessments of their problems and capacities have dictated this approach. If, on the other hand, we succumb after the fact to their importunings for information, what marks these clinical situations as different from others in which our schedules, appearance, or general habitus may have been changed for different reasons, in the wake of which we would be less inclined to provide analogous explanations?

It would be correct to assert that *not* to provide information, or answer questions about the interruption or change in appearance, also has meaning to patients. However, we are accustomed to pay analytic attention to their reactions under those circumstances, and are therefore likely at least to attempt to understand the unconscious significance of not telling. On the other hand, the act of telling something has meaning and reverberations independent of the specific facts revealed. If we think of the communication as simply "realistic," made in response to the clinical assessment of the patient's needs, we may be less likely to pay attention to its unconscious meaning. Telling something can be a way to convey a covert message from the analyst, which may be more or less correctly received; it can also have significance for the analysand quite distinct from the covert communication, and that also would be very important to analyze.

Some of the hidden messages which might possibly be carried by means of giving factual information about the analyst's condition are relatively easy to indicate. For example, when we are ill, or recuperating, or in the aftermath of such disruptions, we do not consciously intend to dilute or deflect our patients' anger at us, but it may be harder than usual to bear when one is, or has been, seriously ill, and frightened or uncertain of one's strength and capacities. We would not intentionally ask our patients to be caring, sympathetic, and concerned about us, but telling them of our troubles may be a subtle way of doing just that. The regressive impact of pain, illness, injury, and danger can influence us unconsciously to invite such responses. Certainly we would not knowingly tell our patients they should or should not worry about our well-being or survival, nor ask them to reassure us. Yet are these not liable to be implicit messages contained in the giving of factual information about our condition, treatment, or prognosis?

Furthermore, the weight we assign to the psychic burden of vivid fantasies of death or mutilation must be affected by our own unconscious conflicts. These elements are enmeshed in the nuclear oedipal and preoedipal wishes and fears in all of us; they are bound to be stirred anew, in analysts as in others, by illness or injury. Under such circumstances, cool, reasoned, objective judgments are not favored. To admit this to ourselves constitutes a fundamental recognition of an analyst's humanity and limitations, which may have more important consequences for the conduct of analysis than does acknowledgment of specific reality events. At times it may actually be easier on the analyst to make patients privy to his or her personal plight than it would be to deal with patients' fully expressed fantasies and feelings; this choice is subject to rationalization on the grounds that the patients' interest is served by such sharing.

This list of possible complicating aspects of the transmission of factual information about the analyst's condition is merely a partial one. Many others will no doubt occur to practicing analysts upon reflection. The above illustrations came readily to mind, based on my own experience and self-observations and on discussions with colleagues.

I had reached the decision before the interruption occasioned by my illness to provide no factual information about the reason for my enforced absence to analytic patients, and indeed was able to maintain this posture and to work productively with their individual transference elaborations of the anticipated break in schedule during that period. If anything, my own anxiety was allayed by my holding on to the familiar and far more comfortable role of physician, attentive to and concerned about the anxieties and illnesses of others, not my own. A couple of psychotherapy patients, both too ill to work with in a conventional analytic mode, and with whom transference interpretation was at all times more restricted, were told some of the facts. My impression was that this knowledge served to limit their freedom to express anger and concern for their own needs, but I cannot be certain that it would have been otherwise had I not given them the information.

I fully intended to continue my nonrevelatory stance with my analysands upon the resumption of work; to my surprise, that proved all but impossible. Like Dewald, I returned bearing clearly visible signs of my recent experience, and I knew that my patients' reactions would be influenced by the change in my appearance. One of my patients was an adolescent whose father died during his childhood; he had repressed all awareness of the visual evidence of the progressive wasting illness that had killed him. I decided, before resuming work, the boy should be prepared for my altered appearance, and so said something about it to him when I telephoned to set the date for resuming sessions. The results were ambiguous at best. This youngster misinterpreted what he saw and what I said. Although some useful analytic work could be done with the reasons for this confusion and for his reluctance to pay attention to the facts, the analysis on this point was not fully satisfactory. However, this does illustrate how imperious the need was to abandon the stance of restricting my interventions to interpretation, and how soon it influenced my clinical judgment.

Within three days after I began to see patients I had found equally compelling reasons to tell all but two of my analytic patients something factual about my illness. Several were in the field of medicine and had obviously noted the evidence of my having been ill. They either drew, or conspicuously avoided drawing, the conclusion that I might be irreparably damaged or even dying. Those I told what had actually occurred; others, I simply informed that I would recover fully.

Those patients to whom I did not tell anything factual did perfectly well. Of those I told, some disbelieved me, others distorted what they noted or what I had said, some complained about being told anything, others about not being told more; in short, each reacted to what I said or did not say in his own way. As I regained a more usual state of mind, I was profoundly impressed by the fact that it had proven impossible to do as I had intended with the majority of my analytic patients. In fact, I had ended by doing exactly as Dewald and many other colleagues had done, that is, I had attempted to assess each patient's needs on an individual basis. In retrospect, however, I believe that my assessments were neither accurate nor objective. I can only reach the conclusion that my own countertransferences, rather than a correct appraisal of what was best for each patient's analysis, decided me to provide factual information.

Consider, for example, one patient, a young psychiatrist,

who had suffered very much in childhood as a result of prolonged separation from her father and repeated brief separations from her mother. Her reactions to my planned vacations and to occasional cancellations at relatively short notice had always expressed important transference material in the past. Much that was familiar, related to separations, had returned to prominence during the period just before the interruption. After we resumed, my appearance reminded her of the ill, malnourished look of her father upon his return to the family. She seemed very upset, but my telling her what had actually been wrong with me led to an unexpected outburst of anger. She interpreted my comments as a sign that I felt she could not tolerate not knowing the truth, as, she imagined, all my other stronger, more capable patients could. With some bitterness, she added that she had done well in my absence, as compared with previous times, and was feeling much worse since my return. This led to the uncovering of the fact that she alone, as she believed, of all her family, had not missed her father much, and had not been altogether pleased and relieved to have him return. She had subsequently felt extremely guilty because of these responses, which she had kept secret. Her guilt had been compounded by his evident illness.

Her initial angry reaction to my telling her what had actually happened to me turned out to be an attempt to defend herself against her unconscious reaction to this communication, which she had perceived as an accusation along the following lines: "I have been very ill, and you alone of all the children did not care enough to cry." That was what was behind her thought that she had been singled out to be told the facts.

A case could be made for the proposition that my telling her what had happened had a beneficial, if serendipitous, effect insofar as it served to bring to light important material. Perhaps the essential material would have emerged in any case, perhaps not; in analysis that question can never be answered with absolute certainty. It may also be true that I had misjudged her situation. I present this incident merely to illustrate how erroneous the basis for a judgment to reveal factual information can be. The assumption of a "realistic" processing of the interchange ignores the inevitable truth that it will be understood primarily in terms of its unconscious ramifications for the patient. In this case, the nature of her reactions led to useful analytic work, and no harm was done, so far as I am aware, to the subsequent course of the analysis. We have no assurance that this will invariably be the case, and no reliable way to predict when the results will be less than desirable.

The factor of visual evidence of the illness presents particular problems for both analyst and patient, but my experience suggests that these, like the meaning of the interruption itself, resist generalization. The meanings evoked, to each practitioner and analysand, are special and individual. While one would naturally expect narcissistic, exhibitionistic, and scoptophilic concerns to be heightened by the phenomenon of altered appearance, their expression is extremely variable, and other related issues may be crucial. As I observed the reactions of my own patients, it was most impressive to me how even those with medical training misperceived and misinterpreted what they observed. Attempting to analyze their distortions was both fascinating and instructive; in my opinion it is doubtful that providing correct information facilitates this task any more than factually correcting other kinds of transference misperceptions is advantageous to the analysis of their significance (Stein, 1966; Abend, 1982).

The analysis of patients' fears that the analyst can no longer function capably or may be at risk of imminent death poses one sort of problem when there is no substantive basis for them, as understood by the analyst, and another, very much more complex problem, when such fears correspond to the realities at hand. Eissler (1975) addressed this problem. He expressed as an ideal that analysts would possess both the capacity and the maturity to assess their own situation accurately and to place patients' welfare above personal comfort. Unfortunately we all recognize (and perhaps have observed) that countertransference may all too often interfere with the attainment of this desirable standard. While consultation with trusted colleagues might be helpful in cases of doubt, the judgment required would be a severe test for the consultant, who is likely to be tied to the inquiring analyst by bonds of friendship. Should the analyst's infirmity be such that he should retire from practice, one can easily imagine the difficulty in making such a recommendation—all the more so if the consultant is no longer young and vigorous. The best one can say is that these are extremely difficult situations, for which there is often no truly satisfactory solution (Brenner, 1981, personal communication).

My own experience inclines me to the view that it is better for the conduct of analysis not to reveal factual information about the analyst's illness. Many colleagues, probably the majority, seem to believe that it is more useful to give some information, at least to some patients. My observations do not support an unequivocal decision in favor of either course, but they do suggest the need for more investigation of this subject.

In discussions with colleagues, I explored the rationale for their various clinical interventions. Some of the reactions to the questions I posed about why and when information is provided included responses which are at least consistent with my view of the role of unrecognized countertransference. A sense of uneasiness with respect to specific clinical instances was by no means unusual. On occasion, my queries seemed to give rise to the misinterpretation that I was suggesting that to give factual information under any circumstances means one is a "bad" analyst, or practices "improper" technique. In clinical work, we are accustomed to similar attributions of condemnation when interpretations bring to light unconscious wishes which are accompanied by hitherto unsuspected shame and guilt. The parallel suggests that similar affects, connected to unconscious countertransference gratifications, are being warded off. Needless to add, we are convinced of the ultimate value of unearthing hidden discomforts in our patients, and in ourselves, because it leads to an improved likelihood of arriving at more satisfactory solutions to problems with which they, and we, must deal.

To state that what we do in analyzing patients provides

us with gratifications, conscious and unconscious, is merely to express a truism about mental life. We do not refrain from making interventions, or decide to make them, because either course provides us with satisfactions; we only hope, insofar as possible, to understand those factors that exert influence on our judgment in each case. The burden of proof ought always to be on the side of justification of departures from standard technique, rather than on that of its maintenance.

I am certainly sympathetic to the dilemma of the analyst who must determine how to deal with his patients' reactions to his serious illness. What I wish to emphasize is that we sorely lack reliable data to guide us in making assessments and decisions in managing these situations. Furthermore, the inescapable influence of countertransference factors operates precisely against the very objectivity on which we are accustomed to rely in reaching clinical judgments.

Dewald's pioneering effort, and the discussions to which it gave rise, were received with much interest. The paucity of such studies cannot be explained by denial and narcissistic avoidance alone, although these surely contribute in a major way to the discomfort this subject seems to arouse. My own experience suggests an additional element may be at work. The transmission of factual information about the analyst's illness subserves unconscious needs in the analyst which may not always be recognized and acknowledged. This is so even when the analyst is convinced it is technically correct to provide such information, and independent of whether the conviction is warranted, even if subsequent analytic work appears unimpeded or even enhanced by the analyst's divulsion.

Analysts are understandably reluctant to disclose to colleagues what gratified them, even unconsciously. In part perhaps this is because of guilt at transgressing an analytic ideal, and in part because of residual discomfort about personal exposure of deep, nominally hidden aspects of their own psychological makeup. If I am correct in my assumptions, this reluctance helps to account for the evident disinclination to study, describe, and report on the problem of the technical management of the analyst's illness. This is especially unfortunate since such observations are needed in order to provide reliable and convincing answers to the questions I have attempted to highlight. Under what circumstances, if any, and for which patients, if any, is it advantageous to provide factual information about the analyst's illness? What are the advantages of doing so? What are the difficulties attendant thereon, and what problems ensue if information is not provided? We do not have definitive answers to these questions as yet. A thorough and honest attempt to illuminate this topic is long overdue, and its investigation will be of benefit to many analysts and their patients.

References

Abend, S. M. (1982), Some observations on reality testing as a clinical concept. *Psychoanal. Quart.*, 51:218–238.

Brenner, C. (1976), *Psychoanalytic Technique and Psychic Conflict.* New York: International Universities Press.

Eissler, K. R. (1975), On possible effects of aging on the practice of psychoanalysis: An essay. *J. Philadelphia Assn. Psychoanal.*, 2:138–152.

Stein, M. H. (1966), Self observation, reality, and the superego. In: *Psychoanalysis—A General Psychology: Essays in Honor of Heinz Hartmann,* ed. R. M. Loewenstein, L. Newman, M. Schur, & A. Solnit. New York: International Universities Press, pp. 275–297.

——— (1981), The unobjectionable part of the transference. *J. Amer. Psychoanal. Assn.*, 29:869–892.

6

Illness in the Doctor: Implications for the Psychoanalytic Process

HARVEY J. SCHWARTZ, M.D.

> "How agreeable it is that I, the patient, am really healthy, whereas he, the doctor, has a serious illness!"
>
> The Wolf Man [Brunswick, 1928, p. 445]

Becoming seriously ill activates powerful fantasies of punishment, mutilation, and abandonment. The fact of physical injury transiently reifies universally present terrors derived from the oedipal period and earlier. Mechanical invasions of one's body ego, such as diagnostic procedures or surgery, similarly rent one's repression barrier, leading to a magical blurring of the reality/fantasy distinction. The hard-won confidence in the safety of fantasy is temporarily supplanted by the instinctualization of the metaphorical experience.

Similarly, for patients suffering from neuroses, the past intrudes in the present. By definition, neurotics are unable to simultaneously recognize and tolerate inner-derived drive fantasies while observing and responding to outside reality. To that extent they share with the physically ill patient the burdens of omnipotent thinking. For both, historically derived perceptions challenge autonomous ego functioning.

When a patient's neurosis coalesces around the figure of the analyst, the latter becomes the bridge that both connects and separates the infantile neurosis from the present. As both the object and observer of childhood derived impulses, the analyst or therapist must be able to maintain a simultaneous immersion in the subjective and objective experience. This contradictory capability is made possible through the analytic neutralization of his own time-warping drive energy. The stance that results—both taxing and meditative—is known as empathic neutrality.

The dimensions of the analytic space that each practitioner's neutrality creates is continually being challenged by patients' defensive efforts to either deny the regressive pull it exerts on them or insistently transform it into a familiar arena from their past. Patients' continual discovery of the ever-widening boundaries of the firm analytic frame derives from their deepening awareness of increasingly crystallized and dystonic infantile drive-derived wishes and the characterologic compromises they have formed. One element of a successful analytic process is the patient's discovery, through the vehicle of the repression-undoing transference illusion, of his own intrapsychic analytic space.

This space, more accurately seen as a catalytic nucleus for an evolving process of derepression, suffers distortion not only from the patient's unconscious resistances to self-observation, but also from the analyst's or therapist's failures to continually define its integrity. Transference–countertransference reenactments are the most frequently recognized impingements on the otherwise deinstinctualizing process. Therapist-initiated transferences to the patient are also common, but less spoken of contaminants to the position of even-hovering attention. My focus in this communication is on how real life events, in this case severe illness in the doctor's life, may contribute their own particular difficulties to maintaining an affectively receptive analytic instrument.

This concept of an analytic space serves as a metaphor for a peculiar real–not real relationship. It is initially painstakingly created by the analyst throughout the opening phase of treatment, though in middle phase it is variously a conjoint undertaking. To construct a bilateral condition of participant observation requires first and foremost a thorough analysis of the doctor. This provides him with the experiential capacity to work in a psychic arena otherwise ineffable, that is, beneath the repression barrier. In addition to thorough technical knowledge, an analytic ego ideal is required in order to withstand the inner and outer temptations to nonsublimated gratifications, and to sustain a lifelong fascination with a relatively aim-inhibited search for truth. A coherent and consistent personal identity is the foundation for this dependable professional self.

An honest self-respect and confidence in one's clinical competence stand at the immediate interface between the personal and professional identities. Underlying supporting structures ideally include a gratifying intimate life, a retrospective and prospective sense of personal history, and a view of one's mortality only slightly clouded by denial. Accordingly, a sudden breech in one's lifelong experience of physical intactness and health makes impossible an uninterrupted capacity for self (and other) neutralized observation. The very tool of self-awareness is based on the a priori condition of physical safety. When this is threatened, the developmentally advanced analytic space gives way to a hypercathexis of survival reflexes.

The sick role with its institutionalized regressive functioning and supporting social network is an exquisitely adaptive framework for the tribulations of illness. The demands of advanced ego functioning are forgiven as responsibility for memory, motility, and even elimination is assumed by gentle caretakers.

The recuperative period, assuming it occurs, has its own conditions. Externally, regressive behavior continues to be sanctioned, but is now understood to be time-limited. A gradual recathexis of others and their needs is expected. Internally, with the immediate threat over, and assuming no latent predisposition to passive dependency, self-observing capabilities are reactivated and the meaning of recent events begins to be processed. Given adequate prior analytic resolution of regression-reinforcing conflicts, one may expect a gradual return of the capacity to create an analytic space. Considering the potential plasticity of the compromises that create one's character and hence one's analytic fingerprint, a slightly altered and, ideally, enriched postillness psychic homeostasis can be hoped for. However, while such an advance in functioning may be possible, dependent on a host of genetic and identificatory circumstances, lapses in one's professional proficiency are not to be unexpected.

One's usual tolerance for almost all transference-directed fantasies may be temporarily supplanted by a reflex preference for some and suppression of others. The resultant size and shape of the analytic frame, defined as it ultimately is by one's personal capacities, may transiently be distorted by postillness inclinations toward denial, suppression, as well as gratification. This effort to forget the unpleasant past may result in an acting out in the clinical situation of one's own (fantasied) prior relationship with one's medical doctor and his mind-altering medications. This could lead to overactive efforts to reassure patients as well as to an excessive denying stance based on an ambivalent transferential identification with one's perceived powerful and dangerous physician–surgeon.

In this communication, I shall discuss the brief literature on this topic, focusing on two recent papers; describe the meaningful details of my own sudden hospitalization; and present case material that sheds light on the clinical issues that arise in these circumstances.

Literature Review

The paucity of reports discussing the clinical implications of illness in an analyst or therapist has been noted, somewhat critically, by all who have written in this area. There are less than ten such reports in all the psychiatric and analytic literature. There is consensus among them on the meaning of this oversight. It is, they feel, an expression of avoidance and denial that is invoked by practitioners when faced with the anxiety, guilt, and vulnerability that accompany incapacitating illness. The frequently resulting countertransference discomforts and technical ambiguities are said to have led to a preconscious suppression of the clinical study of this phenomenon.

My own experience and discussion with colleagues inclines me toward a more generous view. The implication of the critics is that an absence of published reports reflects denial in the clinical situation. I would suggest greater parsimony in the conclusions drawn from the absence of public documentation. It is quite conceivable to me that the considerable efforts one must exert in honestly and carefully working clinically with this delicate material may in itself be a more than sufficient challenge and reward as to make a literary recapitulation unnecessary and burdensome.

Other than the report of the Wolf Man's postanalytic encounter with an ailing Freud (Brunswick, 1928), there are no specific reports in the first half-century of psychoanalysis on the impact of the doctor's illness on the analytic situation.[1]

More recently, in the psychotherapy literature, Goldberg (1984) reported on the consequences of her terminal cancer on her work with patients in group psychotherapy. She noted that questions of how much information about her illness to tell them became intertwined with her own feelings of helplessness and wishes to be cared for as well as the group's increased difficulty in recognizing both sides of their ambivalence toward her.

[1]Other life events may similarly intrude on therapists' more usual presence in the clinical situation. Givelber and Simon (1981) studied the impact of the death of therapists' spouses on their empathic and interpretive attunement. They noted a frequent mourning-induced tendency to more primitive and concrete cognitive functioning, as well as reparative overidentification and narcissistic nonrelatedness to patients. They feel that telling or not telling patients the facts of one's trauma should be decided on whether that will or will not reenact a pathogenic sequence from the patient's past. Telling one psychotherapy patient of the death of her therapist's mother was seen as not interfering with the flow of fantasy material and served as a "correcting" experience for a prior incompetent self-image. Significantly, the authors note that patient curiosity about such private events may often be both energized and inhibited by its association with primal scene schemata. This has not been noted elsewhere in the literature, but is in accord with my own clinical experience.

Chermin (1976) described his guilt in becoming ill and abandoning his patients, and through his reflex apology to one of them came to recognize his underlying assumption of omnipotence. His child patients' fears of their magically empowered death wishes troubled adult patients no less than their younger counterparts. (In fact, in one report's biographical information [Little, 1967] *the reader* is even reassured that the author is alive and healthy!)

Lindner (1984) documented his experience of life-threatening cardiac surgery and its impact on his therapeutic work. Unusual in his report is the "fabrication" he initially communicated to his patients regarding the reason for his sudden absence. As it came one week before an already announced vacation, he had his secretary inform his patients that a family emergency had arisen requiring him to be out of town one week earlier than anticipated. Following confirmation of the necessity of surgery, he then wrote to his patients and told them the factual details of his illness and the approximate date of his expected return. Surprisingly, no further mention of the meaning or implications of the discrepancy between these two explanations is given.

Upon return to practice, Lindner encountered in his patients intense morbid curiosity, dramatic acting out, and powerful defenses against patricidal wishes with fears of retaliatory aggression. He underlines the importance of monitoring countertransference reactions, although he recommends hypnosis to "remove" defenses.

In the analytic literature, Little (1967) described the regressive impact of a myocardial infarction on his analytic functioning. His unconscious fear that his analysand's aggression would lead to a second infarction led him to defensively reinforce her conscious and unconscious defenses against her hostility. He also insistently interpreted away from the here-and-now transference and focused exclusively on her presumed rage at her mother. Ultimately, Little resumed his own analysis following which he was able to safely acknowledge with his patient her feared "lethal" hostility.

Hannett (1949) reported on the meaning to her patients

of her sudden absence for two weeks due to a miscarriage. She used this event to study the relative importance of the repetition compulsion as compared to the interpersonal relation in the formation of transference. At the onset of her hospitalization, patients were informed simply that she was ill; no more specific information was given. Of the six analysands described, the five who were able to relate to her transferentially all experienced major conflict over their hostile fantasies. They all guessed the nature of her illness quite accurately. One patient, after hesitantly exploring his fantasies, specifically asked her what had happened. In reply, she told him the actual facts. Unfortunately, there is no further discussion of the effect on this patient of having been given the details either as it related to his ongoing analysis or as compared with patients who were not told.

Hannett concluded from her experience with illness that both irrational and rational elements make up the transference. She feels that the repetition compulsion is the overriding determinant "with particular details added because of the particular character of the analyst in relation to the particular history and character structure of the patient" (p. 81).

Regarding what she described as the "gratuitous question" of what patients should be told about one's illness, she reiterated that her practice was to inform those who specifically ask. She concluded, somewhat enigmatically, that "the countertransference in such a critical situation is of crucial importance. It is sometimes difficult to integrate what might be technically valid and what is humanly possible" (p. 81).

What is common to all these reports is the therapists' illness-induced uncertainty about the boundary between their personal and professional selves, and the ratio of reality to illusion in the transference. Similarly, patients become confused by the apparently blurred reality–fantasy distinction, and experience a deepened sense of unconscious guilt over their hostile impulses. This in turn further diminishes the capacity for autonomous (from the drives) observation. One may say that for both participants there has been a breech in the analytic frame. The more usual metaphorical level of consciousness, which serves as a subliminatory "container," is supplanted by what appears to be instinctual damage (castration) and omnipotence. Behaviorally, the reassuring ground rules have been broken by the doctor's sudden and unprepared-for absence. More important, the therapist's experience of a rent in his own intrapsychic "container"—a product of infantile holding experiences, drive neutralization, syntonic benevolent parental–analytic introjects—leads to structural defects in the integrity of the analytic frame he can offer the patient. The therapist's highly developed capacity to reflectively "contain"—in both meanings of the word—the disparate affects of infantile drive fantasies is transiently weakened by the traumatic reinstinctualization of his own psychic autonomic nervous system. Derivative of this injury to the analytic form, though not in themselves unimportant, are the numerous content questions that arise postillness, that is, what to tell the patient, how to deal with the reality basis of his fantasies, whether the point of urgency is in the present or in the past. I conclude the literature review by focusing in detail on two recent analytic contributions that thoroughly and thoughtfully address these issues.

Dewald begins his 1982 paper, "Serious Illness in the Analyst: Transference, Countertransference, and Reality Responses" (see chapter 4) with a detailed and dramatic account of the beginning and evolution of his life-threatening illness—meningoencephalitis with a cavernous sinus thrombosis. The immediacy and power of this unusual opening of an analytic paper informs the reader of the exceptional nature of the events to be described. Dewald's gripping description of his illness draws us into his poignant and private moment in his life and mobilizes in the reader elements of curiosity and voyeurism along with their underlying libidinal and sadistic components.

The initial communication to his patients of his sudden incapacitation introduces the central technical issue of the paper—what does one tell patients? An initial benign diagnosis of his disorder led him to have his secretary contact his patients and tell them that he hoped to be back in the office in one week. As his condition worsened, he put off informing his patients of this fact in the reportedly rationalized interest of protecting them from undue anxiety. Finally denial gave way and patients were told he would be away from his practice indefinitely. With the deepening of his illness, regression into a state of narcissistic preoccupation precluded further concern about patients' anxieties.

The question of how much factual information to provide to patients while in the acute phase of illness was raised in Dewald's case by the early dissemination of rumors and miscommunications. Concern that detailed factual information would harmfully shrink the analytic field was balanced against the fear that in the absence of the reality of the analyst's presence, which contributes toward defining that field, fantastic fantasies (or the defenses against them) could become reified in an antianalytic direction. While noting the difficult set of choices, Dewald resists making specific recommendations on this issue.

Convalescence provided the opportunity to regain his self-observing capacities and take stock of the psychic impact of his illness. Successfully traveling "upward" from his illness-induced regression permitted the affective recognition of the impotent helplessness that had been thrust upon him. As a foil, this experience highlighted the opposing characterologic assumption of invulnerability that had previously been unrecognized. Simultaneously, his concern for patients reemerged, and with it a desire to return to work. He understood this wish as containing both sublimated interests and a need to redefine himself as a competent, intact professional. Castration fears had been activated, though the regressive pleasures of the invalid status had their own seductive satisfactions.[2]

[2]The collusive denial by one's treating medical doctors of the emotional impact of one's illness can play an important role in an incomplete recuperation. In the absence of an analytic attitude toward recognizing and mourning prior self-images and omnipotent fantasies, the medical doctors' exhortations to forget the past can interfere with the meaningful self-analytic resolution of the unconscious impact of the illness. Given their inevitable role as transient transference figures, their unconscious resistance to the slowly evolving psychic reequilibriation can inhibit one's self-analyzing function and lead to characterologic encapsulation of the trauma, with attendant malformation of one's analytic space.

Returning to practice reintroduced the question of how much information about his illness to give to patients now that he was available to recreate the analytic frame and process. The eye patch he wore for a residual oculomotor palsy highlighted for both analytic participants the issue of his physical and emotional competence. Central to his renewed professional functioning was the discovery in himself of powerful illness-specific countertransference wishes toward his patients and their reactions to his absence and dysfunction. A search for appreciation, a tendency to masochistic exhibitionism, and an overidentification with the powerful medical doctor can all be expected to intrude on and imbalance the otherwise functioning compromise formations that create one's unique analytic character.

The meanings to patients of their analysts' or therapists' absence and illness vary widely. They are the product of earlier life history, state of the transference, depth of treatment prior to interruption, capacity for regression, and amount of factual information available. As Dewald notes, equally contributory to the fantasies and their analyzability is the analyst's recognition, tolerance, and monitoring of his inclination to use the patient as a need-fulfilling and esteem-enhancing object. The Herculean task of dissecting and exploring patients' transference fantasies, even as they touch on the very raw concerns of the only recently recuperated therapist, highlights the necessity for at times painful self-scrutiny. Added to the usually manageable task of tolerating transference-derived challenges to one's competence and therapeutic strength, is the new consideration that the patient may be observing accurately one's postmorbid less than optimal functioning.

The recent loss of the fantasy, as Dewald describes, that one's personal analysis offers (perpetual?) immunity against illness, lends greater immediacy to the therapist's responses to patients' illness-related reactions. While tolerating if not envisioning his own mortality, the therapist must simultaneously be able to delicately dissect patients' resistances to their affective experience of the illness. What is introduced for the therapist is not only the reality of the debilitating illness and whatever sequelae remain, but also the perhaps new recognition of physical vulnerability. The temptation to use the fantasied relationship with the patient to fulfill a grandiose wish of having been missed or of being important and irreplaceable, may emerge from a reluctance to fully accept the possibility of one's demise. A collaborative denial of death may lead to premature closure on such fantasies or a resistant preoccupation with them. The seed of eventual termination, analytic and physical, that the ending of each analytic hour portends may be seductively swept aside by the wished-for timelessness of the infantile pleasure principle.

In response to the specific technical question of what one does or does not tell patients about one's illness, Dewald concluded with a somewhat flexible approach. For those in supportive psychotherapy, complete and detailed information should be given. Those in the opening phase of analysis should receive a moderate amount of factual data, following brief transference exploration; those in the middle phase should receive the least information; and those in termination will not need factual information. The principle employed by Dewald is that to be evasive or secretive at an inappropriate phase of treatment would interfere with the establishment of the therapeutic situation.

Abend's (1982) paper, "Serious Illness in the Analyst: Countertransference Considerations" (see chapter 5), is intended as an alternative perspective to Dewald's. While agreeing with most of Dewald's findings, Abend differs on one key conclusion—what patients should be told about one's illness. Simply put, he feels that since one's very analyzing instrument is what becomes most distorted by postillness countertransferences, the analyst is not capable at such a time of objectively evaluating whether patients would be better off knowing the details of one's illness or not. Further, since clinical experience at other times invariably attests to the advantage of not informing patients of the details of one's life, the same is true after an illness. That is, if one should feel it to be in the best interest of a patient to tell him some facts about one's illness, one should resist that inclination and assume oneself to be under the sway of countertransference wishes or resistances. Abend's intent is to challenge the "common-sense consensus" on this question and highlight the subtle and not so subtle gratifications that lead one away from the standard technique of focusing on patients' fantasies in a neutral field.

What is perhaps most evocative about Abend's paper is that throughout it *he tells us nothing about his illness.* We the readers are left to experience along with his patients the same insisted-upon vacuum of information, as well as the scoptophilic fantasies it gives rise to. The induced discomfort in the reader, that is, the frustration of one's voyeuristic and sadistic impulses, differs considerably from the experience of reading Dewald's paper. Equally telling is the realization that knowing the facts of Abend's illness is irrelevant to comprehending his thesis, as it may very well be to the progress of an analysis. More important, through the differing experiences with these two papers, the reader has the opportunity to affectively sample the unique size and shape of the analytic spaces these two experienced clinicians create. It is more than likely that each is optimal for himself and his patients.

This suggestion at first blush may seem to border on a nihilistic relativism that is not intended. Indeed, the issue of how one comes to decide what if anything to tell a patient of one's illness is quite important. Furthermore, I am in agreement with Abend that departures from standard technique require an understanding that is different from that of its maintenance. What I wish to add is that just as all facets of one's analytic functioning may be influenced by postillness countertransferences, so too, and I would suggest especially, one's relation to standard technique may be distorted in a nonanalytic direction.

Specifically, the illness-reinforced role of regressive submission to medical authority may extend temporally and emotionally to include a tendency to retreat from the affective ambiguity of the analytic encounter. To decide, as Abend suggests, a priori that any clinical decision one makes to tell a patient some facts of one's illness is necessarily born from a contaminated understanding runs the risk of advising in a direction away from analytic recuperation and toward continued invalidism. While great caution and self-scrutiny are indicated in the postillness period, such a retreat from the immediacy of the transference–countertransference interface would presumably be a dramatic change from one's more usual mode of working. This would, despite any verbal reassurances to the contrary, be unconsciously communicated to the patient, justifying concerns in his mind about the doctor's ability to fully reengage in analytic work.

One may in fact use the extent to which one is prepared to trust one's groundings to reenter the analytic arena, informed certainly of any inclinations toward gratifying overinvolvement or self-protective arbitrariness, as a yardstick of one's recuperation. In my experience, errors committed as part of this effort to reengage the analytic encounter are more remediable than those derived from an excessive hesitation to carefully trust one's bearings. The latter tends to concretize patient fantasies of one's continued fragility and defectiveness.

As I am about to discuss, I decided for reasons quite similar to Abend's that it would be in the best interest of my patients if I did not reveal to them the details of my illness. I am under the impression, to the best of my awareness, that this decision to withhold information was arrived at from an experience-near, yet objective, evaluation of each clinical situation. This is not to say that I did not struggle with what I felt to be a continuation of my somewhat comforting illness-reinforced deference to perceived authoritative stricture. The behavioral similarity of my decision with what I felt one is "supposed to do" made the differentiation particularly difficult, though in retrospect probably aided in my regaining a sense of competence. I felt, after an adequate recuperation, I was able to cautiously reinvest myself in the vicissitudes of the clinical encounter and trust that I was capable of informed decisions.[3]

[3]Casement (1982) emphasized the differing routes by which one can arrive at the abstinent position and, in a sensitive accounting, revealed the clinical value of reach-

The Illness

A Friday afternoon, after a full morning of patients, I went to my internist because of a worsening pain of five days' duration on my right side. Radiologic examination revealed a large mass of unknown origin in my right chest cavity. Initial impression was that it was "probably benign," but an immediate thoracotomy was indicated. Hospitalization was scheduled for that Monday. It was estimated that with chest surgery and convalescence, I would be able to return to work in six to eight weeks. I returned to my office to close down my practice and delegate my administrative responsibilities. I called all my patients and told them that a medical problem had arisen that I must attend to and that I expected to be fine. I said I anticipated being back at the office in approximately two months, and that I would call them some time before to schedule appointments. Patients were variously shocked, did not ask the details of my problem, and wished me well. I made arrangements with a colleague for coverage of my practice and in case I would not be able to return to work.

As the implications of what was happening to me grew more apparent, I became terrified, for myself and my family. Closely parallel to my personal feelings, I developed a concern of panic proportions for my patients. Under the traumatic impact of these events, my initial realistic concerns for their well-being mushroomed into projecting upon them my own distress, as well as reliving through them a painful event from my past.

Some years earlier, in my own experience as analysand, I felt abandoned and profoundly shaken by my analyst's repeated hospitalizations and ultimately his sudden death. This perceived new version of an old trauma reawakened my grief, sense of loss, and guilt. While a subsequent analysis essen-

---

ing that equidistant stance *experientially* through appreciating its specificity and meaning to each patient. He detailed the richness of encounter that emerges from foregoing a safe commitment to "correctness" and instead advised, through trial emersions into transference complimentarity, a continual rediscovery of the therapeutic correctness of one's neutrality.

tially resolved the traumatic impact of that experience (and of the earlier sudden death of my father), it remained a piece of my psychic history, and in my overidentification with my patients, was renewed.

I experienced again an overwhelming sense of loss that transcended my self-observing or fantasy functioning. As a projection, my patients' abandonment temporarily became my near-exclusive focus of pain. A potential empathic link with my patients became instead a regressive identification in service of my own repetition compulsion. The more usual fluidity of cathexes that would have permitted deidentification, acknowledgment of aggressive fantasies, and attention to reality was frozen when faced by my reawakened grief and by my increasing awareness of the real medical dangers that lay before me.

By the next day my emotional investment in my patients' fears rapidly waned as I left the past behind to face my frightening future. While I looked and generally felt perfectly healthy, I began to enter the regressive role of the self-involved medically ill. As all personal relations began to be measured in the degree to which they attended to me, I found myself inclined to mentally turn to others, including patients, in search of objects who would be concerned for me. As a consequence of my deepened narcissistic functioning, "as-if" relationships lost meaning and latent, and not ordinarily problematic, countertransference fantasies emerged. Just as the day before I had lost awareness of patients' complex individualized fantasied reactions to my illness, I now was losing any meaningful awareness of the metaphorical basis of the relationship—it all seemed "real." Now I wished for their feelings of abandonment.

With a prolonged but inconclusive diagnostic workup and with my mental preparation for the surgery, most all relationships other than those immediately involved in my care fell away in importance. My attention was exclusively focused on my body and my future.

One week after what turned out to be successful surgery for a noninvasive tumor, I returned home for recuperation. As it now seemed that I would be able to return to work in two to three weeks, I had my secretary call my patients and inform them that I was fine and would be returning three weeks earlier than anticipated.[4] As I healed and reinvested an optimistic and object-related attitude toward my future, I began to become reinterested in the technical aspects of dealing with my patients' reactions and with my administrative responsibilities. I was, despite temptations to the contrary, reassuming my professional identity.

The specific question of what I would tell patients of my illness emerged quickly. Initially it seemed best to tell them that I had a tumor removed that was not expected to return. This would both explain the long absence and indicate that there were no anticipated sequelae that would interfere with our work. Over the time that I was considering this question, I was slowly and only intermittently regaining my physical strength and psychological equilibrium. Continuing narcissistic preoccupations and regressive gratifications formed the emotional backdrop to my renewed clinical concerns. Increasingly able to observe my state of mind, I became aware that regardless of what I said to patients, the state from which I said it would determine its therapeutic usefulness. Recathecting the illusory basis of the relationship would demand thorough neutralization of my own needs and would clearly prove to be the central and most difficult issue in my resumption of clinical work.

My ability to deaggressivize the experience of becoming ill, that is, to free the reality of serendipitous sickness from the inevitable linked fantasies of primary-process causality, would be necessary in order for me to be able to recreate an arena where drive-derived fantasy could flourish and be observed without fear of magical enactments. This would also serve to deepen my autonomous appreciation of reality which, as a supporting framework, simultaneously permits a more thorough encounter with the power and ubiquity of unconscious fantasy.

[4]In hindsight, I realized that my desire at this time to actively reassure patients of my being well and able to return to work was partially an effort to undo the earlier failure of my analyst/father to return from the hospital.

Given my understanding of the critical importance of my being able to recreate an analytic condition, I set aside the question of what I would tell patients and instead focused on rediscovering that psychic space in myself. Sometime later, in so doing, it emerged there was no need to discuss the details of my illness with my patients. Indeed, it seemed quite beside the point. The issue was, given the reality of my physical health, of which I reassured patients, to resume an analyzing relationship. In that capacity, the facts of my illness were as irrelevant as any other personal information. The *real* question of consequence was whether I could reprovide an uncontaminated analytic space in the present within which they could continue to affectively encounter their past. The answer to this lay outside the issue of the details of my illness.

After considering each patient, I decided to tell them, if asked, that I had had a medical problem that was taken care of and was not expected to recur.

Clinical Material

Mrs. A. is a European-born, childless woman in her late thirties who had been in treatment for seven months before the interruption. Her initial presentation was for an eating disorder that had been a deeply kept secret for two decades. This was soon revealed to mask a severely distorted body image, a fear of mutilating childbirth with a history of repeated abortions, multiple phobias, a preoccupation with cleanliness along with chronic constipation and abdominal pain, and an ostensibly loveless sadomasochistic marriage.

Initial transference imagery consisted of an idealized powerful father who could give to her wisdom and perfection if only she obsequiously deferred to him and feigned helplessness. To be a doll-like extension of him (as she was of her mother) brought relief from terrifying feelings of inner ugliness and emptiness, and spared her from being the object of his anticipated humiliating ridicule. When her efforts at identifying with and controlling men failed, a revenge-filled rage emerged as she feared being left with, and similar to, her perceived defective, deprecating, and intrusive mother. Lifelong anally oriented conflicts with her mother reflected their mutual preoccupation with defecation, money, and inner/private-outer/public boundaries.

The patient's initial efforts to get me to talk and answer her incessant questions were met, to her considerable frustration, by my explaining the benefits of exploring the meaning, history, and apparent pleasure to her of my speaking. In response to this nascent analytic vacuum, she felt frightfully angry and alone as she experienced herself as left with an inner dirtiness that would become visible to me if she could not control me as she did her husband and her father. She recalled her childhood habit of asking her father all sorts of naive questions in order to evoke from him his strong reassuring voice and his preferential attention, as well as in an effort to passively receive and become joined with his omniscience. We learned it also was an unconscious attempt to protray herself as virginally ignorant and nondangerous as she sought to undo her exclusion from his secret, yet partially exhibited, activities with her mother. Memories of showering with father until puberty emerged, and evoked great resistances as she struggled with her "secret" fantasies, affectively screened by her phobic displacements, of wishing to control and possess his awesome and hurtful penis, and her guilt in wanting to bite it off, be filled with it, and deny it to mother and sisters.

Mrs. A., alone among my patients, called my secretary during my absence to inquire as to my health. She, too, was the only patient who insisted on sitting up in the chair at the first postillness session, though she resumed the recumbent position the next day. She wanted *to see* that I was intact. She also sought to avoid the associative situation with the object loss it entails and the guilt-filled fantasies it allows. She renewed her insistent questioning and demanded to know the details of my illness. She was in fact quite distraught. Her initial fantasy was that I had an operation on my back, and later that I had AIDS.

She described feeling abandoned during my absence and said she was not important to me. She struggled with her childhood worry that because she was bad, her father would die and that something, she did not know what, would be left unfinished between them. She recalled her lifelong concern for and protectiveness toward men she viewed as inherently vulnerable, and hence could be easily damaged. Throughout this first session she constantly and anxiously brought up her need to know what had happened to me. Interpretively, this reenactment remained out of range and I wondered if by my abstinence I was asking too much of her at this time. At the end of the hour though it seemed that she felt reassured of my undamaged strength of purpose as she smiled and wryly commented, "Now I remember what it's like to be here."

As we continually worked with her syntonic controlling demandingness to avoid her own thoughts and wishes, and instead to be gratifyingly spoken to and given to by the ambivalently idealized male, her chronic constipation began to clear. Reflecting both her frustration and her burgeoning curiosity about her emerging self, she commented, "I always thought that I would have to work here, but now I really know what that feels like—now I understand it." Her fantasies became available for our observation.

In the days that followed my return, she imagined the couch as an operating table upon which her legs would be cut off. Some time after my return, the patient alluded to an atypical sexual experience she had with her husband—implied was an acting out of a slave scene with the husband being humiliated—but teasingly refused to speak of the details or her feelings. In this way she attempted to undo her feelings of exclusion from my own secret sadomasochistic "scene." She defensively identified with, and simultaneously took castrating vengeance upon, the dangerous phallic father, as she sought to reverse her own growing masochistic impregnation fantasies.

In the context of my strict neutrality, the patient became able to recognize her fantasies as an aspect of her self. Despite characterologic inclinations to alloplastically resist ackowledging the imprint of her overstimulating childhood, she became able to appreciate the consistently neutral analytic arena—a place for "work"—where genuine self-knowledge and autonomy could emerge from affectively based insight. Lacking a meaningful personal set of ideals, the neutralized respect she developed for analytic integrity was of additional value in enabling her to crystallize (and actualize) her own independent viewpoints, capabilities, and initiative from which she could begin not only to experience and observe her own drive-derived fantasies, but also objectively assess her mother's narcissism and her father's seductiveness.[5]

Mrs. D. is a woman in her late twenties who was well into the middle phase of treatment (third year) at the time of interruption. Her initial presentation was for violent outbursts at her boyfriends, mild phobias, overintellectuality and confused thinking, work inhibition, and psychophysiologic dysfunction (Raynaud's disease).

From the first day she took her place on the couch and complained of the hole in her sock she was ashamed of, Mrs. D. alluded to what was to become the theme of a number of years of treatment. Her conflicts around her childhood fantasy that she had been born with a penis but had it taken from her formed the core of her adult neurosis and symptomatology. The initial most frequently focused on cause for this tragedy was the fantasy that when she was an infant her father

[5]The capability that one's coherent neutrality in the face of stress has to represent to the patient an enriching analytic ego ideal may itself be an important factor in treatment. Mrs. A.'s distorted conception of her worth and potential was partially derived from her lifelong functioning as compensatory "perfect" phallus for her mother, and her overwhelming experiences of phallic awe. This contributed to her essentially phallic ego ideal that valued only the peripheral/exhibitionistic—i.e., phallic—facets of her functioning, and devalued as worthless and sinful all that was inner-derived—that is, her feminine and individuating sexuality, creativity, and ideals. Firm inner-created and trustworthy abstinence, as a facilitator of resistance analysis, offered the patient the opportunity for a constructive reorganization of her disrespectful ego ideal (Bibring, 1964). Its insisted-upon consistent metaphorical basis aided the metamorphosis from her wanting to "be proud" of her concretely perceived phallic body to the abstracted pride she felt in her growing self-awareness and ability to transform her expulsive eating symptomatology into verbalizable fantasy. It also may have contributed to her capacity to retain inside herself her subsequent pregnancy.

dropped her on her head and a piece of her skull fell out, damaging her irreparably. (Other explanations that were to be elaborated upon included her being damaged at birth by the cesarean section, her own masturbation, and, ultimately, her mother jealously cutting off her prized ponytail.)

Her life motif was to revenge and reverse her perceived pitiful state of deprivation while masochistically suffering as a result of the defenses against these wishes. The resultant compromise constructions included the belief that she possessed an inner penis that would grow and be visible, but that she must keep secret or else it would be taken from her again; the inhibition of her considerable intelligence and creative talents for fear of being dangerous to men and of damaging them in the competitive workplace; the fear of acknowledging her feminine charms and attractiveness lest she recognize her esteem for men and her wish to be seductive; and the inability to fully engage in genital sexuality without mild depersonalization, which served to avoid the pain and anger of losing the penis when intercourse was completed, and which defended against the underlying incestuous basis of her fantasies and arousal.

The exclusive possession of her adored father and his phallus, whose size and grandeur were boasted of by her mother, was the consuming goal of her unconscious life. However, the shame she felt in acknowledging her wish for him to repair the damage he caused—her "castration"—and her fear of her death wishes toward her additionally demeaning and competitive mother, led to a turning inward to an illusory self-sufficiency with a marked inhibition in her developing femininity.

A repetitive trauma of her childhood that reenacted her fantasied castration with loss of the phallus to mother occurred with her father's frequent, sudden, and prolonged business trips and his royal welcoming home celebrations. When he announced his departures, the patient became withdrawn and sullen and hid in the bathroom until he left. She characteristically refused to acknowledge her hurt, anger, and sorrow at his leaving and her dismay at being left alone with mother. While he was away she often, at mother's request, slept with her in the parental bed in order to soothe mother's loneliness. In this identification with father, her own pangs of missing him were denied and she recalled feeling at those times that he did not exist.

When he returned with great fanfare, she experienced a secret euphoria that quickly turned into disappointment and frustration as she witnessed his showering mother with expensive jewels and attention, leaving her alone and guilt-ridden over her competitive possessiveness. She felt it was forbidden to express her own excitement over his return and to wish to receive from him his precious gifts. She remained the aloof, proud, and well-behaved child.

In the months before my absence, there had been a shift in the proportion of self-disdain and destructive envy to pleasurable fantasy and transference flirtatiousness. Memories of childhood sexual curiosity and coquettishness emerged as she cautiously allowed herself the physical feeling of being as feminine and sexy as her mother without her more usual obsequiousness, intellectuality, and self-punitive inhibition. While vengeance toward men was never far from the surface, and layers of masochistic transference fantasies were often hinted at, but just as quickly suppressed and avoided, sufficient neutralization of her destructiveness and guilt had taken place so that she was able to apply for and be accepted at her first full-time job at a prestigious firm. Despite her fears of becoming too professionally powerful and dangerous, and her fantasy that her father would prefer her now that she was less afraid to dress femininely and succeed professionally, she began her job. One week later, I was hospitalized.

Five weeks later we resumed our work. She began by describing, devoid of affect, that after I had called her about my illness she went to the bathroom and cried, but did not want anyone to know of her sadness, about which she felt embarrassed. Soon thereafter in the session, she denied there was anything wrong with me, but thought instead that it was my "child" that was ill. Indeed, she expressed no overt curiosity about the nature of my problem. She was not sure she could trust me again, but had the physical sensations, again without affect, of sitting in my lap and holding on to me. She described a cold fury at her husband for the entire time of my absence, and casually mentioned she had spent all the money with which she was planning to pay my bill.

The next day she mentioned, for the very first time, her father's prostate cancer, diagnosed while she was an adolescent, that required him for three years to have repeated and painful operations through his penis. She described feeling bad about his suffering, but angry at his rejection of her while he was hospitalized. He reportedly preferred the company of his male friends or the patient's sister who brought him pleasure by showing him her male children. As a childless female, she felt worthless and rejected.

While her professional work continued to go well during this time, one week after my return her husband, with subtle provocation, became abusive and she, reversing her own abandonment, left him and moved in with a close woman friend. This reenacted defensive masculine identification served to avoid her passive experience of loss and, as a result, limited the availability of affect in the transference. It provided as well the reparative illusion of control over the whereabouts, activities, and availability of the missing man.

With this acting out, the patient's associations to my illness dried up, and compensatory phallic fantasies became her focus. She reported that now that she was sleeping without her husband, she renewed her childhood habit of falling to sleep "holding on to my fantasies for comfort." She became preoccupied with the size of her new business briefcase, her competition with men at work, and her new sense of power. Gradually, explicit exhibitionistic seduction wishes and infuriating primal scene imagery of exclusion emerged for the first, though by no means the last, time. The symptomatic coldness of her hands (Raynaud's) began to be reconverted first into the emotional coldness she defended herself with, and then into the original sexual (masturbatory) heat and excitement of her genitals and entire body, and into early memories of being in bed with her parents and touching her father.

After approximately the same number of weeks that I was away, and in a remarkable reenactment of her father's grand homecoming, the patient returned to her husband. Recognizing this, and under the restimulated abandonment of my announcing a future vacation, she began to directly associate to and reexperience my illness and the loss of her father. As the full force of her feelings approached consciousness, she repeated over and over, now as then, "I'm not going to let it get to me." She struggled against the emergence of her transferential longings for her father out of the guilt over her associated competitive strivings with her mother and from the embarrassment she felt revealing her feminine wishes entailed. It emerged that this event screened a series of losses that included her father's preference for mother and his giving her a child, the patient's perceived punitive exclusion from the parental bedroom, her mother and father's vacation when she was two years old, and the loss of her fantasied penis. We learned that her recurrent masochistic provocation of her husband was a projection of her own castrating anger at my desertion as well as self-inflicted punishment for desiring my return and causing my injury. It also sought to recreate the passionate violent "scene" she felt excluded from and thereby gratify her later emerged regressive libidinal wish to be beaten by me. Through analysis of her repeated revenge-filled acted-out reversals of my abandonment, she was able to experience first the fear of and then the content of her lifelong overwhelming yearnings for her father, which came to include her murderous rage and suicidal despair at his repeated departures, the consequent terror at his possibly not returning, and the wish to sexually excite him and be excited by him so that before he left they would finally consummate their union with a child.

In light of the prolonged absence of any expressed curiosity about the facts of my illness, I asked her what she imagined had happened to me. (We later learned she also insistently avoided her fantasies about her father's liaisons on his business trips and any factual information about his illness.) She immediately responded characteristically that she had no idea and had not thought about it since "I don't know about medical things." The next day she revealed that she thought I had prostate cancer like her father did and had to undergo the same procedure. Alternately, she imagined I suffered from infertility. She had the further fantasy that she had caused my illness "because of my periods—because I want a penis—because I'm a girl." The following day she recognized the magical and deeply guilt-filled thought that her father's surgery/castration was the result of her retaliatory anger at him for his damaging her when she was an infant and for having left her that way for all these years.

Mr. L. is a man in his late thirties who was in a thrice weekly vis-à-vis therapy for two-and-a-half years. His initial presentation was for drinking binges, frequent nightmares, Don Juan-type promiscuity, and periodic depressions. History revealed an initially perceived passive and ineffectual father for whom he felt no respect or admiration, and from whom he felt no support or strength. His mother was portrayed as volatile and violent, and on two occasions in his youth threw a knife at him that barely missed. She reportedly debased her husband's masculinity and mocked her son's athletic prowess, all the while provocatively exciting the patient with violence-tinged physical intimacies. When the patient was twelve, the father introduced him to a homosexual friend of his with whom the boy began a passive homosexual relationship that lasted two years and consisted of the patient being masturbated. The patient's vocation, in which he has been increasingly successful, involved considerable grandiose exhibitionism in preparation for which he often would drink compulsively until he became "blind drunk."

Early transference imagery consisted of a passive search for guidance and wisdom from an admired powerful man. He consciously and unconsciously resisted the homosexual feelings evoked by these emerging fantasies and explicitly detailed dreams, and responded to them with an increase in his heterosexual freneticism. These conquests included the seduction of older married women, which was partially in an effort to incorporate their husbands' potency. He transferentially reexperienced his encounter with the older homosexual man, and was frightened of his wishes to be cared for, and of his own fantasies of orally and anally sucking out my strength.

After considerable analytic attention to the resistances against his passive wishes, the ever-present underlying competitive and self-castrating material approached preconscious accessibility. His exciting childhood discovery of naked pictures of his mother that were taken by his father, itself a partial screen memory, formed the nucleus of his erotic fantasies and practices and of his massive castration fears. Women were seen as damaged and dangerous as well as highly arousing and unattainable. He imagined, we learned later, that they were secretly phallic. His own retreat to narcissistic exhibitionism was an attempt to master and reverse his childhood guilt-filled voyeurism and disavowed painful feelings of smallness, as well as an effort to achieve phallic supremacy freed from object-related castration fears. In the transference, his passive and grandiose fantasies increasingly screened competitive impulses as he was slowly able to recognize his preemptive self-destructive punishments and the object-directed triumphant underlying fantasies. At the time of interruption, he was hesitantly becoming able to approach and explore his experience of anxiety and guilt-derived fear from which he had characteristically retreated.

As a result of my prolonged doctor's visit on the day of my initial medical evaluation, I was unable to be at this patient's regularly scheduled session. My secretary informed him when he arrived that an unavoidable emergency kept me from our appointment. When he immediately asked if I was all right, she informed him that I was and that I would contact him. My calling him the next day and informing him of my illness confirmed his fantasy.

Five weeks later, his first question to me upon resumption was, "Am I allowed to ask what happened?" I responded first by telling him that I had a medical problem that was taken care of. He went on to describe his severe anxiety while I was away and his loss of sexual interest in his new girl friend. When I brought to his attention the phrasing of his question—"Am I allowed"—he said, "No one told me anything," referring to when he asked my secretary what was wrong and she replied that he should discuss it with me when I returned: "It was as if I shouldn't know." He was able at that time to explore his lifelong sense of forbidden curiosity for others' secret activities, as well as his feeling that it was wrong to have personal feelings for me. Following this atypically straightforward expression of his wish to actively see, he became frightened and began to describe his feeling that I had not wanted to see him for a while, that I was performing a special experiment on him by manipulating him to see how he would respond to my absence. It also occurred to him that his past repeated romantic failures were the result of a spell an old girl friend cast on him.

The next day, the emerging paranoid fantasies continued: he feared of being attacked by strong men, of their "bugging him," of his craving for the cigarettes he saw dangling from their mouths. He said he felt weakened during my absence, less manly. In detailing his activities during my absence, he described flying to another city, something he usually feared, to receive a lucrative and prestigious award for a professional achievement. When I brought the importance of this to his awareness, his suspiciousness cleared. He became anxious and uncomfortable and, in a manner akin to a confession, admitted he had in fact enjoyed my being away and his success, saying "I did it on my own." He feared, however, that I would be angry at him for this, and for his income which he assumed (and hoped) would be greater than mine, and that I would attack him and take it away.

The association of his success with my debility evoked his anxiety over abandoning his presumably passive father and self. The guilt over the death wishes that were gradually to emerge, and which were intermittently turned on himself in the form of feelings of inferiority, work inhibition, and somatized fears of suffering a heart attack, was additionally responsible for the back pressure on his characterologic regressive slipperiness. He feared that becoming the independent powerful man who would be unafraid to aggressively see and desire his in fact quite beloved, and at times loving, mother, with its parallel violent wishes to make me "smaller" than him, put him in dangerous opposition to me. For his feelings of rivalrous triumph the reality of my illness stimulated, he feared the most terrifying consequences. Succinctly stated, "I feel like I'm becoming too big for my britches and that I'll be struck down for that." The castration concept of my infirmity was represented in the talionic punishment he initially anticipated for his haltingly emerging rivalrous wishes toward me—having his eyes poked out.[6]

Reflections

In 1930, in "Civilization and Its Discontents," Freud described the transcendent pleasures that become possible as a result of neutralization of the drives and the attendant joys in artistic and scientific creative work. He noted that these "finer and higher" endeavors, through displacement of libido, can offer subtle and long-lasting gratifications and sidestep the frustrations of the external world. But he commented sadly, "this method cannot give complete protection from suffering. It creates no impenetrable armour against the arrows of fortune, and it habitually fails when the source of suffering is a person's own body" (p. 80).

The unique richness of the analytic encounter is for many a source of lifelong creative stimulation and gratification. The fascinating opportunity to help create in another person the

[6]One year later, as an anniversary reaction, the patient began losing interest in his new wife and developed a somatized exacerbation of his feelings of worthlessness and depression—involving multiple physical complaints and doctor visits—which ultimately led to the uncovering of the heretofore unconscious and guilt-filled fantasy that my illness had entailed my losing a testicle. This brought to memory previously unspoken feelings concerning his father's life-threatening surgical loss of a kidney, which left a prominent scar, that occurred before the patient's birth. That event, imbued with considerable family mythology, became the initial nidus for extensive comparative fantasies concerning his father's phallic prowess and mother's preference for an intact, powerful man.

capacity to affectively discover his own vast subterranean instinctual life is a rare and rewarding privilege. Participating in the at times elegant unfolding of the infantile experience with its unparalleled rejuvenation of life-enhancing energies is daily testimony to the power of one's work. The preconscious inclination, though, to be somewhat worshipful of the presumed omnipotence of the analyzing process is challenged by one's encounter with organic illness. It is, as Freud well knew from his own experiences, one of the frustrations of the external world that drive sublimation is helpless to avoid.

Freud's own history with illness is worth recalling. His initial surgery for his jaw cancer was in 1923, a full sixteen years and an astonishing thirty-three operations before his death. Despite severe pain and discomfort during these later years, though undoubtedly influenced by it, Freud wrote some of his major works. It is equally noteworthy that although his jaw prosthesis made talking at times almost impossible, and led to unilateral deafness (requiring a reversal of the position of the couch), and that as early as 1926 he commented "I am of course reminded every hour of the mutilation caused by the operation on my jaw" (E. Freud, 1960, p. 224), he made no mention of the clinical meaning or impact of his progressive disability on his patients or himself. Perhaps clinical analysis as a science was still too young to document the seeming technical confusion introduced by real disease in the doctor. It is also possible that in his role as primal father of psychoanalysis, Freud felt that publicizing his disability would weaken the field's organizational structure and interfere with the all-important task of ensuring its survival. (Equally contributory may have been Freud's discomfort with the reported illness-induced reawakening of his passive wishes toward Fliess—his former transference object and physician-surgeon [Shengold, 1972]. It is worth noting that Freud had considerable and ambivalent reactions to Fliess's own earlier illnesses [Schur, 1972, pp. 77–79].) Whatever the case, he left us little guidance from his own experiences with his "dear old cancer."[7]

[7]Even among Freud's analytic biographers, there is only passing mention of the clinical impact of his obvious and incapacitating disability (Jones, 1957, p. 13; Schur,

The recognition and tolerance of human frailty adds a dimension to the as-if analytic relationship. Depending on the therapist's age, the nature of the illness, and the visible and invisible sequelae he brings into the consulting room, the fact of his fragility and mortality is often introduced into the work. For example, as mentioned, Dewald wore an eyepatch when he returned to his office. Patients' scoptophilic fantasies in that case need to be understood as not only reflecting early wishes to see and know and the fear of being seen by others, but also as their wondering about the analyst's current ability to see—meaning, in addition to the implied castration wish, can he see their wish-to-be-hidden fantasies, can he function analytically and can he see?

In my own case, I returned to work appearing well rested, tanned, and in no apparent distress. This healthy visage surprised patients and aided their denial that anything serious had been wrong with me. The differing internal and external perceptions of my condition, as indeed I was emotionally still very much involved with my recuperation, had its own impact on my work.

Some weeks after my return, a woman patient began speaking of the scar she feared she was inflicting on her face by her nervous scratching. While this scar image had in the past, with good evidence, been well recognized by me and partially by her as a reference to her perceived genital wound, at this time it occurred to me that it also contained a transference reference to my own new scar (about which she had no factual information). I inquired as to thoughts she had regarding any scar that I might have from my recent illness. While it was quite possible that her fantasy of a genital scar and my surgical scar were linked in meaning, her associations

---

1972, pp. 382–383), though patient memoirs from that period reveal readily apparent latent references to his fragility and demise (Doolittle, 1956).

Early analytic speculations about the psychogenic origin of Freud's cancer are recorded by Nunberg in his memoirs (1970, p. 41), and Bernfeld (1962) presents a thought-provoking view of the role Freud's 1923 "death and resurrection" had on the development of psychoanalysis.

to my comment produced no evidence to suggest that at this time her reference was transferentially related to my illness. After not very considerable self-reflection, it became readily apparent to me that the only person in the room who was somewhat preoccupied with my recent scar was me.

One's illness differs from most other aspects of the analytic encounter in that it is to some degree a shared event. That is, both participants know that one of them is physically sick, they both do not meet, and both have powerful fantasies about it. While this also holds true when the patient becomes seriously ill—another neglected area of study—particular meaning is added when it is the otherwise anonymous doctor who is disabled.

The nonmetaphorical quality of the event transiently links the two participants and reifies the defensive elements in the real relationship. Accordingly, patients' resistances take the form of a retreat from the apparently dangerous arena of fantasy as they seek to share in the real experience. This concretism may take the form of somatization (i.e., identifying with the illness) or acting out (i.e., motorically reenacting the abandonment).

Under more or less similar pressure from the universal "need for causality" (Nunberg, 1961), the therapist himself may only intermittently be able to "metaphorisize" his trauma. The inevitable instinctualization of the experience of illness intrudes, via depression, on his autonomous capacity to neutrally observe drive-derived fantasies. The resultant concretization of perception, in the form of self-sympathy, can lead to failures in maintaining an empathically defined relationship. The hypercathexis of one's own physical functioning can, as demonstrated, inhibit the receptivity and accuracy of one's empathic data-gathering trial identifications, based as they must be on the premise of a freely mobile and playful imaginativeness. This same narcissistic literalness can also lead to overidentification with one's patients.

Six weeks after my return, I was preparing to announce to patients my usual vacation in August. This became an unusually difficult thing for me to do. As weekend separations had for some patients, this event reawakened for both me and my patients the panoply of emotions associated with my hospitalization. I reexperienced through their renewed pain my own fears and guilts. I felt sorry to be causing that suffering again.

This recapitulation, however, was now one of *fantasied* disability. As such and under the safety afforded by its illusory basis, patients like Mrs. D. became able to explore their historically derived fantasies, freed from the overstimulation of my actual illness. Through the reassurance offered by my physical presence and consistent analytic functioning, we had reentered the metaphorical field.

It is, as mentioned, the boundaries of this illusory field that are challenged and defined through one's illness. Artifically leaving aside the important issues of the postillness intactness of the therapist's intrapsychic analytic space and patients' preexisting ego deformity, the question of what one tells patients of one's illness is not unimportant. Most would agree, and I concur, that for the analyzable patient in the middle phase, sensitive abstinence is of most help in sparing them the burden of one's misfortune and reassuring them of the continued intactness of the analytic field. Assuming one's health is actually no longer in jeopardy, one's illness and absence should be used strictly transferentially as an opportunity to uncover and rework the past. However, if further serious medical problems are expected and the analytic frame is therefore no longer dependable, patients should be told about them frankly and completely.

In the somewhat differing circumstances of the opening phase, for patients like Mrs. A., the task at hand is to begin to create an analytic space out of early interpersonal dialogue and manifest expectations of gratification. Of the innumerable instances that arise which allow one to tactfully demonstrate to the patient the abstinent nature of the work, withholding facts about one's sudden hospitalization is perhaps one of the most difficult to meaningfully define for the patient as helpful. To deprive patients of this information, all the while suggesting to them the importance of their verbalizing their fantasies of curiosity, creates a strange set of conditions indeed for the naive patient.

Faced by such a patient, one who has not yet comprehended the simultaneous demand for affective participation and reflective observation, individualized and "common-sense" recommendations on technique have usually been made. Some would use this opportunity to initiate the patient into the peculiarly evocative but abstinent mode of working. Others, feeling that these circumstances are extraordinary and not representative of the essential frustrations, would answer general questions and await the next set of more usual inquiries to evoke and demonstrate the latent elements in the manifest inquisitiveness.

In my view there are some cases of otherwise treatable patients who early on in these circumstances would experience strict abstinence as painfully rude and rejecting. While this response of theirs is transferentially derived, it is not at that time clinically available for joint study. Short of making a virtue of withholding information for its own sake, it seems that there is little to be gained and potentially much to lose in strict neutrality in these cases. On the other hand, carefully titrating one's responses to the patient's ability to even vaguely recognize the constructive possibilities in one's abstinence would contribute to creating in the patient a deeper capacity for the uncoupling of magical thinking, and ease the development of the transference neurosis.

The nature of the underpinnings of one's abstinence may be decisive in this matter. A clinical stance that is inner-created allows a guilt-free loosening of the abstinent position when deemed appropriate. It is conceivable that this flexibility may itself, not so paradoxically, permit a wider application of the strictly abstinent stance.

Through my own encounter with illness, I came to appreciate Freud's realization of our helplessness at the arbitrary hands of an impersonal fate (*Ananke*). I developed a richer comprehension of a serendipity that is uniquely motivationless. I also discovered ever more deeply the ever-present veil of unconscious fantasy and conflict through which we perceive and respond to that reality. I learned that an analyzing capacity is no less personally valuable when faced by the starkness of real trauma than it is when we encounter the cryptography of screen trauma.

Similarly, the therapeutic power of one's painstakingly developed analytic neutrality is never more revealed to be an exquisite instrument for the evocation of patients' deepest and most feared fantasies as when the frame is momentarily ruptured. This creates a breech universally filled by key infantile conflicts and their magical assumptions. Maintaining one's metaphorical stance at these times makes available to the patient a profound experience of the true depth and ubiquity of unconscious fantasy. This is our gift that will stay with them long after we are gone and will be of inordinate value to them as they face life's tribulations.

References

Bernfeld, S. (1962), On psychoanalytic training. *Psychoanal. Quart.*, 31:453–482.

Bibring, G. (1964), Some considerations regarding the ego ideal in the psychoanalytic process. *J. Amer. Psychoanal. Assn.*, 12:517–521.

Brunswick, R. M. (1928), A supplement to Freud's 'History of an Infantile Neurosis.' *Internat. J. Psycho-Anal.*, 9:439–476.

Casement, P. (1982), Some pressures on the analyst for physical contact during the re-living of an early trauma. *Internat. Rev. Psychoanal.*, 9:279–286.

Chermin, P. (1976), Illness in a therapist—Loss of omnipotence. *Arch. Gen. Psychiat.*, 33:1327–1328.

Doolittle, H. (1956), *Tribute to Freud.* Boston: Godine.

Freud, E., ed. (1960), *Letters of Sigmund Freud.* New York: Basic Books.

Freud, S. (1930), Civilization and its discontents. *Standard Edition,* 21:59–158. London: Hogarth Press, 1961.

Givelber, F., & Simon, B. (1981), A death in the life of a

therapist and its impact on the therapy. *Psychiat.*, 44:141–149.

Goldberg, F. (1984), Personal observations of a therapist with a life-threatening illness. *Internat. J. Group Psychother.*, 34:289–296.

Hannett, F. (1949), Transference reactions to an event in the life of the analyst. *Psychoanal. Rev.*, 36:69–81.

Jones, E. (1957), *The Life and Work of Sigmund Freud*, Vol. 3. New York: Basic Books.

Lindner, H. (1984), Therapist and patient reactions to life-threatening crises in the therapist's life. *Internat. J. Clin. Exper. Hypnosis*, 32:12–27.

Little, R. B. (1967), Transference, countertransference and survival reactions following an analyst's heart attack. *Psychoanal. Forum*, 2:108–126.

Nunberg, H. (1961), Curiosity. In: *Practice and Theory of Psychoanalysis*, Vol. 2. New York: International Universities Press, 1965, pp. 168–206.

——— (1970), *Memoirs: Recollections, Ideas, Reflections*. New York: Psychoanalytic Research and Development Fund.

Schur, M. (1972), *Freud: Living and Dying*. New York: International Universities Press.

Shengold, L. (1972), A parapraxis of Freud's in relation to Karl Abraham. In: *Freud and His Self-Analysis*, ed. M. Kanzer & J. Glenn. New York: Aronson, pp. 213–244.

7

Resuming the Work with a Life-Threatening Illness—And Further Reflections

ANN-LOUISE SCHLESINGER SILVER, M.D.

Suddenly, in July of 1978, I faced a life threatening illness requiring major surgery and prolonged debilitating treatments. My surgeon ordered me to resume work promptly, seeing anxiety and self-preoccupation as stressful. He was convinced that stress interferes with the immune system, this the mysterious but decisive factor in survival. He viewed work as a life-saving distraction. Thus, I was transformed from an ebullient junior colleague to a fatigued, pale, despondent individual as I fought to keep my spirits above the waters of self-absorbed despair. If the ideal therapist serves as a secure container for the projected affects of the patient, I guiltily thought of myself as more a collander or saturated sponge than a container. So, I returned to work at Chestnut Lodge, partly as a therapist, partly as a patient on an occupational therapy assignment. My patients became part of my metaphoric treatment team, giving to this work their best and very effective efforts, replete with the expected ambivalences. It was as if they too had been drafted to fight at the front lines of a confrontation with death. I wish to convey, through a

[1]This paper was presented at the Twenty-Seventh Annual Chestnut Lodge Symposium, October 2, 1981.

series of vignettes, something about this phase of the work, and then to offer a few comments.

Initially, the staff tried to spare my patients the news, but it became clear some patients already knew. For example, among my initial visitors to the hospital was an intrusive twenty-six-year-old borderline woman who had left the Lodge a few months earlier against medical advice. She appeared at the hospital soon after I'd left the intensive care unit. So, the six administrators of my six patients met with each of them, informing them of the situation as they each understood it. Interim therapists were assigned.

I returned to work after a two-month absence. People seemed astounded to see me back. An aide impulsively called out from the tennis courts, "Dr. Silver, you back for a while?" "That's the plan," I answered, groping for my former cheeriness, experiencing his "for a while" as reflecting a shared pessimism. All my patients had elected to continue working with me, understanding that I might, on return, not be working full time, and might not be able to continue with them. I felt their decisions to be votes of confidence.

I will present vignettes from my work with five patients, the one already alluded to, one with whom I stopped working upon my return, and three with whom I am still working three years later.

Prior to my illness, the patient already mentioned had maintained a tenuous idealizing attitude toward me as she attempted to isolate me from her largely despised unit. But when she became physically ill, we met in her room. Suddenly I saw how intensely self-absorbed, obnoxious, and rejecting she could be. The more she needed human contact, or so *I* saw it, the more contemptuous she became. When she recovered from the ailment, she signed out of the Lodge, accusing us of ineptness and malevolence while staying in touch through the invisible but lush Lodge grapevine. The day I was transferred from the intensive care unit to a private room while I was still submerged in the exhaustion and gloom which preceded anxiety, she came bounding past my private duty nurse, giving me a teddy bear clothed in a kindergarten-style dress. It was the only female teddy bear she could find, she said. She stayed a short time, and I appreciated her visit and gift. She returned a few days later, this time with my consent, bringing a non-sectarian religious medal depicting a handshake and inscribed, "The Lord and I together hold you in the power of the healing light." This time she burst into tears saying, "I guess I'll never see you again." I had my first glimmer of returning forcefulness when I answered, "Look, I don't plan to just sink into the woodwork." My tactful private duty nurse insisted she leave. Over the next few weeks, the patient telephoned me at the hospital. While brief at first, the calls gradually grew to monologues of her problems. When I was able to stop these calls on my own, I felt I was once again a therapist, managing the activity of setting limits.

Her expressions of support, immediately followed by statements of total pessimism and appeals for rejection, were patterns I came to experience with others, usually in subtler form, over the coming months. Her style of telephone calls was repeated then with letters. After I recommended psychotherapy rather than the intensive neurological investigation she was pursuing, she had her parting shot in a letter without return address, advising me to change my specialty to pediatrics or surgery so I could do *some* good in the world in my few remaining days. My rage, which she engendered, became an incentive to persevere as a therapist.

On return to the Lodge, I terminated work with three of my six patients since I lacked the strength for full-time work. One of these was a twenty-four-year-old paranoid schizophrenic man with whom I had worked ever since we both had arrived new to the Lodge two years earlier. He had been flamboyantly psychotic, rageful, physically assaultive toward others, and had attacked me verbally during sessions in which he was in cold wet sheet pack. In the months before my absence, he had become calmer. He had met out of pack with his interim therapist, a young athletic male doctor. So, when we met again, the patient was not in pack, and we met in the room where our work began. We sat silently. He grinned fixedly and said, "I still feel like a vegetable. How are you? I heard you had surgery. I heard you had cancer." I thought I was hearing this for the first time and felt like I'd been struck. I told him that because of my illness we'd have to stop working together. Early in treatment he had ruminated on delusional somatic concerns, problems in his abdomen and head, and was under the impression that he was elderly and approaching death. I said that in the ensuing silence I had found myself dwelling on *my* somatic worries and felt he needed a strong and healthy therapist, especially at this time when he seemed to be making definite progress. He kept grinning. I came to experience the grin first as "good riddance" and second as a grimace of profound tension, there having been much evidence of his fondness for and dependence on me, he as my son. Politely, he thanked me for having worked with him.

In the following months when I drove by him on the grounds, as he walked alone no longer requiring a staff escort, and I had to use conscious effort merely to depress the gas pedal, I had the fantasy more than once of driving into him. I envied him his strength and obvious progress. I then recalled that he had once been hospitalized after "dancing in the traffic" of a huge metropolitan freeway, this a psychotic expression of his suicidal despair. I had left our work uncompleted in both its constructive and destructive aspects. I thought, "If I can't have him, nobody can," the "have" here also reminding me of the intensely sadistic sexual assaults he kept promising me when he was in pack. I felt deprived perhaps of them and of whatever satisfaction could be had should he recover. I felt gypped and angry whenever I saw him, these having been his predominant feelings toward me during our work together. By wanting him back I came to discern the highly ambivalent, maternal countertransference surrounding these encounters. I have wanted him back, referred to him too frequently in case seminars, and refused to take certain colleagues' advice to edit the remarks about him from this paper.

Another patient was a twenty-three-year-old, chronically borderline psychotic woman, who had from age fourteen an escalating pattern of runaways, drug experimentation, self-destructive episodes, assaultiveness and fragmentation. She sent me a get-well card depicting a kitten lying on its back with a playful porcupine dancing on its upturned paws. I felt certain she saw herself as that porcupine and me as the kitten. The background color of the card matched the yellow of my office walls. The card said, "To my dear lady-doctor friend, Missing you so much—come back soon please! Lots of love always." She later sent me a book she had talked about during sessions and which she had reassured her head nurse I would not misconstrue. The book was *For Colored Girls Who Have Considered Suicide When the Rainbow Is Enuf* (Shange, 1975). The day I left the hospital I felt terror-stricken, as if the hospital had been keeping me alive. This patient had often described similar experiences, leading to serious suicide attempts. I hoped to have the opportunity to convey indirectly that I now understood her in an experiential as well as intellectual way. I read her book once I was home and it was a comfort, it being a play in poetic form that has the theme of finding life-sustaining beauty amid poverty and despair.

When I returned to work, she asked, "Can I hug you?" I said yes, and we hugged and cried. She later contrasted that with our previous physical encounter, in our second session two and a half years earlier, when she'd come at me yelling, "You hate me—I know you do—get out," and then stabbed at my upraised arm using a white plastic knife she had hidden away. She talked about how the summer had been for her, including a resumption of binge-eating in a futile attempt to combat her feelings of loneliness. Then some weeks later she cautiously asked for details of the treatments I'd been through and we both cried as she said she'd heard I'd need surgery again the following summer and wondered if that were so. She said explicitly that she hated me for getting so sick and frightening her and me so badly. Once she saw that my illness was a permissible subject she repeatedly sought reassurance while apologizing for mentioning it. At first she became alarmed and silent when I looked tired or preoccupied. Once she was able to ask how I felt, and I could, when this was accurate, confirm her impressions that I felt awful, her anxiety diminished. I came to look forward to the hours with her since she, more than perhaps anyone else, soon viewed me as cured. I welcomed her effective use of denial as a means of coping with uncertainty. Her previous sense of humor returned, and I regained a sense of my former healthy self when I was with her. And it was just recently in preparing this paper that I understood why I was so determined to purchase a mobile made of antique prisms which I then put in my office window. In the late afternoon, it casts countless spectra drifting across the walls, subliminally reminding me of her message of hopefulness in rainbows. This patient had been attempting to rid herself of her considerable suicidal potential by projecting it into me. Sending me that book, while well intentioned, perhaps was also a last ditch effort to succeed in this other endeavor.

Another patient, an eighteen-year-old schizophrenic girl, had been struggling for years with denied grief over the death of a relative. She had been flamboyantly suicidal and self-mutilating. During the year preceding my surgery, her father had been seriously ill. The patient had been working on her sense of guilt and sense of responsibility for her father's illness at the time I went on sick leave. On my return I was forced to cancel our first session because of family claims. The patient had just gone to her first day of classes at a local college, and I had been unable to contact or forewarn her. Accidentally, we met at the entrance-way of the Lodge as I was driving home, and talked briefly. This event, my actively deserting her, became the immediate target of her rage. While the sessions went along well enough, whatever the topics were, any silence became awesomely tense. We seemed not to mirror but to magnify each other's anxiety, or to cause it to resonate so that I sometimes thought that the intensity would lead both of us to shatter like cut-glass goblets, or that the atmosphere would shatter like the sky in her previously hallucinated world. Again, I had known intellectually that she had been suffering during the silences earlier in our work together. Now I was experiencing their torture.

Finally, there was a chronically schizophrenic woman about my age, a woman whose first psychiatric hospitalization was at age seven. She had refused to eat and had become cachectic when starting school, requiring tube feeding for three weeks. On return home she refused to eat unless she and her mother went on long walks to the ice cream parlor for milkshakes. She again refused to eat at age eighteen when she started nursing school, and again during her first year here. During our first few months together she was disheveled and mostly silent. But when she did talk, the profound extent of her grandiosity and panic was evident: she had a perfect personality and was a movie star. I treated movie stars and was one myself. Both of us lived a magical partying eternal life, transported anywhere just by wishing it. What she ate determined who would live and who would die, yet at the hospital, she said that "we live in eternal bliss and happiness." She experienced me sometimes as a jealous, ugly, aging woman, a wicked witch imprisoning her because I couldn't endure her triumphing over me; sometimes she and I were characters in a movie and she was bitter that the audience, while empathic during the film (our session) would leave the theater and forget the movie. She wrote the following letter within a week of my surgery: On the envelope she wrote, "Never to Say I'm Sorry. Trust Busters; In Dire NEED OF FLOWERS."

Dear Ann Silver,
I hope you get Iris's, Neurstatiums, Rhodadedrums from Hawaii. Have you received your vanilla shake? Have you met Irate Irene from Nasau from Martin Luther King. I never have received a Bohemian bathing suit. I never had seen the Holy Ghost at night, a midsummer's night dream. I have not received my dream of Over the Mountain Across the Sea there's a boy awaiting for me, and I hope the other side of the mountain works for you too and me both. You bet the ___ family is intact.

From Russia with Love,
I have not received my intinerary
1 Referendum, 1 Memorium, 1
trusted identifier
Trust Buster LILIES OF THE FIELD

Her question about the vanilla milkshake came as a stroke of genius: I felt I had to eat to live, but my appetite was nil. It had never occurred to me to ask for a vanilla milkshake from the dietary department. It became her gift delivered by magic. Her acknowledgment that she had not met the man of her dreams was also a gift to me, as previously she had held tightly to her hallucinated lover. The reiterated "Trust Buster" seemed to be a challenge to me to return.

When I did return, she was the most disorganized I'd ever seen her, while making a few obviously clear statements: "Your legs are so thin. It's a wonder you can stand on them" and "I don't know if there's enough apple pie to last the year." For her, it isn't Mom's apple pie, but Mom *is* apple pie.

I arrived on the unit for one session to find her being put in cold wet sheet pack, a procedure which had not been necessary since the very early phases of our work together. I sat by her bed as she was being secured, she raging wildly, and I experienced the scene with weird detachment, as something like a movie. I felt that she was enacting my panic for me in a dramatic manner not available to me personally. The next day I learned that an aide had received a severe injury to his hand during the work of containing her.

Later on, she referred to "the leukemia surgery" and when I asked if she was referring to my surgery that past summer, she said with unusual directness, "I think we'd best not talk about that right now." She resorted to the defenses of denial and obfuscation with enviable effectiveness: so effectively that even though her administrator and head nurse had gone together to talk with her about my illness, neither of them was sure whether she had been told or not. She began calling me "Honey" in a firm and contemptuous tone, setting me straight on this or that as if she had no real expectation I'd ever amount to anything. When she was seven, doctors had told her chronically depressed mother not to expect much from her. An ambience of "better off dead" pervaded the sessions without a sense of where this feeling was coming from. She alluded to feelings coming through the air vent.

I returned to work with these severely ill patients much sooner than I did with my more functional private patients, even though Lodge work involves a forty-five-minute commute for me and I see my private patients in an office in my home. There, the isolation, the lack of a community of collaborators, and the system of fee for service rather than payment of a salary by an institution made the resumption of private practice more complex, guilt-provoking, and stressful. Decisions regarding whom to tell what, how, and when were made with comparative independence. The idea of obtaining supervision to aid in the transition didn't occur to me, nor did anyone suggest it. I refer the reader to chapter 4 where Dewald documents the complexities of resuming work following a debilitating, life-threatening illness from which he had recovered.

There are many articles and books concerning treatment of patients with potentially fatal illness (Pearson, 1969; Kübler-Ross, 1969; Weisman, 1974). Gradually we are coming to accept the dying patient as a subject for psychiatric attention, as pioneered by Eissler, and are exploring countertransference themes (Joseph, 1962; Hägglund, 1978). Also, attention is given to assessment of functioning of sick physicians by boards of presumably healthy psychiatrists. And psychiatrists and others have written autobiographic accounts of severe stress (Cousins, 1979; Casey, 1978; Fiore, 1979; Rodin, 1980; Dahlberg and Jaffe, 1977). We have begun observing patterns of patients' reactions to the death of their therapist or analyst (Lord, Ritvo, and Solnit, 1978; Shwed, 1980). Concurrently we are exploring aspects of the patient as therapist to the presumably physically healthy analyst, as pioneered by Searles. But, we are yet to document the principles emerging from the process of treating patients when the therapist is significantly ill.

Freud suffered a visually obvious illness that his patients couldn't help but notice. In his letters to friends, he thanked them for not asking repeatedly how he was managing. He apologized to Marie Bonaparte for the factor of his cancer intruding into aspects of analysis of the transference, as presented by Schur (1972). Freud saw the reality of his illness as an intrusion into the psychoanalytic work rather than a part of it. While this is certainly true now with analyses and analytically oriented therapies continuing over five or more years, it is increasingly probable that the analyst will be under significant personal stress at some time during the work with any particular patient. His or her technical abilities are bound to be relatively impaired during such a time and this must then become an unavoidable part of the work.

Fromm-Reichmann (1959) wrote eloquently about the patient's loneliness, the awesome isolation which severely mentally ill patients have suffered, probably without exception. Their current symptom complexes seem to be their individual adaptations to this loneliness. Similarly, she noted, anyone who has faced death also must have endured such loneliness under the impact of diagnosis, situations of war, accident, severe isolation, or whatever. *Anguish* or *anxiety* are terms too vibrant to describe this lostness. I experienced aloneness, but did not feel deserted. But it was the possibility of death and dying that I was facing, my own possible relinquishment of hopes and relationships. I believe that my patients knew this because they had been suicidal or psychotic.

Winnicott (1974), in his paper "Fear of Breakdown," discussed this basic and probably universal human experience, the fear of a return of awesome experiences that occurred before the development in the individual of language and memory:

> The patient needs to "remember" this (that possibly the breakdown has already happened), but it is not possible to remember something that has not yet happened, and this thing of the past has not hap-

pened yet because the patient was not there for it to happen to. The only way to "remember" in this case is for the patient to experience this past thing for the first time in the present, that is to say, in the transference. This past and future thing then becomes a matter of the here and now, and becomes experienced by the patient for the first time [p. 105].

Winnicott then discussed the interrelationship of fear of breakdown and fear of death. This seems to me to approach description of the shattering effect of the silences mentioned previously. Perhaps my patient and I, individually and together, were experiencing that preverbal, prememory terror.

Concurrently, I have come to view patients as individuals who had tried but failed to be therapists to troubled family members as discussed by Stierlin (1969) and Lidz, Fleck, and Cornelison, (1965). The resultant contempt and self-contempt added to their burdens in daily living. If the patient's therapist becomes ill but continues work, perhaps the therapist implies that the patient is, in balance, more constructive than destructive, thus making exploration of the patient's destructiveness less awesome. This was the case with the patient who had sent me the book *For Colored Girls Who Have Considered Suicide When the Rainbow Is Enuf* and the patient whose father had been ill. Each of them said repeatedly that they had been sure I'd stop working with them on my return from sick leave because they'd been so much trouble. I then interpreted their implied *wish* that I had done so. These patients in their initial meetings put out their worst verbally and through action. I, in a way, echoing my analyst, found myself saying, "You seem to think Silver's a quitter," thus conveying that I planned to see the work through to completion. My patients remembered this and reciprocated.

Actually, and this I realized only very recently, I had a very definite notion concerning which patients I would continue treating. I resumed work with those patients who actively had reached out to me, who sent me written personal notes. But that was not the only criterion since I knew I would not resume work with that patient who had actually visited, phoned, and written to me. I returned to those patients who prior to my illness had given me to feel that I was, in balance, a constructive force, a good enough mother in their own life struggles. I stopped treating those who viewed me predominantly as a murderous force from which to escape. I did not resume work with those patients who engendered too much rage or despised and despising feelings for my limited tolerance. The final criterion was that the patients and I had stood a test of time together prior to my absence. Ultimately, it was not the degree of paranoia or impulsiveness or violence that had existed in our previous work, but rather the degree to which at some time we had mutually acknowledged a pleasure in our work together.

These patients came to be constructive loving forces in my life struggle. I do not wish to limit "loving" to tender, gentle nurturing, but include intensely sexual love. This was as evident to me as was the patients' rage and hatred. Here I refer to the highly original and for me personally helpful article by Ellen Greenberger (1965), "Fantasies of Women Confronting Death." The most prominent theme she discovered in a series of projective tests was evidence of unconscious fantasies of death as a lover. She mentioned, as did one of my patients, the Greek myth of Pluto's abduction of Persephone into the underworld. My patient used this myth as a metaphor representing her abduction into psychosis, then as her seduction into forbidden sexuality, and later as metaphor for my being carried off into gloom, despair, and possibly death. I suspect that Pluto may have come to represent her fear–wishes to kidnap and possess me, preserving me in eternal psychotic hell. These metaphors then form a continuum with the unconscious fantasy of death as lover. This fantasy could be seen more easily as part of a universal human effort to find something good or hopeful in any situation, a desperate attempt to form an I–Thou relationship with death, having been raped by fate.

I found, and hope the vignettes conveyed, that the patients' acts of caring carried with them unconscious expressions of hatred. Whether these acts stirred in me feelings of tenderness or rage, either of these feeling states was far more comfortable than the alternative loneliness which would have been mine had I tried gradual recuperation at home, once my family members all resumed their daily work and school activities after that grim summer.

I assume that we all imagine that gradually we are gaining in effectiveness as we continue working and studying. Suddenly to find oneself doing the worst work of one's career, to know that one's first error simply is greeting the patient at the start of the session with that panicky, horrified look one is shocked to see on catching a glimpse of oneself in a mirror: all this contributes to a considerable burden of guilt, anxiety, and rage. I had seen my role as therapist as an agent of diminution of anxiety through gradually evolving shared understanding. Suddenly my very presence became a major source of anxiety. I was sustained by the realization that my patients were far more forgiving of all the resulting errors than was I. They set an example for me of getting through as best one can, and indirectly helped me to become aware of the neurotic components in standards of excellence in the work and to experience the intense helpfulness of simply being together.

Analogously, I struggled in writing this paper against a sense of confusion. At first, it was diffuse and unrecognized, then an embarrassment, then a stubborn confusion, persisting through revision. Finally, I realized that this sense of confusion would always be in the paper. It just needed to be recognized to find its rightful and deserved place. I was then pleased to discover that the roots of the word *confuse* mean "to pour or mix together." This pouring or mixing together then called forth the image of swirling smoke, of my patients and me in the hellish situation of sitting in my office watching as our work together seemed to be going up in smoke.

Now that I am regaining strength and health, I can recall, but thankfully cannot recapture, my mental state those first months back. It has faded like any experience of pain. But I do remember vividly that my patients were striving to work with me, working to get through the sessions, then to get something from them, then to reestablish the former equilibrium. That is, they worked to rebuild the holding environment and I struggled to assist them. I observed their efforts gratefully, and am confident that they perceived my being grateful. I have a special fondness for the patients who saw me through those months. We are like veterans who fought together at the front lines. Sometimes, when they reminisce about those times, I imagine we are like ex-G.I.'s sitting over beers at a local bar. And I, like a returning veteran, feel that my more traditional work with my newly assigned patients is bland, pale stuff by comparison. They have the burden, which they may well sense, of being thereby second-best. But this too seems to be resolving.

All this took place in the holding environment of an established and stable institution. Without such a group or setting, the therapist must struggle in comparative isolation, burdened with the guilt and apprehension engendered by the dramatic decline in his or her effectiveness caused by severe illness. These feelings then make it more difficult for him or her to resume the work and thereby to obtain the sustenance which dyadic work provides.

References

Casey, J. (1978), A psychiatrist's experience of terror. *Psychiat. Ann.*, 8:250–254.

Cousins, N. (1979), *Anatomy of an Illness, as Perceived by the Patient.* New York: W. W. Norton.

Dahlberg, C., & Jaffe, J. (1977), *Stroke: A Doctor's Personal Story of His Recovery.* New York: W. W. Norton.

Eissler, K. (1955), *The Psychiatrist and the Dying Patient.* New York: International Universities Press.

Fiore, N. (1979), Fighting cancer: One patient's perspective. *New Eng. J. Med.*, 300:284–290.

Fromm-Reichmann, F. (1959), On loneliness. In: *Psychoanal-*

ysis and Psychotherapy: Selected Papers. Chicago: University of Chicago Press.

Greenberger, E. (1965), Fantasies of women confronting death. *Consult. J. Psychol.*, 29:252–260.

Hägglund, T.-B. (1978), *Dying: A Psychoanalytic Study with Special Reference to Individual Creativity and Defensive Organization.* New York: International Universities Press.

Joseph, F. (1962), Transference and countertransference in the case of a dying patient. *Psychoanal.*, 49:21–24.

Kübler-Ross, E. (1969), *On Death and Dying.* New York: Macmillan.

Lidz, T., Fleck, S., & Cornelison, A. (1965), *Schizophrenia and the Family.* New York: International Universities Press.

Lord, R., Ritvo, S., & Solnit, A. (1978), Patients' reactions to the death of the psychoanalyst. *Internat. J. Psycho-Anal.*, 59:189–197.

Pearson, L., ed. (1969), *Death and Dying: Current Issues in the Treatment of the Dying Person.* Cleveland: The Press of the Case Western Reserve University.

Rodin, E. (1980), The reality of death experiences, a personal perspective. *J. Nerv. & Ment. Dis.*, 168:259–263.

Schur, M. (1972), *Freud: Living and Dying.* New York: International Universities Press.

Searles, H. (1975), The patient as therapist to his analyst. In: *Tactics and Techniques in Psychoanalytic Therapy*, Vol. 2, ed. P. Giovacchini. New York: Jason Aronson, pp. 95–151.

Shange, N. (1975), *For Colored Girls Who Have Considered Suicide/When The Rainbow Is Enuf.* New York: Macmillan.

Shwed, H. (1980), When a psychiatrist dies. *J. Nerv. & Ment. Dis.*, 168:275–278.

Stierlin, H. (1969), *Conflict and Reconciliation: A Study in Human Relations and Schizophrenia.* New York: Science House.

Weisman, A. (1974), *The Realization of Death.* New York: Jason Aronson.

Winnicott, D. W. (1974), Fear of breakdown. *Internat. Rev. Psycho-Anal.*, 1:103–107.

Further Reflections

Over the past eleven years, I have become younger, moving from the psychological age of a premature octogenarian. In the year following my surgery, when treatment outcome was uncertain, I felt a bitter rage seeing gray-haired couples in a restaurant or shopping mall. I resented their years as if they had stolen mine. Gradually, I regained aspects of the buoyant optimism which accompanies "normal denial," and now have regained my chronological age. My doctors have put my current prognosis right there with anyone else's, whereas my original cohort had a five-year survival rate of less than 15 percent, of whom many were desperately ill at the time of that large study.

I was surprised at my intense resistance to reviewing my 1982 paper. I had put the experience behind me. Perhaps during much of my long personal analysis, I have attempted quite literally to put the experience "behind me," into my analyst back there. I lived my anxiety in the sessions, probably in part attempting to give to him my apprehension that I might feel young again, experiencing only neurotic anxiety.

Even before my physical illness, I had dimly in mind the agenda that he was to be vulnerable for me, and was to wish to rely upon me, as if I were then the stronger of the two. A children's book that I especially like (and one I had referred to often in my analysis before physical illness struck) depicts this in metaphor. William Steig's *Amos and Boris* involves a spunky mouse, Amos, who builds a sailing boat, following instructions in a library book. He sets out to sea, taking along sextant, yo-yo, compass, and playing cards. One night, while lying on his back, admiring the phosphorescent night sky, he rolls off the deck and watches in dismay as his boat scuttles out of sight. (I enthusiastically refer the reader to R. Waugaman's paper [1987] "Falling Off the Couch.")

Amos treads water, wonders what it is like to drown, and then, to make matters worse, it starts to rain. He is saved and returned home by a sounding whale, Boris, who is traveling to a whale convention off the Ivory Coast of Africa. Years later, a storm washes Boris up on shore, breaded with sand, near Amos's home. Amos repays the favor, getting two elephants to roll the beached Boris safely into the ocean. They part tearfully.

I had entered analysis with the clumsily stated narcissistic goal of "maximizing my creativity." Now I recognize my underlying objective was "minimizing my destructiveness." I had tried to see myself as a harmless sweet young thing, traumatized by an anxious and temperamental mother. But what barred more effective use of my creative efforts was my working rather frenetically trying to convince myself I was not as destructive as my unfocused fantasies would have me be. As I owned my destructive potential, my constructive efforts became more efficient: One can't make an omelette without breaking eggs.

Initially, I had told my analyst I needed "reparenting." My father had died almost exactly one year before I telephoned my analyst to set up an appointment. It took me a few years to recognize this anniversary phenomenon. Even when I was very young, my father was predicting that he would suffer repeated heart attacks. Yet, when he actually did suffer his first attack, he kept this a secret from his two physician children. Our mother told us after his death that he didn't want to interfere with our busy schedules. His seemingly sudden death barred me from any possibility of helpfulness or harmfulness. That experience inextricably influences my views on the topic of this book. But I am *not* recommending that the analyst who has suffered a heart attack tell his or her patients about it. Instead, I would recommend we stay alert to the themes depicted above: the patient's strongly ambivalent wish that we become sick, thus providing an opportunity for the two to grapple with the patient's simultaneous wishes to nurture and terrors of destroying his or her parents in the transference.

Over the years of my analysis, I have attempted to convert my analyst into my father, who then would be preoccupied with apprehension lest he suffer such a fate. It was not in my script that I would be the one in jeopardy (although *Amos and Boris* conveys otherwise). I have been like Freud's joke in *Jokes and Their Relation to the Unconscious* (1905), quoted here by Thomas Wolman (chapter 12), "If one of us dies, I shall move to Paris." Somehow, fate had played a mean trick on me. I wasn't "old enough" for all these troubles, which were "supposed" to happen to people much older than I.

My private fury toward those a generation older represented displacements from my analyst whom I dreaded subjecting to the full intensity of my bitter rage. I am "undyingly" grateful that he did not decree that my situation of suffering a life-threatening illness made me unanalyzable. He did not write me off. Nor did my boss at Chestnut Lodge, Dexter Bullard, Jr., who could similarly have shunted me aside, to do work which was not directly patient-related.

At the time I wrote the original paper I had just begun analytic institute training. Even though I delivered the paper at the annual Chestnut Lodge Symposium, to an audience of about four hundred mental health professionals, the vast majority of whom work in the Washington area, none of my control cases was to learn of my illness, nor did they subsequently discover it, even though some had regular associations with people who probably had heard that paper, and each of whom had access to the professional literature.

Thus, I have been impressed with both the community's respect for the anonymity of the analyst and the patients' desire to create an image of a strong vibrant analyst who is not self-preoccupied. I wonder how I may have colluded with them in keeping their awarenesses of my times of difficulty off-limits for their associations. Perhaps my best defense was a good offense. I have been chided by more than one of my patients for "reading things into" their associations, interpreting their anger, which they experienced as diffuse, as directed at least in part toward me. I sometimes interpreted their seeing me as seeming too weak for the task at times when these feelings were not yet clearly in their awareness.

Now, patients are seeking me out for analytic treatment *because* they have heard that I had come through a harrowing experience of illness. I am interested to see how this feature of their selection impinges on the unfolding of their analyses.

Within the Chestnut Lodge community, the staff made a concerted effort to help me put this episode of severe uncertainty out of the picture in the work with my current patients. Once it seemed very probably that I had recovered, the nursing staff began telling patients on a unit where a newly admitted patient had been assigned to me, not to burden that new patient with the information that I had been very sick. There was a *community* consensus that I now needed not the direct support and sympathy they had given me, but that I would be more supported by being seen simply as recovered.

The only unit where patients violated this has been the one specializing in borderline personality disorder, which I experience as a hornet's nest. On two occasions, one and then another of my schizophrenic patients has improved to the point of being able to socialize with someone from that unit. In each case, the patient was told I had been very sick, and might become sick again, and might die. My patients became gradually more disorganized, self-defeating, and enraged, then were able to reveal what had happened and to ask for some information regarding my situation. I have said that I went through a rough time, and am now out of the woods. Each patient's regression promptly abated, and they resumed their prior level of functioning. Again, were that not the case, their regressions might have deepened.

With one exception, I am no longer treating any of the patients with whom I worked during the phase of chronic uncertainty about my own outcome. But the three women whose treatments were referred to in the paper have kept in touch with me, and each of them has married. The woman who wrote me the letter asking if Irate Irene had delivered the vanilla milkshake is now living in her home state far away. She had reminded me of her dream that "over the mountain, across the sea, there's a boy awaiting for me." And that proved to be the case. She is now helping her husband in his business, as well as attending a mental health center regularly. She at least intermittently is quite delusional. She contacts me when the hallucinated creatures are stealing her glasses or food or pencils, or are putting words in other people's mouths, but not supplying her with words.

The woman who sent me Ntozake Shange's book has now embarked on her own business venture, assisted by her husband. She is no longer in therapy; we reached a mutually agreed upon termination. Now I have the pleasure of occasionally being a customer of hers; she does not give me bargains.

The then eighteen-year-old girl, whose illness emerged in the context of denied grief over the death of a relative, moved back home after we had worked together for seven years. I had wanted her to continue with me, but she felt strongly that she wanted to have a more constructive relationship with her parents than had been possible during the years of her illness. She worked for a few years as a licensed practical nurse, caring for the terminally ill. I felt guilty about this, feeling that she was doing penance, if she did experience herself as having left me in the lurch. She is now pursuing training as a registered nurse. She contacts me from time to time. She had most forcefully resisted the strongly stated counsel of her administrative psychiatrist that she allow herself to be reassigned to a healthy therapist. Perhaps she knew that my illness had created an opportunity for her to rework her experience with the intensely loved and hated deceased relative.

On return from a two-month sick leave, I had met with the Director of Psychotherapy, with the agenda of reducing my clinical obligations by half, that is, treating three rather than six patients, still scheduling four sessions per week. One patient worked with his interim therapist, having only just met me the day before calamity struck; another was soon to move out of the hospital, to a Washington suburb where his interim therapist had an office. The third was ragingly violent, had responded well to the formidable male therapist assigned as his "interim." The first of these three had wanted to return to me, and I told him it wasn't possible. The other two really wanted to make the switch. The three women adamantly chose to stay with me.

The most startling misunderstanding of my paper has come from readers who feel that I recommended that analysts reveal to their patients when they become ill. These readers have similarly misread Searles' (1975) paper, "The Patient as Therapist to His Analyst." I did not, and do not, recommend disclosure or role reversal. I was describing the situation of severe illness occurring in a member of a very special *community*. The analyst in private practice is subjected to a similarly special and quite opposite *absence* of community. One cannot readily generalize from one situation to the other.

However, I believe we use massive denial when we believe that we are effective in keeping our personal suffering secret. Our patients, by their very dependence on us, have a heightened scrutiny, both conscious and especially unconscious, of our aura of well-being.

I am reminded of a highly esteemed analyst who kept working while knowing he had an untreatable terminal illness. Some of his colleagues, myself included, knew of his plight and his wish that the information remain confidential. Each time I arrived at his office door, I saw on his face an expression of terror, reminiscent of Edvard Munch's "The Scream," the same look I had seen on my mother's face during her terminal illness, and the same look I had been appalled to see on my own, when I came upon my image suddenly, when walking by a mirror. My colleague would then reflexively assume a look of bland neutrality, or pleasure at greeting me. I was certain that his patients had also seen this look of terror.

His presentations of ongoing clinical material indicated to me that his patients were unconsciously absolutely aware of the situation and by their specific regressive actions were trying desperately to get the situation out in the open, or to have their own efforts in his behalf recognized in some way.

I am not suggesting that he should have told them, but rather that he should have stopped denying the effectiveness of his secretiveness. And yet, paradoxically, I recall visits my parents made to my home in the year after my father's first heart attack about which he, too, was secretive. I knew he looked tired, even weary, and annoyingly preoccupied. I felt sad that he was aging but never guessed he was ill.

Also, I am not implying that the terminally ill analyst should have been forced or encouraged to stop working. One of his patients, who seemed to regress during the time of his final illness, when no longer in analysis, subsequently had to endure a comparable situation of chronic life-threatening illness. The patient endured the situation remarkably well. It is impossible to assess to what extent this strength followed from the work with the terminally ill doctor. I disagree with the statement that analysis stops when the analyst becomes seriously ill. The analysis changes.

I feel strongly that the analyst who thinks she is being effective in keeping her own precarious physical (and by extension, mental) incapacities and uncertainties secret from the patients is operating with considerable denial. Denial, a primitive defense mechanism, keeps close company with projection and projective identification, all of which are weighty baggage as we try to "hover evenly." Fromm-Reichmann (1953) stated:

> Life ends with death, the timing and causes of which are unpredictable. This fact is, actually and symbolically, the last expression of the fact that there are unknown forces which govern our lives. A psychotherapist who does not know and integrate this fact and who dreams about complete emotional security, an unreal attainment in life, cannot guide his [her] mental patients to wholesome, constructive testing and evaluation of reality or to a constructive adjustment to it. In other words, acceptance of emotional insecurity, which is the acceptance of a certain amount of anxiety in the lives of the psychiatrist and his [her] patients, is one of the constructive forces in the psychotherapeutic process [p. 101].

She elaborated on these ideas later (1955) saying:

> Awareness of his [her] anxiety, not freedom from or denial of it, and sufficient emotional security to accept and handle it constitute the philosophical attitude toward anxiety to be expected of a compentent, mature psychiatrist. . . . A state of mind permanently free of anxiety is a utopianism for the psychotherapist by the same token that it is for anyone else [p. 317].

I resumed my private practice quite a few weeks after returning to the Lodge. This is very significant, in that my office is in my home, while the Lodge is almost an hour's drive away. I couldn't imagine whom to tell what, and amazingly, never considered the possibility of seeking supervisory advice. I made some clumsy statements, having mentally reviewed alternatives so many times that I came to believe I had already actually talked with particular patients. Nor did anyone in my professional community volunteer or suggest supervising me, although I received enormous personal support from my friends, most of whom are mental health professionals. They offered professional counsel, too, from their experience working with the physically ill.

Even though I was in supervision regarding my Lodge work, and there were ample opportunities to talk with colleagues about clinical matters, I was unable to connect my private practice life with my hospital life. There were no other patients in my hospital or private practice with whom I elected to discontinue work. Only one patient chose to terminate her weekly psychotherapeutic work with me. She had asked her husband, a doctor, to find out what was going on, and he did so, with apparent accuracy. She came to her first session after the interruption to say firmly that she had too many other burdens at this time. Her mother was sick, and she had to visit and help her, and that was all she wanted to handle right then.

There is a metaphoric wall around the private practitioner's office. This wall is discernably in place in some of the papers in this book, most notably for me in Firestein's paper, in which he says that things worked out best for those patients who were told by a family member of the death of the analyst. We emphasize the need for anonymity in our life's work, and yet would have our families be the ones to tell our patients that the work has come to an abrupt halt. Where is the professional family at that moment of need; are we all too busy maintaining our own walls of denial?

Perhaps I had not thought of seeking supervision because of the aspect of risk to my private practice. Firestein suggests that we each entrust a couple of our colleagues with the responsibility of removing us from work if they see us as unfit. As I imagine whom I might choose for this, I am struck by my eliminating from possibility everyone whom I know well.

Alternatively, I suggest we consider a system of on-going supervision, continuing right through our analytic careers. This would seem feasible if supervisors were directed by the analytic societies to keep the actual material confidential, as is the situation for training analyses. Further, I suggest there be a stipulation that the supervisor *not* take over control of the supervisee's professional life, just as we strive not to do so with our patients.

I would like to refer the reader to Samuel Thompson's case report, "Prognosis, Hopeless," (1966). He illustrates the surprisingly positive outcome in a patient who had been written off. We should avoid determining the professional destiny of our colleagues, but should strive to collaborate in a further understanding of the human condition. Additionally, if such a system were in place, the supervisor would be the logical person to notify the analyst's patients in the event of his or her sudden severe illness or death, stepping in as "interim" or arranging this as seems indicated. Perhaps my suggestion aims toward making our institutes increasingly effective as our professional communities, a task that is nearly impossible when we each work in solitary offices.

The subject of privacy regarding the ill or healthy analyst requires its own study. Many may feel I was wrong to write explicitly about features of my personal history and psychodynamics, that this will influence in inexplicable ways the work with future patients who may read this. However, I am partly convinced that the patient is far more influenced by the analyst who is present in the patient's sessions than by the material gleaned from a printed page, written under the analyst's name, addressing the unknown reader.

We need to review the history of the effects of illness in the analyst in shaping the structure of psychoanalytic practice. While we approached a few psychoanalytic historians, they declined to take on this assignment. Freud's reaction to his father's death, and then to his own chronic, evident, and painful illness have affected our style of working in ways yet to be defined (Schur, 1972; Krull, 1986). It was not until July 1982 that coincidentally four papers on this subject appeared in analytic journals.

Some of the literature on death and dying tends to glorify the survivors, describing them as having found in the process of confrontation with death some firmer and more substantial philosophy of life, and a quest for knowledge less neurotically encumbered by immediate competitive strivings. I know I have gotten nervier. I don't mind confronting someone who just happens to be a few years older than I am, since so recently I experienced myself as quite a few years older than my chronological age. But this does not constitute a philosophy. Raft and Andresen (1986) describe an analysand whom they saw as having undergone something of a saintly transformation following a near-death out-of-body experience. I found the report intriguing, but have not myself been so transformed.

I have found that, once robbed of health, I can less easily separate myself from "them," the sick weaklings. Once we become ill, we are left to grapple wth countertransference toward this new patient who neither pays us nor leaves at the end of the session—our new sick self.

References

Freud, S. (1905), Jokes and Their Relation to the Unconscious. *Standard Edition*, 8. London: Hogarth Press, 1960.

Fromm-Reichmann, F. (1953), Personality of the psychotherapist and the doctor–patient relationship. In: *Psychoanalysis and Psychotherapy: Selected Papers of Frieda Fromm-Reichmann*, ed. D. Bullard. Chicago: University of Chicago Press, 1959.

——— (1955), Psychiatric aspects of anxiety. In: *Psychoanalysis and Psychotherapy: Selected Papers of Frieda Fromm-Reichmann*, ed. D. Bullard. Chicago: University of Chicago Press, 1959.

Krull, M. (1986), *Freud and His Father*. New York: W. W. Norton.

Raft, D., & Andresen, J. (1986), Transformations in self-understanding after near-death experiences. *Contemp. Psychoanal.,* 22:319–346.

Schur, M. (1972), *Freud: Living and Dying*. New York: International Universities Press.

Searles, H. (1975), The patient as therapist to his analyst. In: *Countertransference and Related Subjects: Selected Papers*. New York: International Universities Press, pp. 380–459.

Silver, A.-L. (1986), Discussion of "Transformation in self-understanding after near-death experience," by D. Raft and J. Andresen. *Contemp. Psychoanal.,* 22:346–356.

Steig, W. (1971), *Amos and Boris*. New York: Farrar, Straus & Giroux.

Thompson, S. (1966), Prognosis, hopeless. In: *Psychoanalysis and Pyschosis*, ed. A.-L. Silver. Madison, CT: International Universities Press, 1989, pp. 271–286.

——— (1977), A sequel. In: *Psychoanalysis and Psychosis*, ed. A.-L. Silver. Madison, CT: International Universities Press, 1989, pp. 271–286.

Waugaman, R. (1987), Falling off the couch. *J. Amer. Psychoanal. Assn.*, 35:861–876.

8

Keeping the Analysis Intact When the Analyst Has Suffered a Catastrophic Illness: Clinical Considerations

RICHARD LASKY, Ph.D.

One Friday, after my workday was finished, I fell seriously ill. With no prior warning I suddenly found myself in a life-threatening situation and by that evening I was hospitalized in an intensive care unit where I would spend a few days being stabilized in preparation for a surgical intervention. It was fortunate that I was able to contact my patients the next day without having to use an intermediary. One patient was away on business and I chose to leave a message on her answering machine, reasoning that whatever I had to say—no matter how disturbing to receive it on a machine—was better communicated by me than by a stranger. It was necessary for me to cancel all appointments with no preparation either for me or for my patients, and to reschedule them for a time three months in the future. I must admit to having been rather at a loss as to how to address the special issues of clinical management raised by this sudden and unique situation, in part because I was stunned and disorganized by my personal sit-

I am very much indebted to Dr. Judith Lasky for her thoughtful and thorough criticism of this essay. Her help in the preparation of this manuscript was invaluable.

uation, and in part because I was not then familiar with the literature on illness in the analyst. Indeed, as has been described elsewhere in this book, there is only a very limited literature available on this topic. I was no exception to the rule (also documented in other chapters) that analysts do not seem to concern themselves with this material unless forced to do so by necessity. Thus, I had to rely, in a highly stressful situation, only on my general clinical skills as a psychoanalyst.

Having had neither preparation nor any special knowledge at my disposal, I chose to act as much as was possible in accordance with the general "rules of thumb" of my therapeutic orientation (which is "mainstream" or "classical" Freudian). From my subsequent reading of the literature, and from discussions with colleagues, I have formed the impression that this is the way most clinicians react when confronted with catastrophic illness. The novelty of the situation does not ordinarily lead one to novel approaches but, rather, seems to reinforce one's traditional way of working. How should we understand this? It seems not unreasonable to assume that under extreme stress one finds some comfort in the familiar; and, in addition, that the familiar serves as a defense and exerts significant counterforce to the impairments in one's judgments that are often triggered by having become rapidly and severely ill. As discussed by Dewald (chapter 4), and Abend (chapter 5), and by Schwartz (1987), one's technical equilibrium is severely stressed by a catastrophic illness. A resort to the familiar, most especially if one recognizes but cannot control a deficit in one's clinical judgment, is not necessarily to be understood as being maladaptively regressive. Certainly it need not be seen as problematic so long as it is not done in a purely reflexive fashion. In addition (and this is no small consideration), there is no need, automatically, to create a novel therapeutic intervention simply because a situation may be highly unusual. Thus, while sometimes a sign of rigidity, the analyst's conservatism need not necessarily be seen as evidence of inflexibility. Serving a variety of defensive purposes, it also serves to protect the integrity of the psychoanalytic situation; and if it is true that increased conservatism is a reflection of the stress the analyst is under, it is also true that it reflects some ways that ego autonomy and superego maturity can remain undaunted by the trying circumstances. I make this point because I have been impressed by how difficult it is to maintain an analytic milieu under the pressure of such massive narcissistic injury to the analyst, and I am as interested in what makes it possible as I am in what can tend to get in the way. I will have more to say about the stress-related complications for the analyst, but let us first examine what I chose to tell my patients, and why.

The general "rule of thumb" in the Freudian model is to be as noninformative as possible about oneself and one's circumstances. First, this model presupposes that the patient can tolerate a considerable amount of ambiguity and frustration. Second, while acknowledging that analysts are not able to control what patients can independently learn about them they are obligated, nevertheless, to the extent that they *can* guide participation, not to inhibit the production of fantasy and transference material by informing patients about their personal realities. Ordinarily this model does not present a problem when the analyst implements it in circumstances which are unremarkable. But it may be considerably more difficult to put into practice when the unusual, the unexpected, and the disruptive takes command of significant aspects of the situation. In deciding what to tell patients I first needed to ask myself how much each person needed to know, given their differing abilities to tolerate ambiguity and, more importantly, frustration. Following the model, I should only have said: "I am canceling your sessions, beginning immediately, and will resume sessions with you on *(giving the date of my return to work, three months later)*." I could not then, nor can I now, imagine interrupting an analysis in that way. I find it hard to imagine any patient accepting such treatment. Theoretically, if the patient has sufficient ego strength he should be able to tolerate such a minimal intervention and he will know that the analyst would never behave in a totally irrational or cavalier fashion with him. But in reality, I can only imagine behaving that way if I were going to be there the next day so as to start analyzing. It is hard, except in theory, to imagine anyone who could tolerate such a sudden, unexpected, interruption, followed by a three-month hiatus in treatment, without some better explanation.

The concept of the "average" analytic patient includes considerable ego autonomy, superego maturity, and resistance to reinstinctualization in the patient's character. And while this is undoubtedly the case for many patients we would not wish to confuse the concept of an "average" analytic patient with the concept of an "ideal" analytic patient (who could tolerate *any* amount of frustration and uncertainty). Just as importantly, we must be aware that there is no such creature as a "standard" analytic patient to whom all the "rules" of technique could be applied uniformly in "set-piece" fashion. Our theoretical model of the "average" analytic patient is modal and hypothetical; in the same way that we recognize Freud's depiction of the oedipal conflict as an idealized theoretical construct which is always subject to considerable individual variation, we must also recognize that the architecture of the analytic undertaking is not unalterable and fixed but varies considerably from patient to patient. Therefore, I found myself asking for each patient: "How much do they need to know, and how much can they tolerate not knowing, in order to preserve the analytic relationship intact while I am going to be away for three months?"

If one looks at this question abstractly it seems a simple enough task to assess each patient's ability to tolerate little or no information. But a question arises as to whether an analyst can be as objective as usual under such disorganizing circumstances. A catastrophic illness that threatens the analyst's life and disrupts the treatment of patients so drastically is a narcissistic injury of major importance. It raises many narcissistic conflicts (including exhibitionistic conflicts); engenders considerable guilt about the abandonment of patients; intolerably sharpens castration anxieties (and other phallic fantasies as well as prephallic body damage fantasies); exacerbates long-standing countertransference difficulties;

heightens conflicts about dependency needs; and is so disruptive that it may interfere with the analyst's ability to objectively determine the patient's needs and to separate them from his own.[1] Thus, we can see that the task is not simple, and it may even be impossible in some cases. At the very least the analyst must seriously question his judgment and include the possibility that he may not be in a position to assess his patients' abilities and tolerances objectively.

Given all these considerations, which were immediately clear to me (but not in as much depth as they would have for me after a few years of reflection), I found myself in the position of not feeling secure about my ability to objectively determine each patient's strengths and needs and, at the same time, recognizing that it would be inappropriate to ignore their differences and retreat into an abstract theoretical stance about neutrality and abstinence. It occurred to me that there could be a modification in the model that might not undermine the basic treatment paradigm, much in the way that Eissler (1953) developed his ideas about parameters. I asked myself whether it was possible to give patients *some* information about the interruption while, at the same time, withholding enough information so that patients would be able to reshape the experience in conformity with their inner needs. I also needed to develop a compromise that would be equally applicable to *all* my patients since I had such strong reservations about my objectivity. My solution was to give patients about the same amount of information (actually, just a little bit less) as I used to open this chapter. My overriding consideration was to give (to my patients and to the reader) enough information to make the situation comprehensible without being more self-revealing than seemed necessary. On that Saturday

[1]I have elaborated these conflicts and their effects on the analyst's functioning in "Catastrophic Illness in the Analyst and the Analyst's Emotional Reactions to It," presented at a scientific meeting of the Institute for Psychoanalytic Training and Research, on April 21, 1989, and at the fall meeting of the American Psychoanalytic Association, December 1989. The manuscript is in press (*International Journal of Psycho-Analysis,* 1990, Vol. 70), and I am indebted to Drs. Sander Abend and Theodore Jacobs for their thoughtful comments. The integration of their insightful discussions of that paper can be clearly observed in this essay.

I told patients that I had fallen ill unexpectedly and needed to cancel sessions, beginning Monday; and that I would be having some surgery, which I was told would involve a three-month recovery period. I apologized for the suddenness and inconvenience, and said that I would see them again on such-and-such a date (*giving the date and time of their next session, three months in the future*).

One of my concerns was that giving patients the specific information that I was ill would channel (or even dictate) their fantasies too narrowly, and although I do think that this does ordinarily take place to some extent, it is not inevitable. One patient steadfastly refused to believe that I was ill and insisted that I was going on an extended vacation for which I needed a plausible excuse. I was concerned as to whether it was necessary to apologize for the suddenness with which I had to interrupt their treatments, and for the inconvenience it would cause them not to have analytic hours for three months.

There is always a tension between the ordinary rules of courtesy and the respectfulness which every patient is entitled to, and some of the technical requirements of analytic treatment. For example, we make an explicit agreement with patients not to answer certain questions when we think it is in their best therapeutic interests. The agreement is made explicit when we explain our intention not to respond on the first occasion in which it seems appropriate. Even when the pressures of transference cause the patient temporarily to forget, there is an unconscious area of the ego in which there is a clear recognition that we have not suspended the common rules of courtesy in a cavalier or disrespectful fashion. Every time we do something socially unorthodox (like sitting behind the patient while the patient reclines on a couch) it has the original agreement of the patient; and it is on the basis of our patient's understanding that we are using an artificial device to implement their progress that they acquiesce to behavior which, in other circumstances, would be unacceptable to them. Suddenly interrupting a treatment which they had every right to assume would be continuous, and being away for three months outside of regularly agreed upon vacation times, is not a standard part of analytic technique, has never been explained to them, and has never received either their tacit or explicit agreement. It is a disruption, not part of analytic technique, and reflects the personal requirements of the analyst rather than the needs of the patient or the demands of treatment. Based on this reasoning I decided that a neutrally expressed apology, without going overboard, was warranted. This is not an event, after all, which takes place within the analysis but is, in fact, imposed by the analyst (even if the analyst has imposed it involuntarily) without regard to the best interests of the patient. I think it would be deleterious to the analysis for the analyst to make believe it is just another facet of the treatment since it does not even include the implicit agreement of the patient. It certainly is possible for the masochistic needs of the analyst to be met in making an apology, but less likely to be the case when the apology is given in a "matter-of-fact" way.

It is interesting to note that not a single patient asked me what was wrong with me, and I have a few ideas why that occurred in the way it did. First of all, I think that they were very much taken by surprise, and if they had had a second or a third opportunity to speak with me perhaps they would have asked. Second, and this I know from what happened when the analyses were resumed, some patients chose not to ask so that they could fantasize the worst possible situation for me, and others chose not to ask so that they could deny to themselves the seriousness of my situation. Third, I had in effect prepared a little "speech" for them and I think that they not only picked up my anxiety in it but that it also gave them the tacit message not to force me outside of the boundaries that *I* had decided upon. And finally, my patients do not have the expectation that I will reveal anything about my personal life. Insofar as their character structures and the quality of their transferences permit, my patients *will* ask questions of me, but their experience is that, in response, I analyze the questions rather than provide answers. Both transferential forces, and force of habit, may have led them not to question me about my circumstances when I originally called them. I might add, parenthetically, that they felt no such compunction when I returned and, although many then expressed a wish to know what had happened to me, none indicated a belief that they were realistically entitled to that information.

I might, at this point, describe a clinical situation, and then a possible clinical situation, that raises some very interesting questions about informing patients of the details of one's situation. Two analytic siblings, Mr. X. and Dr. Y., both worked at the same institution. They never came across one another at my office but they discovered at work that they both had the same analyst. When I fell ill Mr. X., who was intensely rivalrous, told Dr. Y. that he had, through personal sources, found out what was wrong with me. I was, he told Dr. Y., suffering from a progressive neurological disorder which would cripple me totally within three months and which would so severely affect my mental functioning that within a year I would be completely demented. None of this was true, as Dr. Y. found out, when she frantically began to make inquiries in the professional community about what had actually happened to me. But suppose she had not been in the same field as me and that she had no way to find out what my true condition was. Suppose that upon my return she was in a panic about this, and wanted to know if it was true. What then might my posture have been about giving out factual information? Should it be different from what I have thus far suggested? In that situation, which is only hypothetical (and it is hard to be certain that one would behave in a particular way when things are only make-believe), I think I would opt not to provide any clarifying information. My reasoning is as follows: first of all, Dr. Y. had very considerable ego strength, and it had always been my belief, before my illness, that she was capable of functioning well even in the presence of extreme anxiety, deprivation, and uncertainty. I would interject at this point my expectation that evaluations of the patient which are consistent with one's *prior* assessments have some possibility of being more reliable than evaluations that change during a serious illness; but they should still be treated with at least a modicum of caution. Next, I would have to ask myself what Dr. Y. was doing with the evidence before her very eyes. According to Mr. X., I should have been crippled and well on my way to being demented. If Dr. Y. saw that I had no physical or mental sequelae to my illness, why would she be asking me if what Mr. X. said was true? In the light of such disconfirming evidence it would be naive to respond factually. Her question would seem to have a rather complex psychological meaning which would deserve, and require, analysis rather than information. A response about the actuality of my condition would deprive her of the opportunity for an analytic advance.

One might ask what makes this hypothetical case any different from the initial decision about how to inform patients about the interruption, and why one should act differently in either instance.[2] I think that there are two very significant differences. First, although the interruption and the false information she was given were events which were not part of the analysis proper, the question *to me in a session* which ignored something which she could perceive and evaluate, *also in a session,* classifies the event as something which was now occurring *in* the analysis and not outside of it. And that being the case, analyzing the material (as opposed to giving any information) seems clearly to be indicated. Second, when the analyst falls ill the analysis becomes suspended; in some cases, for a considerable span of time. In the interim patients have no opportunity to work through the fantasies and conflicts which are generated or intensified by the situation. A total lack of information at the onset of a crisis, which then exists in the absence of any analytically moderating influences for many months, can lead to a disorganizing regression with which one has absolutely no opportunity to constructively work. But when a patient raises a question, no matter how unrealistic, in the context of an ongoing analytic procedure (which is the case after the analyst has returned to work), even the most malignant fantasies and transference configurations have the opportunity of becoming accessible and understood, precisely because the procedure *is* available for

[2]I am indebted to Sander Abend, M.D., for raising this question.

that purpose. In that case there is no need to resort to treating the question nonanalytically.

Thus far I have been addressing the question of what (if anything) and how we should tell our patients about our situation. These are the most frequently raised questions in the literature. Another important question has to do with how we work with the event after the analysis *has* been resumed. Under ordinary circumstances, ignoring for the moment our need to consider the disequilibrium the analyst feels at his return to work, one can maintain an analytic stance and work with the event with no alteration of one's technical approach. The patient expresses curiosity, concern, or other interests regarding the illness, and the interruption of treatment; and more often than not, this comes up almost immediately upon one's return. Assuming that patients do not return to the treatment in a decompensated condition there would appear to be no rationale for engaging in anything other than the model of psychoanalysis in use before the interruption of treatment. I began to touch on that question in the (hypothetical) case of Dr. Y. but would like to focus my discussion on a frequently raised facet of this question, which is, whether or not the analyst should introduce material about the interruption, or his illness, if the patient acts like it never happened.

Before moving to that question I would like to make some brief comments about the disequilibrium the analyst experiences, since it plays a powerful role in influencing his perceptions, thoughts, feelings, and conduct. It is not always easy, or even possible, for an analyst who has been through a catastrophic illness to readily maintain a comfortably analytic stance on his return to work. I mentioned earlier in this chapter some of the narcissistic and exhibitionistic conflicts that can be triggered and which then interfere with the analyst's judgments about what patients need to know. The problem, obviously, does not exist only when one is initially informing patients about the interruption. In addition, there are regressive needs and dependency conflicts which surface in these circumstances, and which can be enacted with one's patients. Given these pressures, one might solicit and reject, at the very same time, the sympathies of one's patients. Or one might feel threatened, insecure, and guilty (if patients trigger off one's own unresolved or irrational questions about one's analytic adequacy) when they inquire, even with some sympathy, whether the analyst really feels ready to be back at work. Callous and rejecting patients, and patients who are openly sadistic about one's situation, may elicit a level of counter-reaction from the analyst (as Silver reports) of equal or greater magnitude. This can be personally stressful, and possibly so disruptive that it can make it impossible for the analyst to conduct the treatment even-handedly and with neutrality. Peculiar physical sensations while at work which ordinarily might be ignored can throw the analyst into a panic if he cannot be sure whether or not it signals a relapse, or it may serve as an unwelcome reminder of painful and traumatic procedures connected with his illness. To say that these may be distracting would be the height of understatement. I think it is also true that analysts are under different kinds of stresses depending on whether they return to work from an illness from which they have been completely cured, or from a chronic illness that is not currently acute but could become so again, or with visible signs of their illness, or with a permanent disability. And it is also worth noting that the psychic trauma lasts considerably longer than the physical illness and may exert a substantial influence even years after the analyst is back to work.[3] Although I have by no means exhausted this subject matter I would now like to return to the technical question I posed in the last paragraph.

Much of the literature on illness considers its effects on dynamic psychotherapy (Adler, 1972; Chermin, 1976; Rosenbaum, 1977; Meissner and Wohlauer, 1978–1979; Dahlberg, 1980; Gilveber and Simon, 1981; Cohen, 1983; Stoudemire, 1983; Goldberg, 1984; Kriechman, 1984; Lindner, 1984).

[3]I recently found this to be the case when a patient informed me that she found she was able to regulate my responsiveness by talking about illness or injuries; I was totally unaware of the fact that, despite the passage of a number of years since my illness, I "seemed to perk up" when she described an illness or an injury to herself or to one of her family members.

Within the literature that specifically addresses classical psychoanalysis, and some of its principal variants (Grotjahn, 1952; Little, 1967; Tower, 1967; Weisman, 1967; Halpert, 1982; Anisfeld, 1984; Dewald, chapter 4; Rosner, 1986; Abend, chapter 5, 1986; Schwartz, 1987; Weinberg, 1988), one finds some agreement that when a patient does not include any manifest reference to the analyst's illness (or to the interruption of the treatment) one ordinarily attempts to analyze the meaning of this conspicuous omission. Views on this are not entirely uniform, however, and there are some notable exceptions. Anisfeld's (1984) work is a good case in point and I would like to closely examine his ideas as a counterpoint to my own.

Anisfeld describes how a patient was helped through a mourning process by using the analyst's coping mechanisms (regarding his physical condition in which there was a visible disability) as a model for resolving conflict. He then suggests the applicability of this approach to other patients in analysis. Strongly influenced by the "communicative imperative" in the work of Robert Langs, Anisfeld does not let his disability go unremarked upon, and when patients seem to ignore it he shows them how it is represented—in derivative form—in what they are saying even when they did not know that they were saying it. Thus the specific content, his disability, and its possible unconscious representations, are always brought immediately into consciousness. My approach was very different. I, too, had some patients who did not make explicit reference to my illness and to the disruption of treatment except in highly derivative form. It seemed to me that there were a number of possible explanations for why this was happening. For example (and I think this cannot be emphasized too much), the patient simply had more pressing personal concerns which eclipsed all else for the moment; the patient was too anxious about it to even think about it consciously (let alone to discuss it with me); or the patient was too intent on acting something out in the transference—using this event in the symbolism of that context—to be able to immediately subject it to analytic examination. From my point of view, then and now, none of these possibilities is mutually exclusive. It is of course very tempting to seize upon patients' references to one's own situation, even when they are highly derivative, because of the analyst's narcissistic investments in his situation. However, to do so raises some technical problems about which I have some concerns. First, I am concerned that the patient may derive only intellectual benefits when unconscious rather than preconscious material becomes identified for the patient by the analyst, and not as a collaborative effort in the working through process. When the patient is so strongly defended that the material is not yet even preconsciously represented, I think it may be premature to force the issue by immediately interpreting. The fact that one is objectively correct does not seem particularly relevant when the patient does not seem ready to use the information effectively. At best, a compliant or overintellectualized patient will accept the analyst's educational efforts, and at worst (which is my second concern) the premature information will create so much anxiety that the patient will need to be even more guarded and heavily defended. Given the fact that I view that as "wild analysis," I chose to let patients consciously talk about the situation at their own pace, and it was my experience that patients who delayed explicit examination of it ultimately analyzed it just as effectively as those patients who brought it up immediately. In my view, we learned as much from examining why it came up when it did, and not before, as we did from examining it in terms of its content when it was, finally, addressed by the patient.

I can illustrate this by describing the case of Ms. V., who, at the time of my return to work, was deeply involved in a consuming and very destructive love affair. All of her energies were devoted to coping with the stresses of this relationship, and it was all she could talk about. She often discussed her fears that her lover would leave her, and eventually spent considerable amounts of time deciding to leave him. It is true that the latent content of these concerns were also references to my illness and my interruption of her treatment, and to her rage and her wish to abandon me in retaliation, but this was so far from consciousness that a restatement of the issue along these lines would have been incomprehensible to her. For about a year she was consumed by the vicissitudes of that relationship, and were I to interpret her productions as being related to me, she would have thought I was wrong, self-centered, and incapable of understanding her (and if I pushed all this on her prematurely, I believe she would have been right). In fact, it was not until three years after I was back at work that Ms. V. could directly approach this subject.

Ms. V. came from an environment where she was the object of considerable sadism, and grew up in a rage which could not be expressed because any show of anger on her part stimulated further attacks upon her. In consequence, Ms. V. developed numerous reaction formations that caused her to have to express exaggerated love and concern for the very objects of her anger. She bought cards, presents, and flowers, and baked cakes and cookies for the people at whom she was most enraged. She, not surprisingly, bought get-well cards for me. Once, early on, she said that she hoped I was cheered by them, and then went on to obsessively discuss her stormy love affair. Why did I not interpret this? I did not think it was appropriate to ignore the overdetermination of her obsessiveness, the power of those reaction formations, or the combined fury and terror she would have been subjected to without those defenses at her disposal. She had no idea that anything she was doing was an expression of rage, and at the time I fell ill she was not yet sufficiently advanced in her analysis to have recognized any of her hidden motives, for example, in sending those cards to me. She had bought three cards to send to me, and ended up sending two of them and keeping the third. The first card had a note from her expressing her wishes that I have a speedy and comfortable recovery. On the outside cover was a picture of a bear, in bandages, asleep in a deep armchair. Inside it said, "Make sure to get as much rest as you do when you're working," below a picture of the bear—this time with no bandages—asleep with his head on a desk. This card was sent about a week after I notified her of the interruption. About a month later, I got the second card. The outside had the words "HANG IN THERE" printed in bold relief. The card opened to a picture of a cat hanging upside down from a tree limb with its hair standing on end. Underneath the cat a pack of vicious dogs is circling. The second card also had a friendly and concerned personal message written on the back.

Three years later, having made major analytic advances which included quite a reduction in her obsessionalism and modifications of the use of her most extreme reaction formations, an event occurred that evoked the earlier experience of my absence and enabled her to bring into the treatment the feelings she had previously obscured. Mrs. V., herself, had to undergo some surgery. During the first week she was back it felt to her as if, for some inexplicable reason, I was angry, even furious, with her, and she thought that I was very detached and withholding. Next, she recalled that, just as she was about to succumb to the anaesthesia, she thought about my illness and my surgery. Because the material was so close to the surface all I had to say was, "You needed surgery, disappeared for two weeks, and came back to find me in a rage about it?" and Ms. V. recognized that this was what she was feeling at the time that I had to be out sick and also when I came back. She thought at first that she was over it by now, but came to see how intense and lasting it was when I asked her why, if she was over it, did she now imagine *me* to be feeling as she then did. She responded to that question by bringing to mind once again the two cards she had sent me, this time with a profound sense of the hostility behind the gesture (and in the symbolism of the cards). All of her thoughts about those cards were about her anger in the past, but we quickly moved into her continuing anger in the present when she brought to mind the third card—acknowledging that it really was the feeling of anger, and not the card itself so much, that she had been secretly attached to for all these years. On the front of this card one sees a very (almost terminally) ill horse all covered with blankets; the message says, "Cheer Up. If you were a horse they would shoot you!"

This triggered an embarrassed and painful admission of both what she had been feeling all along, as well as how she had been able to keep it hidden from herself. These issues took on life as they were enacted now in the transference. It revived her pain and fury at the hands of her sadistic family, and her frustration and transformation of all of that under the threat that it would cause an escalation of her mistreatment. It exposed her identification with them, as well as her defenses against knowing it. It also clarified the fact that she had been, and still was, harboring a long-standing grudge and resentment against me: she was waiting, like a cat with a mouse, for me to fall ill again so that she could tar me with accusations for returning to work with less than my full resources. Her fury gave way to a serious depression as the analogy broke down and Ms. V. began to review the inadequacies that her family had brought to the task of child rearing. I think it unlikely that we would have learned so much, and in so emotionally charged a way, if she had not hoarded those feelings, and kept them a secret from me and from herself, for a number of years. The very fact that it took so long to emerge was a powerful and convincing measure for Ms. V. of just how disturbing all of this was to her, and I do not think I would have wanted to trade that in for a premature elucidation of her unconscious (with which she could have done very little, if anything at all).

It seems to me that when the analyst's situation (or the disrupted treatment) is preconscious it should be treated like any other preconscious material and moved into consciousness via careful and tactful interpretation, but even then, only when it seems to be the leading fantasy material in the hour. Too quick a tendency to exploit a preconscious representation (when it is not the central fantasy constellation in the material, or when it would inappropriately interrupt the flow of free association), and a readiness to make "depth" interpretations of material which seems to be quite unconscious, may signal the analyst's need to deal with this subject rather than the readiness of the patient to do so. In certain instances this is not simply a technical decision but is reflective of the narcissistic injury and disequilibrium imposed by a catastrophic illness which can impair the analyst's technical judgment.

I would now like to raise a somewhat different point. Despite growing attention to the question of when the impaired analyst should discontinue clinical work (Michaels and Schoenberg, 1966; Eissler, 1975, 1977; Barbanel, Dattner, Fieldsteel, Simon, and Ziman-Tobin, 1989) we are all too familiar with horror stories about sick, impaired, and dying analysts who continued to work despite everything, and about patients who arrived at the office to find the analyst dead or dying, and even about analysts who died in the middle of a session and who, it turns out, had known they were terminally ill and still continued to work.[4] This highlights the moral vacuum in which we work, in part as a result of the extraordinary isolation that our work requires; and it makes it clear how dependent we are on the strength of collegial support and reinforcement.[5] I mentioned earlier one kind of tension that exists between the demands of technique and the rules of common courtesy, and I think there is another powerful tension here that deserves a few words.

In the course of conducting psychoanalytic treatments we generally are successful in sublimating many of our personal interests. But it is also true that this is how we earn our livings, and anything that threatens our ability to analyze also threatens our livelihood. Even when no special circumstances exist we work in tremendous isolation, and we have learned to rely on as many contacts with colleagues as possible to help us maintain an even balance between our need to earn a living, our objective analytic abilities, and the many conflicts this work raises in us. It is an unfortunate fact that the analyst who is chronically ill, or has just recovered from having been devastatingly ill, finds himself working in even greater isolation than is usual. They are, themselves, feeling isolated

[4]I very much appreciate the sensitive handling of this subject by Theodore Jacobs, M.D., in his discussion of my "Catastrophic Illness" paper. He managed to convey the profound importance of such events without a trace of moralization (unpublished discussion).

[5]I am grateful to William Grossman, M.D., for his observation (personal communication) that while the ego functioning of sick analysts has been given considerable attention, examinations of their superego functioning is virtually nonexistent in the literature.

and distanced from colleagues because of what they have been through. They may be further isolated by having been forced out of regular contact with colleagues because of their lengthy illnesses. Aside from personal visits, in which work is not the purpose of the contact, they are often professionally shunned by colleagues who are reluctant to refer to them if they feel that there is any chance of a relapse. In addition, they may also be shunned if there is a possibility of regular interruptions in their work, or of impaired technical ability, or if their colleagues are not feeling confident that the "sick" analyst is really going to live even though he has returned to work. In the absence of close professional contact and under the stress of numerous problems in the management of narcissistic equilibrium and the regulation of self-esteem, it is not surprising (and understandable even if not justifiable) that the need to earn a living, particularly when it is combined with denial or when it is the motive for denial, plays a deciding role in whether or not the analyst resumes his practice.

By way of ending this chapter I would like to address one final point, related to my previous comments on the "average" analysand and the "rules" of psychoanalysis. I am not aware of any analyst who was catastrophically ill, no matter how committed to the structure of the classical analytic treatment model, who has been able *never* to tell any patients anything about his or her circumstances. Abend (in his discussion of my "Catastrophic Illness" paper) has argued that just because we are unable to live up to the demands of the model is no reason to "rationalize" a departure from it. It seems to me that if no one, ever, seems to have been able to fully act in accordance with the "model" that we need to review whether the model is meant to be taken as an unconditional absolute. I do not think we should alter the framework of psychoanalysis casually or for reasons of personal convenience, but when the model proves impossible to follow I think we must ask why this is so. We have seen the development of parameters in treatment to cover special, temporary circumstances imposed by certain patients, and we have seen the development of modifications of analytic technique in order to accommodate the more permanent needs of character-disordered patients, without the suggestion that the very psychoanalytic model has been undermined. We do not now have any special (formal or informal) "rules" to cover the conduct of an analysis when the analyst suffers a catastrophic illness, and we are really unfortunate in not having a record of the specifics of how Freud dealt with his illness in the analyses he conducted. Knowing how often Freud modified his theory of mental functioning when the clinical data seemed to demand it, and knowing how much the evolution of his technique depended on his practical experiences with patients, I harbor the fantasy that he would not look unkindly on my raising the question of whether an unfollowable approach should not be reevaluated so that it falls into conformity with what is realistically possible under the circumstances.

References

Abend, S. (1986), Countertransference, empathy, and the analytic ideal: The impact of life stresses on analytic capability. *Psychoanal. Quart.*, 55:536–575.

——— (1989), Discussion of Catastrophic Illness in the Analyst and the Analysts Emotional Reaction to it. Presented at IPTAR, April 21, 1989.

Adler, G. (1972), Helplessness in the helpers. *Brit. J. Med. Psychol.*, 45:315–326.

Anisfeld, L. (1984), The therapist's disability as an adaptive context. In: *Listening and Interpreting: The Challenge of the Work of Robert Langs,* ed. J. Raney. New York: Jason Aronson.

Barbanel, L., Dattner, R., Fieldsteel, N., Simon, N., & Ziman-Tobin, P. (1989), The death of an analyst. *Contemp. Psychoanal.*, 25:412–447.

Chermin, P. (1976), Illness in a therapist—Loss of omnipotence. *Arch. Gen. Psychiat.*, 33:1327–1328.

Cohen, J. (1983), Psychotherapists preparing for death: Denial and action. *Amer. J. Psychother.*, 37:222–226.

Cooper, A. (1986), Some limitations on therapeutic effectiveness: The "burnout syndrome" in psychoanalysts. *Psychoanal. Quart.,* 55:576–598.

Dahlberg, C. (1980), Perspectives on death, dying, and illness while working with patients. *J. Amer. Acad. Psychoanal.,* 8:369–380.

Eissler, K. (1953), The effects of the structure of the ego on psychoanalytic technique. *J. Amer. Psychoanal. Assn.,* 1:223–254.

——— (1975), On the possible effects of aging on the practice of psychoanalysis: An essay. *J. Phila. Assn. Psychoanal.,* 2:138–152.

——— (1977), On the possible effects of aging on the practice of psychoanalysis. *Psychoanal. Quart.,* 46:182–183.

Givelber, F., & Simon, B. (1981), A death in the life of a therapist and its impact on the therapy. *Psychiatry,* 44:141–149.

Goldberg, F. (1984), Personal observations of a therapist with a life-threatening illness. *Internat. J. Group Psychother.,* 2:89–96.

Grotjahn, M. (1952), A psychoanalyst passes a small stone with big troubles. In: *When Doctors Are Patients,* ed. M. Pinnar & B. Miller. New York: W.W. Norton.

Halpert, E. (1982), When the analyst is chronically ill or dying. *Psychoanal. Quart.,* 51:372–389.

Jacobs, T. (1989), Discussion of Catastrophic Illness in the Analyst and the Analyst's Emotional Response to It. Presented at IPTAR, April 21, 1989.

Kriechman, A. (1984), Illness in the therapist: The eye patch. *Psychiatry,* 47:378–386.

Lindner, H. (1984), Therapist and patient reactions to life-threatening crises in the therapist's life. *Internat. J. Clin. & Experiment. Hypnosis,* 32:12–27.

Little, R. B. (1967), Transference, countertransference, and survival reactions following an analyst's heart attack. *Psychoanal. Forum,* 2:107–126.

Meissner, W., & Wohlauer, P. (1978–1979), Treatment problems of the hospitalized physician. *Internat. J. Psychoanal. Psychother.*, 7:437–467.

Michaels, J. J., & Schoenberg, M. L. (1966), Some considerations for retirement policy for training analysts. *Psychoanal. Quart.*, 35:199–216.

Rosenbaum, M. (1977), Premature interruption of psychotherapy: Continuation of contact by telephone and correspondence. *Amer. J. Psychiat.*, 134:200–202.

Rosner, S. (1986), The seriously ill or dying analyst and the limits of neutrality. *Psychoanal. Psychol.*, 3:357–371.

Schwartz, H. J. (1987), Illness in the doctor: Implications for the psychoanalytic process. *J. Amer. Psychoanal. Assn.*, 35:657–692.

Stoudemire, A. (1983), The onset and adaptation to cancer: Psychodynamics of an ill physician. *Psychiatry*, 16:377–386.

Tower, L. (1967), Discussion of Little, "Transference, countertransference, and survival reactions following an analyst's heart attack." *Psychoanal. Forum*, 2:120–122.

Weinberg, H. (1988), Illness and the working analyst. *Contemp. Psychoanal.*, 24:452–461.

Weisman, A. (1967), Discussion of Little, "Transference, countertransference, and survival reactions following an analyst's heart attack." *Psychoanal. Forum*, 2:116–117.

9

Patients' Responses to Pregnancy and Miscarriage in the Analyst

SUSAN G. LAZAR, M.D.

INTRODUCTION

In this chapter I shall present some of my own experiences of conducting psychoanalysis while pregnant. My experiences were both typical, as have been presented in a recently expanding literature on the topic, and were also unique in that several of my patients experienced analysis over the course of a number of my pregnancies. While practicing psychotherapy and psychoanalysis with patients ranging over a diagnostic spectrum from hospitalized psychotics to highly functioning professionals, I had seven pregnancies, five of which I lost, including two at five months. Pregnancy is a unique life event which interferes with the analytic space. Unlike the analyst's illness that Dewald, (chapter 4) Abend (chapter 5), Schwartz (chapter 6), Silver (chapter 7), and others have eloquently discussed, it is a gradually evolving situation of ambiguous meaning for patients. Not an obvious disaster, like life-threatening illnesses, it is nonetheless an unwelcome intrusion on the patient while being a deeply personal and meaningful event for the analyst. A pregnancy stimulates both intense positive and negative feelings in analysands over many months, and when a pregnancy is lost at a late and obvious stage patients feel deeply involved and react strongly, especially in the face of their own covert and explicit hostility. Thus my clinical experience confirms the findings of Lax (1969), Braasch (unpublished), Fenster, Phillips, and Rapaport (1986), Penn (1986), Bassen (1988), and others, that pregnancy in the analyst intensifies the transference, as my clinical material will illustrate. An article by Frances Hannett (1949) documents the same transference intensification with a therapist's miscarriage. A recent article by Bridges and Smith (1988) emphasizes that a pregnant therapist's sicker patients are at an increased risk for treatment disruption and serious acting out, which my own experience also tends to confirm.

The loss of anonymity both with an obvious pregnancy and the loss of an obvious pregnancy also have a strong countertransference effect. Very deeply felt affects are obvious or implicitly so and the analyst is in some measure emotionally exposed to the patient's observation, which in turn is transferentially distorted and magnified. Nadelson, Notman, Arons, and Feldman (1974) mention increased emotional vulnerability, mood swings, and counterdependency in pregnant therapists. Penn (1986) mentions the analyst's anxiety, hostility, and withdrawal in reaction to transference anger. I found myself feeling more intensely during each pregnancy about myself, about my unborn child, and increasingly with each pregnancy, about the threat of loss. However, I also felt more intensely about my patients, about the course of their analyses, their connection to me, and about their welfare. I experienced both great joy with the birth of my two children and intense grief over the babies that I lost. Many of my patients were alert to issues of my feelings, especially with my miscarriages, and the case of Mrs. C. will illustrate her preoccupation with transference–countertransference themes of loss which connected for her to repressed grief for her dead mother.

The issue of what to tell patients about an illness or a death as discussed in chapters 4, 5, and 6, and Givelber and Simon (1981), is also obviously very different with either a completed pregnancy or a very late miscarriage which eventually become evident to all patients. My own method was to wait for each patient to notice my pregnancy and in each case I found that the timing of the patient's perceptions flowed naturally from their individual dynamics and the state of the transference. The latest that any patient ever noticed one of my pregnancies occurred in the analysis of a woman who was herself pregnant and who only noticed *my* pregnancy when she and I were each in the seventh month. In addition, my own experience with patients sensing a pregnancy early and reacting strongly, in fact, runs counter to the common wisdom documented by Lax (1969) in her report that men tend to become aware later and react more superficially than women patients. In this chapter (in addition to one female patient), I shall present in some detail the transference reactions of two male patients, one a hospitalized psychotic and one a highly functioning professional analytic patient, each of whom became aware of my pregnancies early and reacted profoundly to them. The first patient, Mr. A., elucidated for me the great importance of a male child's primary identification with his mother. The reactions of the second patient, Mr. B., parallel in many ways the experience documented by van Leeuwen (1966) of the male's intense "woman-envy."

Several issues raised in chapter 6 are also worth discussing and rethinking in the context of pregnancy and miscarriage. Schwartz maintains that the analyst's neutrality is distorted by her life events and that "one's tolerance for transference becomes disturbed" (p. 118). He also feels that analysts experience an "illness-induced uncertainty about the boundary between their personal and professional selves, and the ratio of reality to illusion in the transference" (p. 121). In pregnancy, however, the more well-documented regressive aspects in the woman are also accompanied by a heightened generativity, as she becomes engrossed with the welfare of a dependent other. This attitude of concern can also extend to the dependency and conflicts of her patient and increase her tolerance for transference expression. This intensified attunement has also been noted by Fenster, Phillips, and Rapaport (1986). In other words, in a pregnancy the mother is not necessarily only *narcissistically* preoccupied. The issue of the boundary between reality and illusion is also special in an obvious pregnancy or pregnancy loss. As I experienced multiple pregnancies, I gradually accepted the fact that I was in *reality* providing an intense stimulus to transference reactions, but I felt also that *all* of my patients' reactions were meaningful in terms of their conflicts and developmental histories. To put it in other words, the fact of repeated pregnancies and even repeated pregnancy loss did not shift my position on what needed to be analyzed or my vision of the integrity of the analytic work over time, probably because I personally was not facing a life and death crisis that would threaten the continuity of the treatment.

Clinical Material

A thirty-one-year-old white schizophrenic male came to Chestnut Lodge after ten years of progressive disorganization after multiple hospitalizations elsewhere. His personal history was remarkable in that he was highly intelligent and exquisitely attuned to his mother's feeling states which made his early apprehension of my pregnancy and his reaction to it peculiarly intense. Mr. A. was the second son and third child of a fabulously wealthy self-made man who was warm, flamboyant, alcoholic, unfaithful, and who had died suddenly five years prior to the patient's admission. The mother was a very narcissistic woman and preoccupied with her own pleasure and appearance. She tried both to care for her children and to keep up with her husband's jet-set life-style, but ended up leaving her children more and more in the care of servants. On her son's admission to the hospital she reported with pride that he had always been aware of her clothes and makeup and treated her tenderly "like a date" when they went out to dinner. When the patient was an adolescent the mother used to bathe and undress in front of him and had him bring her sanitary napkins to her bathroom. As recently as age twenty-seven Mr. A. had slept in her room if he awoke with a nightmare. Just prior to admission the patient insisted that there was nothing seriously wrong with him and if he could just have sex he would feel well. His mother obliged by procuring a prostitute for him. She then promised him $20,000 if he would stay in the hospital for one year.

The patient was admitted to Chestnut Lodge and began four times weekly dynamic psychotherapy. Despite his severe and chronic psychosis Mr. A. established an intense level of connectedness to me which he sustained despite increasing regression. After two months of positive and polite feeling during which he gave me many details of his disturbed history, Mr. A. demanded that I give him an "analysis" of his case. He said he had given me enough time to study him. As I attempted to respond and to understand this demand, he declared that I was lacking, stupid, and contemptibly female and he marched out of my office. Later, he explained, "I am too brainy for you. You can't handle me. You can listen and listen and listen, but you can't handle me. And you won't do anything." When I questioned him about what he meant by "handle," he blew up. I had proved to him my incapacity. He said, "You are a Jewish-American Princess. You have been spoiled with education, and you are talking to me like I am out of a book. You don't listen to me and you are not like most girls who want to be spoiled with clothes and money and houses and cars. You want to play with minds and the murder of minds." I said, "You were talking about murder yesterday as if you were afraid that was what I wanted to do." Mr. A. replied, "No, you are confusing yourself with my mother. She is mad and vicious and mean. You are not. You are just spoiled. You have it all over her. If you weren't so spoiled, you could KO her in just an hour. You have it all over her if you could only see the difference between the two of you." He explained at length how women were incapable of treating men and if I could just accept it I would be a better person for it. Women were physically, emotionally, "glandularly," "menstrually," and "for reasons of pregnancy" unable to handle men. He wanted and needed a man doctor. With a man, if he wanted, he could kick a wastebasket in his hour or build things with blocks. I asked if he felt I was too fragile to sit with him. He replied that he didn't want me to take it personally. It was just that I was spoiled and had been getting away with things all my life which was why I would now insist on having my way in seeing him for our sessions. He said that he was crazy and would die crazy but he didn't want to hurt anyone. He also said he had overheard me speaking to the other doctors in the hospital cafeteria and, "I liked it. You should do that more with me. You should lean on me a little bit. You should stay at this hospital a while." I said, "And you?", and he replied, "Oh, I don't know. It's not that we don't get along and aren't friends. That means a lot to you, but not to me. I make friends easily. I need a doctor."

Thus Mr. A. both projected his conflicts from the relationship with his mother directly onto me while simultaneously somehow still distinguishing her from me. He went on to explain his fears about the power and destructiveness of women and how his selfish mother had emasculated his father. He hoped I was in psychoanalysis for support because of the burden he placed upon me and he admitted a terror of hurting me and of infecting me with his illness. He talked about the vicious battles between men and women and the wars between husbands and wives, and when I asked him to elaborate he said, "You are trying to blame me. I don't know anything about that. If I listened to your questions I would go blind. You are Delilah, but I'm not a dumb Samson. Your questions are meaningless and I chop them up and discard them." When I pointed out the contradiction if my words had so much power and yet were meaningless, he replied, "Yes, you have lots of power. You don't mean to hurt, but if I weren't watching you, you would, if I danced when you said to, just like my mother. You shouldn't be healing a young stud like me and cure him of an illness he doesn't have. I feel fine. I have never felt healthier. I am just staying here because I am comfortable. You should give this up and be at home having babies. I want to see your babies." Unfortunately I became ill with pneumonia at this time and was out for several weeks. Given his talk about Samson and Delilah just prior to the interruption, I felt I had some understanding when upon my return I saw that in my absence he had shaved his head.

In the year of treatment prior to my pregnancy Mr. A. developed an increasingly close, symbiotic, powerful, and psychotic transference. He kept close track of my schedule and vacations and wanted me to report to him on my activities. He continued to denigrate me as a hopeless, uneducated, and simple-minded woman, whose curiosity and arrogance would do great harm. He became increasingly anxious and enraged sitting with me and was clearly confusing me more and more with his mother, until one day he knocked a coffee cup out of my hand and our sessions then began to be held with him restrained in a cold wet sheet pack. The felt tie between us and his anxiety about our damaging each other were so intense that he would sometimes kick his feet frantically and pound his heels into the bed for an entire hour with a rhythmic and hypnotic quality. When he spoke, his contempt and sarcasm were extreme. One day I was fighting a cold and after fifteen minutes of silence in session with him I sneezed. He screamed, "You come in here diseased? You come to me diseased?" I asked if he were afraid he would get ill and he said, "Yes." There was a silence and then I coughed. He screamed, "GET OUT. YOU GET OUT OF HERE." and he began to call for the aides, "COME GET ME OUT OF HERE. GET HER OUT OF HERE," and he began to rant at me, "No money for you, no money for you—if you come to me for money, forget it. How long do you think you would last in here if I weren't tied down?" and he badgered me until I responded, "I am sure not very long, that's why you are in pack." After a long silence he said, "All you do is fuck and shit," and as I left he informed me, "You stink!"

Although he was increasingly regressed and preoccupied with men and women hurting each other and enraged with me, he would talk at moments of wanting to get me presents. He spoke of a special shop in his hometown from which he wanted to buy me a new dress. He was also increasingly self-destructive, referred to suicide, and made some cigarette burns on his body. One night he deliberately provoked a scuffle with an aide and spent some hours afterward in seclusion. The next day he was eager for his hour and greeted me in a cheerful mood. When I asked about the fight he said, "Yes, I really enjoyed it." When I asked if he'd been hurt he said, "No, thank God. If I had been hurt I would feel horrible. And if I had hurt him I would feel horrible. But he was a big guy, and no one was hurt, even though I have a small little body, and I felt like a little girl with him." After a long thought-disordered monologue on the physical dangers to little people, it gradually became clear to me how deeply preoccupied he was with his longing for physical contact, both aggressive and intimate, and how very dangerous these impulses were for him to feel with me. When I asked him if it would feel safe to see me if I were a big man (like the aide he'd fought) he said, "Yes, I have to be tied down with you. When I am vengeful to you, it is like being vengeful to myself. Such a small little body." I told him I thought he wanted intense and violent physical contact in which no one was hurt and he agreed and was delighted with me. "But meeting with someone of the opposite sex isn't good. . . . You know what I mean, because you are a little girl too."

Over the next several days he created several beautiful and beautifully executed chalk pictures on his walls of two intertwined snakes, of two men fighting or dancing, and of two women with bows, arrows, and leather breastplates and knee protectors. I felt he was elaborating his great concern about violent physical intimacy. Although he continued to be increasingly psychotic and hostile to me in his hours, he would occasionally interrupt his tirades and ask me for a blanket or a pillow, which I would give to him, and he would thank me. He continued to be very aware of my schedule and once when I went away briefly he inquired, "Was it family or romance?" He also complained that I was close to him but I liked to cause him pain. I sympathized that it must be terribly hard to sit with someone that he felt was so sadistic, but he replied, "It's okay. Your credit is still good."

At this time I was five or six weeks pregnant. I was beginning to have the disturbing impression that he was somehow aware of it. He would lecture me about Jewish women being sent away to deliver babies, and he was making many other references to pregnancy. It was very uncanny, but it was true that he had caught on and that I should have said something to him. When I was eight or ten weeks pregnant he was wild on his unit one day and had been screaming that he did not want to see me. When I came into his room he was agitated in his cold wet sheet pack and had written in chalk on his window, "MA COW NO SHARE SECRET." I said, "I guess you have the feeling I have been keeping something from you deliberately. I hadn't meant to." I confirmed that I was pregnant and he flew into a rage and began spitting at me and screaming that I was unfit to bear children and he wanted me to get rid of it.

We had several weeks of utterly silent sessions after this in which I felt constrained and afraid to annoy him. Finally we were able to talk a little about his feelings about my pregnancy. He accused me, "You have been pregnant for six months." I was so startled I simply blurted out, "That's not true," and he responded, "Yes, you have. Well, then, you were 'prematurely' pregnant for six months!" And as I thought to myself of my own preoccupations during the many silent hours with him in the preceding months, I had to conclude that he was absolutely correct about the content of my thoughts. In the succeeding month, Mr. A. took to walking around with a pillow under his shirt and he asked the staff for a bowling ball and a shopping cart to wheel around on the unit. When I was four months pregnant he asked tenderly, "Did you get the fur coat I ordered for you yet?" The very next day he tried to avoid his session with me by refusing to see "that little girl."

He began to call me by my first name, and the combined emotions of tenderness, closeness, and contempt became poignant and nearly unbearable in their intensity. During one silent session sitting in my chair positioned behind Mr. A. in pack, where I'd taken to sitting so he could not spit at me, I fell profoundly asleep. Suddenly his voice woke me, saying, "Are you hungry?" I was so disoriented that for a moment I couldn't recollect where I was. He repeated, "Are you hungry?" Dazed I responded, "Oh, no, why? Are you?" And he said, "No, but your stomach is growling." I asked if he wouldn't like something himself and he let me give him juice to drink and I had some too in a startling close and unusual moment of sharing.

I found the therapy with this deeply ill schizophrenic man remarkable for his extreme sensitivity despite his regressed and disorganized state. Several themes emerged with great clarity, especially his hopeless entanglement and profound identification with his mother whom he despised as selfish, exploitive, and cruel and whom he also loved and watched closely and solicitously, all of which he relived with me in the transference. Indeed no matter how regressed this particular patient became he never felt remote or out of touch to me. While Mr. A. was contemptuous of women and of little girls, he also felt himself to *be* a little girl, an attitude born out of his symbiosis with his mother and probably sustained through confused homosexual longings for his father. And despite his feeling that his mother had damaged him horribly with her callous intrusiveness and despite his retaliatory murderous rage, he maintained a tenderness, protectiveness, and concern for his mother, which he expressed toward me, along with his wish that "No one would get hurt." This chronically psychotic man was aware of my pregnancy earlier than anyone in my life outside of my immediate family, a perception doubtless informed by years of living in an unbearably close relatedness with his mother's conscious and unconscious ideation.

My countertransference with Mr. A. was always one of deep concern and involvement. While he could anger me and frighten me intensely, I always felt his pain. I heard his attacks on my pregnancy as his reaction to the damage he had suffered in his relationship with his mother. But more than any other countertransference feeling, I experienced a great respect and even awe for his uncanny perceptiveness.

A thirty-six-year-old man, a highly intelligent and educated government employee, came to analysis because of anxiety, depression, feelings of personal inadequacy, and severe marital distress. He was neat, short, slight, and extremely obsessional. He related in a distant, deferential, dependent, and covertly hostile posture and talked about his felt helplessness and seemed to expect my protection and affection to compensate him for the many sacrifices he'd made of his masculinity. He was the younger of two children and had an older sister who was his father's favorite. His father was warm, loving, and much more affectionate than his mother but he treated his children as narcissistic extensions of himself and was also quite competitive with his son. The patient's relationship with his mother proved to be extremely important both in understanding his deepest anxieties and also for his very intense and deeply intuitive responses to my pregnancies. The mother was a cold, detached, and increasingly depressed woman in the patient's childhood. She seemed to have enjoyed the patient's infancy—in fact memories and dream images of a very early, warm maternal–infant bond emerged very late in his analysis and seemed to have provided him with the inner core of security and object constancy that put the patient in the analyzable, neurotic rather than borderline diagnostic range. Nonetheless his mother was severely and increasingly emotionally ill during the patient's young life. Her mother had moved into the family home to care for the children when the mother returned to work, which the patient experienced as an abandonment at age two.

For the first two-and-a-half years of analytic work the patient was preoccupied with competition with his father and his chronic sense of failure and inadequacy as a man. Then early during the first trimester of my first pregnancy, the patient's material became increasingly involved with dreams and associations related to fertilization and pregnancy which he understood as connected to a passive homosexual tie to his father. In one particularly vivid and disturbing dream he was coming back from running and went to the garden at the side of his house where he'd planted some eggplants that were too soft or too ripe. It seemed he had planted the wrong variety. With disgust he noticed a line of ants emerging from a hole in the ground. The hole was very well-defined and the smoothness and definition of the hole were somehow part of what he found disturbing. The ants emerged and walked across the patio and into another hole from which they were also coming and going. At the mouth of the second hole was a leaf or a grasshopper which was even more disturbing. As Mr. B. talked and thought about the dream he was uncomfortable as if his "skin was crawling." He felt panicky and fearful. The eggplants he associated to eggs, reproduction and parasites living in his body, and "bugs laying eggs inside of me that are growing." He once had had a friend who feared a spider would lay eggs in her ear. He felt both "very uncomfortable" and "mesmerized" by his associations and had an image of "openings in my tissue." When I asked him where, he said "my penis" with a nervous laugh. He also thought of drawings of muscles that resembled freeways and roads, and openings in his body in his ears, nose, penis, and anus. He associated to his parents' controllingness as parasitic and to his terror of being dominated like his envied older sister who never moved far from home. He then had an image again of holes, of worms infecting children's intestines, of a childhood fear of potatoes growing in his unwashed ears, and then explicit images of being anally impregnated by his father. Father had always tried to stuff him with food, he said, and he had "funny thoughts" that he had to seduce his father because he wanted to be like his sister in her closness to him. Would father have liked him better if he had been a little girl? He then nearly wept saying he couldn't live on the basis of wanting to have sex with his father. I interpreted his characteristic difficulty in tolerating intense fantasy and impulse separate from a need to take action, and he felt some relief.

In this one particular remarkable session, themes stimulated by the patient's preconscious awareness of my pregnancy led to an intensification of very central neurotic conflicts. The passive homosexual longings and the envy and competition with his sister were connected in turn to a powerful idealization, fear, and envy of his mother and of women in general. These further themes would prove to take several more years to elaborate and work through, but they emerged with particular clarity and force in connection with my pregnancy.

In subsequent weeks the material relating to pregnancy continued. In one dream the figure of a woman coworker looked "thicker" to him and he associated to his envy of women's capacities to bear children. He and his wife had elected to remain childless for a number of reasons, mostly connected to his wife's extreme emotional fragility, but his wife had also commented that she was afraid to have a child with him lest he become consumed with a child and feel himself to be both mother and father much as his own father often acted. When I asked the patient directly what he thought was stimulating all the pregnancy material he replied that his life was barren and that he was unable to *feel* something inside of him. People talked about pregnancy that way—as an internal stirring. The very next day he announced that he'd decided I had no children but that I might decide to, in which case he would be jealous of my being pregnant. He connected these thoughts to a fantasy of renouncing his masculinity in favor of being a woman. The next day he said he felt competitive with me because I was "clever." He would also be very envious if I had children and he would then feel "so alone."

I pointed out he was repeatedly mentioning bad feeling connected to ideas of my having children and he responded quickly, "Yes, I think you don't and that is very satisfying." A few days later he complained, "I'm foolish and you're smug and serene. I want to draw you into my upset, frustration, and dislike." He said he wanted me to give up my role, my sex, and my pleasure in sex and he wanted me to be as frustrated as he felt. These themes reached a crescendo until one session, three months into my pregnancy, he recalled with rage an incident in which his father had met the patient's future in-laws and responded to their praise of Mr. B., "But wait 'til you meet his sister!" The envied older sister had been pregnant at the time. Mr. B. said, "My sister does get pregnant and produce children and I don't . . . I'm so jealous of his affection for her . . . I haven't had children as a father and I think I have a secret hope of having them as a woman." He made several more associations to me as a sexually experienced woman who, however, was not fertile, and he was glad because if I were pregnant he would be "overcome with envy." At this point I told him that I was in fact pregnant and that I felt he had noticed it preconsciously but had needed to avoid acknowledging it.

His initial reaction was bland, "Really. That's interesting. No, I had not consciously noticed." When he came in the next day, however, he looked at me directly and said, "I guess it is pretty evident." He said it was "a shock having to acknowledge the reality of your life. It's so obvious you *do* have another life. I go on thinking you don't and you just exist for me. I have no perception of you as an *other* person. I do that in all my other relationships. I have the feeling that I'm the only one that counts. When you asked what prompted all my references to pregnancy, it never *once* occurred to me you might be pregnant, *not once*. I make myself oblivious to what other people are doing, but somehow the information does get through. My wife insists I don't acknowledge things until she screams at me. It is true. She has to bludgeon me to get me in contact with my feelings."

His first reaction to his conscious knowledge of my pregnancy was to oscillate between an intense envy of my baby and a denial of his envy and sense of being excluded. He said, "I have a very strong feeling that somehow I'm part of the process of your having a baby." He also wondered what the impact on him and his treatment would be and concluded that I would be away only briefly and the interruption would be minimal. Later he had outbursts of rage and sadistic fantasies of damaging the baby. Very occasionally he also had tender and loving reactions to the idea of my being pregnant. With this first pregnancy, most of Mr. B.'s reactions seemed to be focused on his envy of the baby. Later in his analysis, with subsequent pregnancies of mine, his rivalry with my husband and his envy of me as a woman who could produce a child were more explicit and sustained.

My initial countertransference during the stage of Mr.

B.'s preconscious awareness was of bewilderment and uncertainty as to whether or not Mr. B. could actually be aware so early of my pregnancy before most other people in my life. As it gradually became impossible to deny his awareness because of the persistent and pointed nature of his associations, I nonetheless "drifted" for several more weeks before deciding to confront the patient with his own preconscious perceptions. I think every pregnant therapist is faced with a sense that she is introducing a gradually increasing intrusion into the patient's analytic space. Unlike other more discrete events in the analyst's life that interfere with treatment, the course of a pregnancy is more subtle and difficult to trace in its beginning impingement on the treatment and more slowly evolving over many months. Also, while I was working in a state of suspended animation trying to decide if I should make the situation explicit, a colleague with whom I consulted accused me accurately of being smug. After all *I* had the baby while the patient was envious, childless, and speculating that I was sterile. My continued silence preserved my comfortable, safe, and faintly superior position as the enviable one, deferred my experience of his more directly expressed disappointment and anger, and was overly protective of the patient's defenses against the pain of his own envy.

Later when the patient expressed sadistic wishes toward the baby, I felt both irritated and sympathetic toward his rage and sense of deprivation. This pregnancy was the first of the seven I eventually had, five of which I lost. At this point, however, ideas of miscarriage, loss, and death did not yet occupy the central position in my life experience and associations they were later to assume. From my naively optimistic and innocent position, I felt I could contain the patient's envious attacks, secure in my sense of safety. I was also at the time on the staff of Chestnut Lodge where murder was an important, necessary, and conscious transference theme in the treatment of desperately ill inpatients, compared to which this patient's hostility was pale indeed.

Over the next several years the transference evolved into a vivid and painful reliving of his constricted relationship with his depressed mother. He experienced me as like his mother who was cold, contemptuous of men, including father, and repulsed by sexuality. He was his mother's "bright, shiny little penny" and needed to be asexual and compliant to continue in his favored position, which was a kind of oedipal victory. I felt like a large and frightening presence and I experienced the patient as helpless, clinging, and sucking. His dreams and fantasies elaborated the notion that he was his mother's possession and in one dream he was hanged and bound by an angry woman who prevented his escape. Most of the transference issues related to these themes were worked through and the patient had in fact felt well and terminated analysis only to return twenty months later in a state of panic over a flirtation with a coworker. It quickly became clear that he still had unresolved oedipally based transference longings, expressed in the flirtation, along with some remaining fear and envy of powerful women. I mention the hiatus in treatment because it coincided with four of my miscarriages, three of which were early and one late, none of which this patient witnessed.

Soon after his return, during the first trimester of another pregnancy of mine, the patient began complaining about a pregnant woman at work. He felt her showing off was "cloying" and "too much." Was it because he was envious? Two weeks later he felt enraged and cheated in comparison both to his older sister and to me. His sister and I had it all. She basked in their father's affection and had a beautiful house and children and I had work, children, and a husband while he felt he had been too willing to forego children. He continued with these themes for two more days and reported, "I keep looking at you to see if you're pregnant. I don't think you are." When I corrected this observation his response was, "This feels like déja vu. I guess I'm so upset by it that I don't want to see it. *I feel envious of your husband* and I have some thought, 'I've lost again. I've lost you again.' " Although the patient had again blotted out his conscious awareness of an accurate perception, his conflict had shifted. Instead of the envy of and identification with the baby during my first pregnancy the patient's considerable growth was evidenced now by his rivalry with my husband.

When I lost this pregnancy at a relatively advanced stage, the patient's first response was relief that he would not have to tell his wife about the pregnancy. He then was afraid that I would retaliate for this reaction. Next he felt concern for me but not drawn up into my life issues and concluded that he was feeling very much more separate from me. It was a genuine relief to realize that he had neither guilt nor responsibility for what had happened and that his reactions, in any event, were his own and were not fundamentally important to me personally. I felt momentarily enraged with the patient's initial reaction to my loss but was fortunately able to contain my feeling without betraying it. When the patient subsequently went on to express his guilt about his sense of relief and then to conclude that his reactions were fundamentally unimportant to me personally, I had to agree with him silently and to reflect that his initial rage was really over the blurred boundary between his mother and himself. As he felt more entitled to his own reactions and to his own life, free of a guilty omnipotent sense of responsibility for her and for me, both his rage and my responsive outrage were diminishing.

As the analysis continued, Mr. B. continued to improve dramatically with the exploration of his envy, passivity, and castration anxiety, the reliving of his idealization and fear of his mother, and his experiencing more and more openly positive oedipal longings in the transference and a solidification of a more autonomous and masculine identity. He was more conscious of his commitment to his wife and finally coaxed her into pursuing a fertility workup. When I was again pregnant at this time the patient noticed it quite early and asked me directly and matter of factly for confirmation, in marked contrast to his earlier split between preconscious awareness and conscious denial. He again openly expressed jealousy of the pregnancy and possessiveness of me, and fantasies that the child was his, but he felt the envy and possessiveness were much less intense than with previous pregnancies. As he was experiencing himself as more capable and assertive, his position of envious passivity was giving way to a new generosity of spirit. After half-hearted envious references to my pregnancy and my new car he commented, "You know these things don't really grip at me. I *like* the fact of your new car and I imagine you enjoying it—somehow—why shouldn't you?"

Just before I was hospitalized abruptly for premature labor, the patient was steadily revealing his affection and sexual feelings for me. When I returned, he and his wife had experienced a tragic turn of events. She had finally conceived only to become overwhelmed with panic at the nausea and discomfort. She insisted on an abortion to which the patient finally acquiesced with great reluctance. Both his grief over their loss and the guilt that he could somehow have prevented it were intense and continued over many months. The full extent of his wife's fragility was newly revealed, though the patient was now unfaltering in his devotion to her. This disaster had occurred in the context of an unusually long, abrupt, and unplanned absence of mine lasting ten weeks due to my premature labor, hospitalization, and the premature birth of my second child. The patient missed me desperately in his hour of need, but at this point in his analysis he was able to express this reaction directly and feelingly, in marked contrast to his hostile, covert dependency at the beginning of his treatment.

My countertransference was one of concern. I felt that I was witnessing a tragedy and one of great personal meaning to me since I had myself lost many more pregnancies than this patient knew about. In fact over the remaining eighteen months of Mr. B.'s analysis he worked on a consolidation of his self-esteem in the face of loss. Previously he had experienced the idea of having children as a narcissistic reflection on his status in life, as a way to compete with his sister for his father's affection, and to compete with his father himself as a man. Tragically, as his growing maturity made him more capable of nurturing and appreciating children in a more genuine way, Mr. B.'s hopes for a family were reduced to nothing. Mourning this painful loss and working through the competitive and narcissistic meanings left him feeling that he was no less valuable as a man by virtue of being childless.

The termination of this patient's analysis was marked by the gradual expression and resolution of his envy and idealization of women's abilities and his castration anxiety, and the solidification of his masculine identity and self-esteem. Toward the end of the analysis Mr. B. no longer felt in awe of powerful women in his life. While he had great respect for my skills, he felt that he also possessed considerable professional skills in his own field. He reported a vivid dream of many little cells that he associated to growing embryos. He said it reminded him of the work of the male painter, Robert *Motherwell,* which indicated to him a sense of his own integration and sublimation of the maternal aspects of himself. I have the strong impression that my repeated pregnancies provided an intense stimulus to the transferential expression and working through of these crucial themes.

Mrs. C. was a forty-year-old Catholic woman with two teenage girls who came for analysis for depression, extreme swings of ambivalence toward her husband and children, and bouts of loss of confidence and extreme self-consciousness. She was the older of two children and had grown up in a wealthy home. Her father had been a handsome, engaging, and successful businessman and town leader but was also a womanizer and an alcohol and drug abuser who spent regressed periods drunk and incontinent in his bed. Most of the time, however, he was hyperfunctional, domineering, and totally dominated his wife and two daughters. The patient's mother, whom she revered as perfect, was a submissive Catholic woman. She had been very beautiful, talented, and pious and had given up a career as a scientist to marry the patient's father. She suffered greatly in her marriage to him and became ill with breast cancer when the patient was twelve, dying a few months before the patient graduated from high school. The patient's younger sister was severely emotionally ill, had led a chaotic life, and lived with her illegitimate daughter on welfare. The patient's first marriage had broken up several years prior to analysis when her rakish, self-centered, and philandering first husband deserted her and her daughters. After an initial collapse the patient began a successful concern of her own and established a second marriage with an older, stabler man.

At the beginning of treatment, although referred for psychoanalysis, Mrs. C. was unwilling to come more often than once a week, pleading insurmountable difficulty in leaving her job or her family for more frequent sessions. Her reticence also coincided with a pregnancy of mine to which she had little reaction except a polite positive feeling and some pleasant memories of her own pregnancies. In retrospect, since this patient came to experience intense oedipal rivalry in her analysis, it seems highly likely that a fear of her own aggressive competitiveness contributed to her delay in beginning an analytic schedule. Since her mother had died during the patient's adolescence after an unhappy marriage with an unfaithful husband, this patient had a very particular fear of damaging a maternal figure with her rivalrous striving. This fear was to prove fateful for the course of her analysis, as she eventually left prematurely after I lost an advanced pregnancy. In any event, at the beginning of analysis, Mrs. C. began a four times weekly analytic schedule only after the safe delivery of my first child. Analytic material related to rivalry and fear of damaging me was not available at this time but emerged years later in the work.

In the first three years of treatment the patient made substantial gains. She established an idealizing and dependent transference punctuated by a hostile, sabotaging, passive–aggressive, and envious attitude fueled by her self-image as a damaged, incompetent and degraded female. Obsessional issues about autonomy, money, and control were prominent. Dreams and associations elaborated castration themes, conflicts about voyeurism and exhibitionism, and intense oedipal longings for her compellingly attractive but frighteningly seductive father. With the eludication of this material the patient's self-confidence and assertiveness solidified considerably.

At the beginning of the fourth year of treatment the patient was tentatively approaching what I felt to be the core issues of her oedipal rivalry, which I felt she had unconsciously experienced as the cause of her mother's death. She was much more assertive with her female boss and was able to set firmer limits with her daughters as we interpreted her fear that conflict between teenage girls and their mothers could be fatal.

I also repeatedly interpreted to the patient that she must be experiencing much envy and competition with me, although it was rarely explicit in her material. She then immediately produced a dream in which she described a house near mine, with an office and waiting room much like mine, only this was *her* house. She commented that it had begun to sink in how panicked she had been since the death of her mother, and how her fear had touched everything in her life but was now beginning to loosen its grip on her. She began to recover discrete traumatic memories. One was of mother confiding in her tearfully when her cancer recurred, that she did not want to die and that she was sorry to burden the seventeen-year-old patient, but that she had no one else with whom to talk. I interpreted that the patient had never come to terms with her grief over her mother's death and over mother's emotional isolation and unhappiness. I interpreted that instead of feeling her grief directly and because of her guilt over competing with her, the patient had for years identified with mother by expecting her own life to fall apart with disasters in her marriage and with her children, for all of which she felt vaguely but definitely culpable. The next weekend the patient walked alone by herself sobbing for hours in the woods. She felt really that her tears were connected to her mother's death. She said she could not have mourned it at the time for father had fallen apart and drunk heavily and she often had to care for him. Her younger sister had also fallen apart and begun to run wild. In a subsequent dream I terminated her analysis because I felt she and her children led an immoral life. She associated my leaving her in the dream to her mother's decline and death, alone and unsupported by father, which had of course left the patient alone and unsupported. The interpretation of her own sense of guilty responsibility for mother's death was confirmed when she had a sudden thought, "If I'm a good girl, *I* won't get cancer."

After the elucidation of this material the patient was able

to feel a more direct and conscious hostility toward me in the transference. She began to express openly her rivalry and her resentment of me as a professional who was somehow superior to her. She felt unequal to me and assumed I gloated over her progress and took credit for it and she felt a spiteful wish to spoil my success. I felt that her guilty fear had decreased enough for her to risk a more direct expression of her aggression with me in a way that she had been unable to express to her mother.

During the fourth and final year of the patient's analysis the patient was more confident and assertive at home and at work and her depressive periods were greatly decreased. During this year I was again pregnant. The patient was grateful to me for her improvement, admiring of all I seemed able to manage, and was also challenging and envious. She said, "You haven't completely fixed me yet. I also envy your example. You never cop out. You show up every day. You're pregnant, you have a little baby, you teach and have a practice. It almost has an unreal quality to it." I asked why, if she envied me as someone she felt was better organized, did she feel it was unattainable for her? "That's true," she said, "I've spent so much time thinking I can't handle things ever, but I do feel it much less and I do handle a lot of things."

Unfortunately, as the patient was struggling with her competitive and envious strivings and her conflicting wishes either to identify with me or to defeat and devalue me, I lost the pregnancy at a fairly advanced stage. I informed her of this development a few weeks later and she felt devastated. Her first reaction was of guilt that she hadn't noticed although she always looked to see if I was any bigger. She said, "How could you have continued to work and to look so cool? How can I possibly talk to you when a much worse thing happened to you?" I replied, "I wonder if that feeling isn't also one you felt frequently with your parents?" She said, "I wonder if you can really pay attention when you've had such awful things going on—I couldn't." She felt reluctant to discuss her reactions out of a fear of "putting me through it over and over again." I pointed out she had felt the same about her mother and her disease. For the next several days the patient was tearful about my loss and also felt increased distance from her husband who she felt was rejecting her. I pressed for her thoughts about me and with extreme reluctance she said she wondered how long I had known my baby was dead. Had I been sitting with her during that time? She just couldn't believe it. *She* couldn't have done it. It made her feel inferior by comparison. I interpreted that instead of feeling the grief stirred up by this death, which evoked her grief for her mother, her sadness was expressed as a sense of lowered self-esteem. This observation had an immediate effect, for she spent the next several days weeping openly and thinking for the first time, "I want my mother." She was now also fighting viciously with her husband and complaining to me about his coldness, which I interpreted as her great difficulty staying focused on her tears and her wish for her mother. I also said that "the mother–child tie shattered by a death resonates with deep issues in your life. You are also worried about my availability to you now." She agreed. She had been happy about my pregnancies. She said, "I think you're remarkably available and better able to talk about all this than I am." I linked her positive feelings about my pregnancies to her wish that I could show her how a woman could successfully combine work with home, children, and a husband. She now felt something positive had been lost abruptly which felt like a repetition of her mother's death.

At the time I myself was feeling intense shock and grief at this loss of an advanced pregnancy, which was my third miscarriage, the first two of which had been early and unnoticed by this patient. I had the distinct impression that in addition to the fact that I was accurately interpreting my patient's old, repressed grief for her mother; the fact that I was actively experiencing similar affects of my own made her feelings more accessible to her consciousness. There was a powerful unspoken assumption in the room that unlike her self-absorbed and oblivious father who was no emotional help when her mother died, I knew on a deep level what her grief was like. Of course she had reached a certain point after three-

and-a-half years of analytic work with a strengthened ego and self-esteem that were also crucial to the derepression of such intense and conflict-laden affects.

A few weeks later another blow fell in that her medical insurance psychiatric benefits were drastically cut, and she insisted she would have to draw the analysis to a close. She was able to continue an analytic schedule for another three months. Despite the very real financial pressures, I understood and interpreted to the patient that the real reason she was leaving her analysis was her fear of the intense feelings it had aroused and her fear of experiencing even more vividly her destructive feelings and rivalry with me. My loss had magically confirmed her sense of her own dangerousness. In fact her marital discord became severe again for a while which I interpreted as a distraction from her sense of loss and as a punishment for her imagined destructiveness to me and to her mother. Nonetheless Mrs. C. stopped her analytic schedule when her benefits expired but continued to see me once weekly for a number of months during which she continued to work in an attenuated fashion on issues of rivalry and aggressiveness. She stopped treatment altogether when she noticed that I was again pregnant, although I interpreted vigorously her unconscious fear of harming me yet "again." While some important work of mourning for her mother was accomplished, the patient was unable to face the full depth of her guilt, rivalry, and felt oedipal triumph to complete that important task. The loss of my pregnancy became an insurmountable disturbance which contributed to the interruption of her analysis.

Additional Clinical Material and Conclusion

In addition to the material presented above, others of my patients experienced reactions to my pregnancies, some of which bear at least brief mention. Several other patients were exquisitely attuned to even early pregnancies of mine, in particular one highly competitive woman patient with narcissistic and hysterical features. This patient always knew very early when I was pregnant, was intensely jealous of my baby, my marriage, and my professional status, and finally quit her treatment prematurely after witnessing six of my pregnancies before the seventh one concluded successfully. She had struggled intensely with her fear that her spiteful envy had led to my miscarriages, and as she left she anxiously insisted that I notify her of the outcome of my last pregnancy. I decided to accede to her wish and did indeed send her a note about the birth of my second child. Subsequently she conceived herself and aborted one pregnancy out of wedlock, and finally returned to treatment four years after her first termination, pregnant yet again, and with deep and deeply conflicted wishes to raise this baby as a single mother. After much agonizing she again elected an abortion in the twelfth week, leaving me with the impression of a disavowed enactment of her murderous rivalry toward me and of her guilt-laden, self-inflicted punishment. I experienced her return to treatment, her pregnancy, her agonized indecision, and her final decision to abort as a kind of Greek tragedy which had been staged for my benefit and which I was forced to witness in helpless horror.

Another brilliant and gifted male patient with an unresolved identification with his mother seemed, like the two male patients already described, uncannily attuned to my pregnant states. In the fifth month of a pregnancy after my unborn child had been killed by an amniocentesis, I was aware unconsciously but unaware consciously for several weeks that my child was dead. Prior to the official diagnosis of the death, this patient reported anxiety about my baby and dreams of a frozen beehive in which the new generation of embryonic bees had been killed. Whether this was an unresolved transference fantasy or an uncannily accurate perception is an unresolved question in which I lean to the latter explanation.

Two analytic patients, one male and one female, both of whom had been in treatment during my late miscarriages, experienced my long hospitalization and absence with the delivery of my second live-born child as a nearly intolerable strain. The woman patient was extremely demanding that I resume a frequent schedule with her before I was ready and able to do so and remained in a rage about the felt abandonment that reached paranoid proportions for most of the next two years. These transference developments accurately reflected her own history, having experienced the birth of four younger siblings at a very young age and in a family situation where she herself was rejected by both parents. However, the sudden eruption of this traumatic reliving almost disrupted her analysis, was attended by much destructive acting out, and was certainly precipitated by my pregnancies more than by a natural analytic unfolding.

The male patient was overwhelmed by my long and abrupt absence and needed to deny his emotional response. The colleague whom he consulted in my absence reported that the patient simply pretended that his interim doctor was me. This patient did not begin to report and deal with his reactions to the "abandonment" until four years later in his analysis. It is possible that his treatment was prolonged as a result, rather than emotionally intensified, as in the other case. Several patients, both male and female, simply left prematurely after years of fruitful work either just before or just after my second successful delivery. In all such instances it seemed clear that the rivalry and anger were too intense to analyze and instead were rationalized and enacted.

In conclusion, pregnancy and miscarriage in the analyst are powerful transference stimuli for analytic patients. Themes of identification with the mother and intense rivalry with her procreative functioning are especially heightened in patients of both sexes. In fact the stimulus of a pregnant analyst may elucidate a male patient's womb envy, an issue that may have otherwise completely escaped notice in our analytic climate that has largely ignored this important aspect of male developmental psychology.

Countertransference responses in the pregnant analyst are often correspondingly intense and other authors have noted self-protective anger, guilt, and partial withdrawal. I discovered through my own experiences that, in addition, a pregnant analyst experiences heightened countertransference concern and dedication to the ongoing work in response to her patients' intensified reactions. In particular, experiencing an analyst's repeated pregnancies and repeated pregnancy loss can create a special, often silent, transference–countertransference climate in which the analyst's survival of repeated loss and yet continued functioning becomes a powerful reassurance while it also reality tests her omnipotence.

One final point I came to appreciate is that in modern life we have come to expect continued health over extended periods of time and that loss through death is viewed as an abnormal "life event." These privileged assumptions and expectations have surely not been the norm for most of humanity for most of history until very recently and then only in the highly industrialized world. With repeated pregnancy loss, along with other deaths in my life, I came to feel more of the tragedy in everyone's life and to feel that loss and death are normal even though they are commonly denied and disavowed. I became aware that, at least in modern times, health, success, and fertility are taken as givens and are all too often experienced as essential contributors to self-esteem. Feeling intact as a worthwhile human being in the face of illness, loss, and death became a developmental challenge and goal, both for myself and one to which I became sensitized in my patients. I found myself, for example, interpreting more frequently how life's reversals and losses were experienced as narcissistic mortifications and as oedipal defeats that diminished a patient's self-esteem. And, again, in an extraanalytic sense, knowing that I had experienced repeated loss, along with some success, yet continued to work with the same analytic attitude, was something that several of my patients reported was a powerful incentive and support to their self-esteem in their own difficult times.

References

Bassen, C. (1988), The impact of the analyst's pregnancy on the course of analysis. *Psychoanal. Inqu.,* 8:280–298.

Braasch, L. (unpublished), The analyst's pregnancy and the course of psychoanalysis: A "Special Event," 1979a.

Bridges, N., & Smith, J. (1988), The pregnant therapist and the seriously disturbed patient. *Psychiatry. Interpers. & Biolog. Proc.*, 51:104–109.

Fenster, S., Phillips, S., & Rapaport, E. (1986), *The Therapist's Pregnancy*. Hillsdale, NJ: Analytic Press.

Givelber, F., & Simon, B. (1981), A death in the life of a therapist and its impact on the therapy. *Psychiatry*, 44:141–149.

Hannett, F. (1949), Transference reactions to an event in the life of the analyst. *Psychoanal. Rev.*, 36:69–81.

Lax, R. (1969), Some considerations about transference and countertransference manifestations evoked by the analyst's pregnancy. *Internat. J. Psycho-Anal.*, 50:363–372.

Nadelson, C., Notman, M., Arons, E., & Feldman, J. (1974), The pregnant therapist. *Amer. J. Psychiat.*, 131:1107–1111.

Penn, L. (1986), The pregnant therapist. Transference and countertransference issues. In: *Psychoanalysis and Women*, ed. J. L. Alpert. Hillsdale, NJ: Analytic Press, pp. 287–315.

van Leeuwen, K. (1966), Pregnancy envy in the male. *Internat. J. Psycho-Anal.*, 47:319–324.

10

Doing Psychotherapy While Living with a Life-Threatening Illness

AMY LICHTBLAU MORRISON, M.S.S.W.

> Since almost all of us think as savages do on [the topic of death], it is no matter for surprise that the primitive fear of the dead is still so strong within us and always ready to come to the surface on any provocation. Most likely our fear still implies the old belief that the dead man becomes the enemy of his survivor and seeks to carry him off to share his new life with him. . . .
>
> —Sigmund Freud (1919, p. 242)

> Depend upon it, sir, when a man knows he is to be hanged in a fortnight, it concentrates his mind wonderfully.
>
> —Samuel Johnson

While dealing with cancer for the past six years, I have felt paradoxically interested and challenged by the implications and issues raised in the work with patients. For reasons stemming from my own history, I am personally and professionally committed to dealing with matters of separation and loss, and to helping others with their feelings on these matters when appropriate. Over the years, I have known many instances in which patients were abandoned by ill or dying therapists, who denied the gravity of their own illness or impending death, and did not attempt to say goodbye or help their patients connect with another therapist. Most of us have known of these sometimes horrifying tales which, often enough, have brought about a repetition of past traumatic losses. While we cannot prepare for every eventuality or protect our patients from all disruptions stemming from our own lives, we can pause for thought about the meaning and implications for the treatment of how we handle these situations. From my own experience of living with a life-threatening illness and the vantage point of six years' survival, I can speak to how this experience can enrich and inform the work, as it also poses new and difficult dilemmas.

Six years ago I was stunned and my life disrupted by a diagnosis of breast cancer. Two years, and then one year later, I had recurrences, locally manifested. I've been treated with various combinations of surgery, radiation, and chemotherapy. Interruptions in my work have varied from no time (third occurrence) to five weeks. Other than for the effects of the treatments themselves, to date I have not felt ill, but rather have felt physically healthy and energetic. (The loss of my hair as a direct consequence of chemotherapy during the second episode was the worst effect of all of my treatment. More than the hair loss itself, I experienced wearing a wig as a major narcissistic embarrassment. I managed this phase with the image of going through a tunnel, knowing that in time I would emerge and there would be light.) Prognostically, the outlook for me has moved from optimistic, to guarded, to grim; and now, with time elapsing, to more hopeful. Emotionally, I have gone through a number of stages: the predictable feelings of shock, sadness, anger, depression, worry. But there has also been another side: an energizing, a greater attunement to my patients, a sense of myself as courageous and as physically and emotionally strong; an experiencing of this siege as providing a strangely useful opportunity.

In the context of a recent return to a personal psychoanalytic psychotherapy experience, an early life event known to me during my own psychoanalysis of twenty years ago and subsequent stints of psychotherapy, came "alive" and yielded understandings which had escaped me and my previous therapists. When I was two and a half, I witnessed the violent, suicidal death of a close maternal relative. I was subsequently kept out of the family's grief process, and the topics of this death and of suicide were "forbidden" for discussion. My mother's unchanging position was that this traumatic event occurred to her and not to me, for I was "only a baby" who couldn't understand. Now, fifty years later, I've come to understand the meaning to me of this event and how it was handled, and the intimately connected resonance of my illness, which, in turn, bears on how I have felt and conducted myself as a therapist.

My illness became the traumatic event in the present, which echoed and rekindled the traumatic event of the past, and provided both an opportunity to grieve and to derive the gratifications which had been denied me in the past. More explicitly, I got from friends, family, and my doctors the affirmation of self (through expressions of love and concern) and validation of my experience as horrible and terrifying, and as happening to me, all so important and missing for me in the earlier traumatic loss. While I hope I have not sought these gratifications from my patients, this understanding explains to my satisfaction the paradox of the greater sense of attunement rather than of depression or anger, which has permeated my life and work since the cancer. In a secondary way, the illness served a corrective emotional function for me. With patients, who so often provide for us the way to self-understanding, I often felt that I was able to listen with a "fourth" ear, particularly for issues of loss and meanings around my absences. (This aspect of my experience is like that of therapists in mourning who reported that their own suffering deepened their ability to listen and to respond to loss in a patient's life "in a keener and more sensitive way" [Givelber and Simon, 1981].) This is not to say that my illness has not interfered with the work with some patients, and sent some persons away.

PATIENTS' REACTIONS TO DISRUPTION

In the first episode of my cancer, I was away from work first for a week for surgery, and then, six weeks later, for three days (plus a weekend) for a radium implant as the final stage of radiation treatment. In each absence I had some lead time, and told my patients that something had come up such that I had to be away for the determined time; then I listened. There was, of course, a range of response, from denial to concern. Not surprisingly, people reacted in ways that reflected their own experiences and defense patterns. For example, Ms. W.'s parents had made innumerable moves around the globe, in some instances moving the family, and in others moving themselves and sending the children to American boarding schools. The children were always told that these moves, which were for financial gain, were for their sake, that they would reap the financial rewards in the future. Ms. W. assumed that I had decided to attend a professional meeting, and would return a better therapist for her.

In contrast, Ms. F.'s father was diagnosed with a serious, degenerative disease when she was eleven. This loving, close, and devoted family reorganized itself around the father's increasingly home-bound needs, the mother committing herself first and foremost to her husband. Ms. F., a young woman in her early twenties, had entered treatment a year before the onset of my illness, in excruciating psychic pain, dominated by feelings of enormous rage. About my forthcoming absence, Ms. F. first wondered whether anything was wrong in my family, immediate or extended. The anxiety generated by my announced absence was expressed in a deflected transferential form. She asked if we could meet an extra time in the week before my absence because a lot of "shit" was going on in a current relationship with a man: "He can't take my pain." In the session following my absence, she worried about her self-involvement in relationships, while at the same time saying, in response to my query about her further thoughts concerning my absence, that she didn't want to know—"Maybe a parent [of yours] died." My suggestion that sometimes not wanting to know was self-protective, as with a child for whom it is scary and overwhelming to see a parent as vulnerable, brought a response of tears, along with the expressed wish not to further discuss it at this point. Ms. F. then focused on her and her mother's dependency in relationships with men. Yet, she thought she would be able to manage during my absence, which she decided was to be a vacation; her anger would be about her envy! She had a passing thought, at the end of one hour, as to my health, but though I felt able to help her pursue this, she chose, and I think, at that time needed, to abandon the concern.

Another case vignette took an interesting turn. Mr. C. is a musician, with a highly idealizing, merger transference. The birth of a brother when he was a year and a half had been traumatic for him, both as a loss of his mother and because of his unbearable feelings of envy. He, in fact, had left the treatment for a two-year period, generated by my pregnancy. He also moved to another state, a four-hour drive away. He had returned to therapy around the loss to an early death through cancer of a close male friend. He was narcissistically wounded by the fact that his friend had not brought him into his inner circle in his dying days, and he was unable to grieve or let go of this friend. Since Mr. C. felt unable to work with anyone other than me, we had double sessions on each of two weekend days, occurring at one- or two-month intervals. Thus, he knew nothing of my absence for surgery two weeks earlier, when we met on a late April weekend. I had spent the greater part of that Saturday baking a cake and otherwise preparing for my daughter's fifth birthday party, being held the next day. Sitting with Mr. C. was the first time I had stopped moving that day; I felt very tired, my eyelids drooped, and I think I even nodded off for a minute. Mr. C. was quite alarmed, but struggled with his question as to what was going on with me. I too struggled with my conflict: feeling I had to tell him of my illness, both because I had betrayed myself and because he was so sensitive and vulnerable to loss; also thinking that honest disclosure would be protective and, perhaps, emotionally useful. On the other hand, my more usual analytic stance told me not to self-disclose and to buy time, which is what I decided to do, knowing that we had another meeting the next day. On Sunday Mr. C. was still disturbed about my lapse. I asked for his thoughts. He said that he wondered if I was pregnant, and that if I was, he would have to leave the therapy, as he could not bear to see me so. A wonderful reminder, I thought, that it's what is on the patient's mind that matters.

The Uncanny

There have been numerous, seemingly uncanny coincidences between my illness and aspects of my practice. At the time of my original cancer diagnosis, I had in my practice three people who had been referred as transfers, because their previous therapist, a social worker colleague, had died of complications subsequent to breast cancer. In addition, at the time of my first diagnosis, while awaiting the results of my biopsy, I found myself sitting across from a patient who also was awaiting the results of a breast lump biopsy. She detected from the knowingness of my comments, and I allowed, that I was in "the same boat." My self-revelation was not based upon a carefully thought out decision, but rather emerged as the human, kindred thing to do. I experienced the coincidence as both serendipitous and bonding. We both received cancer diagnoses. While Ms. R., like me, experienced the drama of the coincidence, and a sense of closeness, the more important meanings of her experience were very different from mine, and ultimately led her to disconnect from me and the therapy.

Ms. R., the divorced mother of three children, was the

younger sister in an unconsciously hostile, and extraordinarily dependent relationship with her older sister, whom she viewed as much more competent and successful than herself. Ms. R. had been in treatment with me for four rather slow-moving years before the onset of our mutual illnesses, and continued for another two-and-a-half years. She chose to discontinue therapy a short time after my first recurrence and chemotherapy, some months before the onset of a metastasis to her bones, although she was continuing to work. Already through chemotherapy, she had come in to a session offering me some of her head scarves along with a demonstration of ways of using them. I had chosen to wear a wig only, but think I must have offended Ms. R. in refusing her offer. More importantly, the transference meaning of this offer, as a role reversal in which Ms. R. was the more experienced, "older" sister, escaped me and was thus bypassed. Ms. R.'s life's credo was, "If something bad is going to happen, it will happen to me." While her sense of self-worth and actual life experiences had begun to improve, we had neither understood, nor had she been disabused of this credo when her cancer struck. For her, the cancer became the confirmation of the credo. In the transference, I became the older, more competent and more successful sister, viewed as being stronger (and better) than she in my attitude and handling of my illness. Unfortunately, my interpretations went nowhere, as in much of the work before our illnesses. Ms. R. and I were unable to work on or bridge her envy, which I can only postulate became so unbearable as to cause her to flee. Neither she nor her family chose to notify me of her worsening illness, and ultimate death.

I have in my practice now two women whose fathers have metasticized prostate cancer, and five women affected by breast cancer in their mothers, or, in one case, a sister (my practice is half-time; about eighteen people). I mention this as a further reflection of coincidence and the feeling of the uncanny; perhaps it more truly reflects the ubiquitous aspect of cancer in the population.

The Therapist's Stance Toward Divulgence; Patients' Stances About Knowing

"The readiness is all," is a favorite quote (Shakespeare) and guideline to me, and suggests the stance I came to take, regarding whether or not to divulge my illness to my patients. During the second episode of my illness, when I was away from work for five weeks, I thought a lot about dying. My thoughts included the importance to me of facing it, and helping others including my patients, by allowing them to know, thus enabling them to grieve. However, before my return to work, I realized that I was not at that point a dying person. What mattered most to me was to be able to return to work maintaining a stance of inquiry and openness to meaning. I decided that I would be willing to respond honestly to those who wanted to know, would not initiate any self-disclosures, and, above all, would listen. My experience has been that some people struggle, at a more or less conscious level, about whether or not they wish to know, and the conflict about knowing may become the focus of the therapy. A few people who had a particular historical sensitivity to illness or loss struggled about knowing in relation to whether or not they could bear the news and maintain the treatment relationship, as with Ms. F., mentioned earlier, who had grown up with a loss in parenting because of an ill father, and chose not to find out about me. A few people picked up on changes immediately, and wanted to know. What amazed me was the number of people who both manifestly, and in their latent material, seemed not to notice at all such marked changes as the appearance of my wig. I view this as a manifestation of self-absorption and reflection of narcissism, both characterological and phase typical, as in adolesence.

Patients: To Know or Not to Know

Ms. B. is someone whose first therapist had died of breast cancer. In my first episode, she asked following my absence whether it had been for anything medical, only asking at the end of a session. I said this was a question worthy of more time, and in weeks following we got into her conflict about whether she really wanted the answer, along with my willingness to tell her, or to not tell her, as she preferred. It took three weeks until Ms. B. decided that she did want to know.

Ironically, and back in the realm of the uncanny, Ms. B.'s younger sister had developed and been treated for lymphatic breast cancer in the interim between my first two episodes. The second episode of my cancer occurred shortly before a planned three-week vacation, allowing me simply to add two weeks for, this time, the more major surgery of a mastectomy and breast reconstruction. Chemotherapy was also initiated during my "vacation," and I returned to work wearing a wig. Before my departure, I told my clients that something had come up, such that I would be adding two weeks to the planned three weeks I'd be away. Again, I tried to listen for reactions. Ms. B. immediately guessed that I had a recurrence and this was acknowledged. She made a dire prediction: that my disease would be found to be systemic, at a time when it was being regarded optimistically, as simply a local recurrence. I considered Ms. B.'s prediction a reflection of her anger at me for again getting sick and reviving the threat of yet another death of a therapist for her. While my understanding may have been correct, Ms. B.'s understanding of breast cancer and prediction for me also turned out to be correct.

Mr. J., a thirty-five-year-old, depressed, unhappily single man was another one of the people who came into treatment with me after the loss to breast cancer of his previous therapist. He felt alone and isolated in his loss; he had kept his therapy a private matter and had no one to share in or validate his grief process. This young man was someone whose parents suddenly, from his experience of it, separated and subsequently divorced when he was ten. His father, felt by Mr. J. to be the more nurturant parent, was banished from the home by his mother. Mr. J. later banished him from his life, in contrast to his younger brother's decision as a young adult to seek father out and establish a connection. Mr. J. felt his role in the family was to be the "anchor," especially to mother, feeling he had to be in control and fearing becoming overwhelmed. He also felt and feared that his needs drove people away.

Mr. J.'s prior therapy was experienced very positively. He felt he had just reached a point of trusting his therapist enough to be able to express some anger to her, before the therapist's death. The former therapist's relatively sudden death and the lack of goodbye were experienced by Mr. J. as a betrayal which clearly repeated his earlier parental loss. With me, around the disruptions during the first episode of my illness, Mr. J. had associations to the illness of the prior therapist, and was conflicted: his felt need was not to know in order to be able to do his own work; yet, he also wanted to have advance warning of an impending loss! He elected not to know, and we went on with the work. In the second episode, Mr. J. noticed my hair change, struggled with whether or not he wanted to know, versus "living in limbo." He ultimately asked if I was sick and if it was cancer, and when informed, first laughed at the uncanniness of this happening to him yet again! He conveyed his experience of feeling utter and total abandonment after the previous therapist's death. He decided that he wanted to terminate with me. He did not believe that I would survive and definitely did not want to face my dying. Mr. J. terminated two months after finding out about my cancer, with an agreement to call and return in three months for a termination follow-up, an agreement which was not maintained. (I wonder how he has fared.)

For Ms. W., the conflict about knowing reflected a tenacious issue which my illness brought out and enabled us to work on. As noted, Ms. W. viewed my first absence through the transferential prism, excusing me, as her parents had her excuse them, without anger, viewing the disruption as being on her behalf. At the time of my first recurrence, Ms. W. was in the seventh year of her one session per week therapy, dealing with her fear of her anger and violent fantasies as driving people away. My announcement of adding two weeks to my planned three-week absence dovetailed with the subject on her mind that day anyway, her fear of abandonment. Her associations took her to her mother, as unhelpful, and her own feeling of helplessness. By the end of this hour, she felt "bummed out," listless and depleted, and she requested an additional appointment. In the couple of remaining sessions before my departure, Ms. W. realized her "annoyance" with me for giving sudden notice of added time away, and she moved from wondering whether I was adding more vacation, to concern that her neediness was causing me to take more time off, to wondering whether there was something wrong, whether I was sick, whether I would never come back. These queries led Ms. W. to feelings of sadness, with thoughts about her grandmother's dying, and that her parents would die.

When Ms. W. and I resumed after my five-week absence, I was wearing a wig. She greeted me with a "Welcome back," sharing her anxiety about whether I would return, whether we would reconnect. She described her now familiar to us conflict during the separation, between "going on automatic pilot," or having feelings. She felt she had regressed some during my absence, in the area of her sexual/relationship issues, and only at the end of this hour, said, "You look different than when you've returned from other vacations. . . . I don't like your new hairdo . . . it looks like you have more gray hairs. . . . You don't look tan and glamorous as at other times . . . as I want you to look." In the next session, I was wearing a bandana on my head (as an interim measure, before getting a better wig). Ms. W. wondered whether I was wearing the bandana because of her remark about my hair, but otherwise she focused on her need to "escape from reality" through flirting with men. In a transference deflection, she spoke of her mother's enormous rage, if she or her brother rejected some aspect of mother; for example, a dessert that mother had made. I missed Ms. W.'s fear of my rage for her criticism of my looks, but sought to link her wish to escape from reality with her notice of my less glamorous appearance, asking for further thoughts about my added time away: Ms.

W. stayed with her "escape," thinking that I wanted to spend more time with my husband, and/or more time at the beach.

In the ensuing weeks, Ms. W. had perceptions relating to changes in the therapy or therapist. I sought to help her pursue these clues, but she was not ready. Then she came in with a dream in which she was coming to therapy and saw me on the street, going to a mailbox at the side of a building; I did not notice her. . . . She had to greet me . . . I looked "yuppie," younger, with lighter brown hair, and was dressed in a professional manner. She came in the [my] house, but it was a very different house. She entered the office to wait for her session, but an older, short, dark-haired woman came in ("Your mother?"), wanting her time and space. She got angry, started to fight for it, ready to physically lift and remove the older woman—who looked like an "older, scrappier version of you." "You (therapist) and Dr. M. (therapist's husband) came in to help." By the end of recounting this dream, Ms. W. felt sad and was crying. Her feelings were of "loss" and of "parting." For me, the imageries of this dream called forth Ms. W.'s awarenesses and worries about me, and gave me to feel she was readier to know.

The work from this dream led us to an enunciation of two of Ms. W.'s plaguing issues: a conflict experienced between what she perceives, and whether she wants to know/go where these perceptions lead; and an old, familiar issue for us, expressed by her as, "Who's it for?" (i.e., the telling: for the patient or for the therapist?). Ms. W. was excruciatingly conflicted about whether she wanted to ask, to know, if her therapist had a "fatal or chronic illness." In what became the revelatory session, she said she had already feared this would be "the worst day of my life," and, as the end of the hour drew near, she wrestled with the consideration of whether she would be more anxious leaving the office knowing, or not knowing. She ultimately decided to ask, and when I responded that I did have a serious illness, and yes, it was cancer, Ms. W. became sad, choked up and said, "I'm very sorry . . . for you and for me." She asked about the kind of cancer. I told her the facts of my breast cancer and chemotherapy treatment, with, I felt right afterwards, too much detail. Nonetheless, the hour ended with Ms. W. saying she "felt better knowing."

During subsequent sessions Ms. W. expressed a range of feelings: her concern as to whether my telling was for her sake or mine, that is, to elicit her sympathy; feelings of omnipotence and of responsibility and guilt; concern with the therapist's vulnerability and susceptibility from hereon; conflict about whether it was all right to focus on her own concerns even if seemingly "trivial" compared to therapist's "problem." She, and we together, were able to make connections to earlier events and feelings in her life. She came to some inner resolution, quoting her father's saying, "Welcome to the adult world," and feeling some pleasure in learning to live with and handle these difficult and sad human events, while going on with life.

Our work continued, and a few months later, I, at the earliest possible time, removed my wig, presenting myself with a very short hair style. To my surprise, Ms. W. reacted with alarm and reluctance to talk about her first thought, which was that I looked like a concentration camp survivor. She then thought I had gotten brazen, and wondered whether this radical haircut represented a new step in my life. It unfolded that despite her many earlier perceptions and associations to my changed hair, she had not made the link between my changed hairdo (i.e., wig) and the information given her about my cancer and chemotherapy. When now informed, she was startled and felt "duped," the latter being another familiar feeling which led to further exploration.

With this patient, the subject of my illness and the unknowns of its course became immediately and inextricably linked with concerns about termination and worries about whether I'd be there for her if she felt the need to return. How would she know how her therapist was faring? Her concerns were manifested periodically, particularly at any cancellation of mine, and were worked out through an existential resolution (i.e., we are all going to die; no one knows when), during Ms. W.'s termination, which occurred recently, three-and-a-half years after learning of my illness.

In contrast to Ms. W., Ms. N. is someone who perceived, asked, wanted to know, reacted, and got on with her own work. Ms. N., an extremely perceptive and sensitive person, six years younger than I, when told of my lengthened absence wondered if anything was wrong. However, at her second session the same week she said that she realized that it may just be that "your villa in the South of France had an earlier opening." I did not disabuse her of this more enviable and less worrisome notion, as I too fantasized and wished it were so. When we resumed in September, Ms. N. took one look at me from the waiting area, came into my office where we took our customary positions, and she said, in a way that definitely was not superficial or pro forma, "So, what's been happening with you?" "A lot," I replied. "Is that a wig?" "Yes." "Do you have cancer?" "Yes." And we proceeded to talk about it, my responding to her queries with the facts, then moving on to her material. In the ensuing weeks, Ms. N. was well able to feel and to express a range of feelings, including her deep anger at me for reviving and threatening to repeat her life experience of vacated support from parental–dependency objects, and the consequence of being thrust on her own and feeling so alone. My perception was that our work was enriched, not hampered, by my sharing the facts of my illness with her. I also found that it was freeing for me to have a patient know. Work has been more difficult and constrained with patients who have not known, as I shall next elaborate.

Countertransferential Issues

Since the interventions for the third episode of my cancer required no interruptions in my work schedule, and there were no visible changes, none of my patients were told. I found this very difficult. When sitting with patients I was alone with my most depressing news, and without the particular challenge of listening to hear what was in their material in reaction to a disruption of mine. I was depressed anyway, and I was less "there" for my patients, at least during the first few months. (The silence of my disease was, this time, deafening—for me.) Ms. W. was "right" in her question at least, as to who the telling was for. There had been a "need" to tell, and to "help" people with their feelings about loss, including the loss of me! The preclusion of this opportunity was stultifying for me. While I have tried to contain my needs, I have been aware of a set of exhibitionistic wishes: for others to know of my trauma; to get expressions of love and concern; to get admiration about my strength and courage in handling the whole thing.

Even recently, two years after my last recurrence, an occurrence with a patient reminded me of my continuing need. Mr. C., the man who drives a considerable distance for double session weekend meetings, now comes about once in three or four months. Much of the therapy has also been through letters. After the time, six years ago, when Mr. C. feared I was pregnant, he went through a long phase of needing me to be there for him, signing many a letter "Don't die on me!" Again, I had to contain my own wish to tell, cloaked in thoughts about protecting him through forewarning. Now, he who was in a better differentiated self state, wrote me that his mother was diagnosed with breast cancer. In the session which followed this news, I, once again, got sleepy. I realized that I had anticipated that Mr. C. would talk about his mother's cancer, giving me an opportunity, minimally to be knowledgeable, and perhaps to open the subject as well, to be able to "share" about my cancer. When he did not talk at all about his mother's cancer, I felt doubly rebuffed: in the chance to disclose, and as to the importance of having such an illness.

Hard for me also was the work with a patient who is oncophobic. Ms. D. feared and worried about cancer with each nonmalignant health problem she did have (e.g., a sebaceous cyst which was surgically removed from her back). Ultimately, she had a small growth behind her ear removed and diagnosed as malignant. While she was given an extremely positive prognosis, she was angry and insulted when she felt that the people close to her did not indulge her to the extent that she wished. I felt identified with these others, viewing her cancer as minimal compared to mine. All along, in working with Ms. D., when she worried—unrealistically—about cancer, the thought in my mind was, "Boy, if you only knew!" This is the closest I've come in awareness of my own competitive or angry feelings toward patients for being healthy.

I have a patient now who came into treatment with me since my cancer episodes and does not know about these. She is someone who has had a serious chronic illness since her late teens. She holds basic feelings of being set apart from life, and that people who know about her illness are afraid of her. Along with other projections which keep me at a distance from her, she casts me into the group of the healthy who, she adamantly believes, can never deeply know and understand the experience of the ill. Internally, I have felt an ironic humor about this exclusion. I also found it hard to address, because of its closeness to me. My finding an opening to address this as her projection dramatically enabled this woman to begin to disclose more about her self and her experience.

Complexities and Intrusions

A couple was referred to me a few months after my last recurrence. Both in their forties, the wife was in treatment with the colleague who referred them. They presented initially as an appealing, well-functioning couple, who had some issues for which they could benefit from conjoint work. The husband is an oncologist at the hospital where I am followed. A few weeks after beginning work with this couple, the husband became mildly depressed and said that he wanted to do some individual work and wanted to do this with me. We then spent a number of sessions exploring this request and what it would mean to each partner. During this process, I saw the husband separately a few times. He talked about his work, sounded caring, competent, and committed. My fantasy feeling was about the serendipity of life: now I am your therapist; some day you may be my physician. As such, I felt that each of us was in good hands.

I returned from a holiday weekend away to a phone message to call the husband. He, communicating urgency, asked for an immediate appointment. The next day, with trepidation he revealed that he had followed a "feeling" about me, by getting hold of my hospital record, breaking through a confidentiality "lock" (that, until this, I hadn't known was on my record); he now knew all about my cancer and felt extremely upset. My first feelings were mixed: disturbed by the intrusion, but also relief at my illness being known, and some pride and enjoyment in an awareness of my self-presentation as healthy and energetic, having been through so much! This patient, however, rapidly sank into a severe depression which, along with his intrusive action, made dramatically clear the correctness of deciding to refer him to someone else for individual treatment. I remain the couples' therapist. In addition to the first intrusion, Dr. M. has talked about me at various times with my nurse from the chemotherapy phase; this nurse and I have a warm, mutually admiring connection, and the patient reports that he and my nurse exchange about what a wonderful person I am. My initial diagnostic impression of this patient was incorrect. Along with his idealization of me, he used the information gained from his intrusive action to confirm a deeply felt lack of self-worth: he should die so I could live. The anger elicited by his violations of my privacy have had me at moments with feelings echoing his.

Ms. Y., a twenty-five-year-old graduate student, had been in treatment with me for a year and a half, not knowing about my cancer, when she learned that her mother had breast cancer. I was presented with an excruciating conflict when I felt that, from what I heard from my patient, her mother was not being given sufficient medical information by her doctors. I regard myself as knowledgeable and well-informed about breast cancer. I have a wealth of printed information on file, know something about what is going on at the cutting edge of research, and am fairly often called upon, as a willing resource and counsel to others newly diagnosed with this disease. Obviously, neither my patient nor her mother was asking for the information I so much wanted to share. I wrestled with myself: the idea of intruding, breaking the stance of abstinence, bringing the knowledge of my illness into the therapy in a way initiated by me, rather than by the patient, weighed against the wish to share information that potentially could be life-saving. I realized that this conflict raised a "Who's it for?" question. With the thought that five years hence, if I were alive and my patient's mother dead, I would feel at fault for not having shared the information I had, I decided to err in favor of life, accepting that this was first of all, for me! (i.e, serving the needs of my own conscience).

At the manifest level, my patient was grateful for my disclosure. She went "home" shortly thereafter, armed with a couple of reprints supplied by her therapist. She returned to her next session reporting that her mother and stepfather were not interested in reading these articles, and that her siblings were angry at her for disturbing their mother's contentment with her physicians and their recommendations and highly optimistic prognosis. As for the therapy and the transference, Ms. Y. initially saw my overt good health and strength as a positive example of how things would go for her mother. A short time later, after I announced a forthcoming week's absence (for vacation), we met with "nothing to talk about" resistance. Exploration led to concern about and anger at me for burdening her with the news of my being at risk. The therapy nonetheless goes on, and does not feel in jeopardy.

Terminations

With the termination process and the inevitable question about the possibility of a return to the therapist, the awareness of my illness and unknown future arises, in my mind. With terminating patients who do know about my illness, the question as to whether I will be available in the future can be directly expressed, along with feelings of concern, and wishes to know what will be happening to the therapist in regard to the illness. Among the aspects of loss during the termination process, one that has emerged is the loss of the ability to keep an eye on me!

Some patients, like Ms. W., can deal with this issue in the broader existential context which the termination process often engenders: recognition of the ambiguities and uncertainties of life that need to be borne. For these patients there is acceptance that I either will or won't be there for them in the future, and that we also don't know all of what will befall them. In contrast, I had one terminating patient who has worked with me in three segments for the better part of sixteen years, knew about my illness, and was worried about whether I would be there for her in the future. Somewhat uncomfortably, I acceded to her request/need to have me notify her if I possibly could, if I become seriously ill.

Economic Implications

I have been open about my illness with colleagues and friends in my community. I was living in a state of siege, this was my "headline," and stylistically I could not have done otherwise. I did not give much thought to the "reality" of the likely consequence, that this information would negatively affect referrals to me. I certainly would hesitate to refer a candidate for long-term, open-ended psychotherapy to someone with a known, life-threatening illness and statistically poor prognosis. The threat of financial loss is real and great, when one depends upon one's income, is healthy enough to be working, and not eligible to collect disability income (assuming one even has such insurance).

While having lunch one day with a colleague who is a usual source of referrals but who hadn't referred since my illness, I asked about this. She replied that she would refer some people, not others. I sought further elaboration and she said she would refer people who had not suffered loss, and would not refer those with histories of loss. I thought to myself, "Which of our patients has not suffered loss?" A short time afterwards, this colleague called to refer a depressed young man, emphasizing that he had not experienced any deaths in his family. Within the first few diagnostic sessions I learned that this man's father had been diagnosed with prostate cancer a year earlier, and that his stepmother was then dying of cancer. I have been working with this man for three years. His stepmother has died. His father's cancer has metasticized to his bones. He does not know about my cancer history.

While the number of patient referrals has not been seriously affected, it seems the pattern of referrals changed to more time-limited kinds, such as students and couples. However, as time and my health go on, longer term type referrals resume.

Discussion

At the conclusion of a recent check-up, feeling in good health and good spirits, I asked my oncologist whether I could stop worrying about the illness (*illness* has never felt like the right word, since I haven't felt sick). His response was that this was something we could never stop worrying about. For me the feeling of worry has changed. Earlier I saw it as a dagger, pointing at me, poised close to my face. Then, at some point, I realized that the dagger had moved: it was somewhere in back of me; I had to turn to see it. Now, the dagger has disappeared from view. My paramount feeling is of being lucky, so far. While the awareness of my illness and the risk of recurrence and metastasis is ever present, the worry is not so immediate. The experience informs my life. I postpone things less; I try to live more fully. I think this attitude infuses my work. I feel both freer and more fully "there" with patients.

Ethical questions arise. Should a new patient be told of my cancer history before starting treatment? What if there's a history of and vulnerability to loss as occurred recently with a prospective new patient who at an early age lost his mother to breast cancer? Currently I have nothing known from which I am dying. But what if I do have a metastatic recurrence with an unknown time course? Would there be a greater obligation then to inform my patients? Or to leave or change my work? I do not have answers. I think about these things, highlighted with each new patient. Thus far, it feels right to go on with my life and work, and it seems inappropriate to inform or warn new patients of my cancer history.

Until recently the issue of the therapist's illness and dying had not been addressed. While Freud stressed the importance of honesty in the doctor–patient encounter, from what can be discerned he did not for the most part deal with the impact on his patients of his long, sixteen-year struggle with his "dear old cancer." There is evidence which suggests a conflict between what he felt (shame) and what he thought. In his correspondence he thanks a colleague for not mentioning the evidence of his recent surgery. On the other hand, he is said to have admonished a patient who was withholding her fears about his condition: "We have only one aim and only one loyalty, to psychoanalysis. If you break this rule you injure something much more important than any consideration you owe me" (Schur, 1972, p. 383). This volume reflects and adds to the recent interest and surge in the literature dealing with these matters. These writings attempt to raise and to answer questions. How much of the therapist's "reality" in respect to her illness should patients be told? By whom? When? Which patients should/should not be told? What gets compromised or sacrificed in the analytic work when patients are given facts about therapists' lives and vulnerabilities? There are those who advocate, in the name of analytic anonymity, that patients never be given the facts about the reasons for the therapist's interrupting the work, although these therapists candidly reveal that they told their patients more than they later wished they had (chapter 5). There are those who think how much is told should be titrated, in accord with the therapist's judgment about the best interest of the patient, using criteria of patient vulnerability, or stage in the treatment, or the kind of treatment (i.e., analytic: tell less; supportive: tell more) (chapters 4, 6). There are those who made their decisions about how to handle their illness/disruption in conjunction with their own comfort, varying what they did by the responses anticipated from different patients (Goldberg, 1984; chapter 7).

A premise of this writing is that there is a "real" relationship in the therapist–patient encounter, one that, at least for some patients, is separate from and goes beyond the transferential relationship, or that of serving selfobject needs. A corollary of this premise is the implication that we do our patients a serious and potentially harmful disservice if we refuse to acknowledge certain realities such as of our own serious illness, even when the patient perceives something and inquires. For many a patient, the therapist's refusal to acknowledge the patient's awareness of the therapist's vulnerability becomes a repetition of past, deleterious experience. Most familiar to us are parental efforts to cloak, hide, or forbid talk about "bad" events, in the name of protection, but almost always resulting in confusion or disturbance. On the other hand, I also think it is not for us to impose our "reality" on patients who, for a variety of reasons, are not ready or do not want to know.

We need to consider and balance what is gained or lost, in the adherence to a stance of analytic anonymity when the therapist is dealing with a serious or life-threatening illness. The principal argument for nondisclosure has to do with the purpose of this "rule," which is to optimally facilitate the development and exploration of the transference relationship. We may add that by maintaining a cherished and familiar professional role ideal, one retains one's own cohesion and self-esteem, with obvious advantage to one's patients.

On the other hand, one must ask what gets sacrificed in the therapist–patient encounter if the therapist withholds personal information, even as it may have crucial implications for the patient? Many a therapist in the situation of his or her own illness or dying has chosen to falsify with the rationale of protecting patients or maintaining anonymity, often misnamed abstinence or neutrality.* The patient's feeling of trust may be jeopardized. If the therapist has known about her own condition for a period of time, but the experience of the patient is of a sudden interruption, termination, or death, the patient is likely to feel betrayed. At what point does analytic anonymity become deception? Not to help our patients to face and deal with loss, if we can, is counter to our analytic values and ideals. Patients are likely to be isolated in their grief as it is, since there is no socially sanctioned base for mourning a therapist (Foulkes, 1989). There also may be some real therapeutic advantage for the patient in the therapist's example of the capacity to bear ambiguity, or to face the unbearable. Yet we know that reactions to major life events are idiosyncratic, at the same time that they hold universals. It may not be humanly possible to handle a frightening illness, a threat to one's own life, in a way that is optimal and ideal for patients. We cannot prepare for all eventualities.

References

Fowlkes, M. (1989), The morality of loss: The social construction of mourning. Presented at the annual meeting of the American Sociological Association, San Francisco.

Freud, S. (1919), The uncanny. *Standard Edition,* 17:217–256. London: Hogarth Press, 1955.

——— (1915), Observations on transference. *Standard Edition,* 12:159–171. London: Hogarth Press, 1958.

Givelber, F., & Simon, B. (1981), A death in the life of a therapist and its impact on the therapy. *Psychiatry,* 44:141–149.

Goldberg, F. (1984), Personal observations of a therapist with a life threatening illness. *Internat. J. Group Psychother.,* 35:289–296.

*Along with Hoffer, I regard neutrality as the therapist's stance in relation to the patient's conflicts. Anonymity is the therapist's stance in respect to his/her own self-disclosure, whereas abstinence, as used by Freud, pertains to the therapist's stance in respect to the transference love of the patient (Hoffer, 1985; personal communication, 1989).

35:289–296.
Hoffer, A. (1985), Toward a definition of psychoanalytic neutrality. *J. Amer. Psychoanal. Assn.*, 33:771–795.
Schur, M. (1972), *Freud: Living and Dying*. New York: International Universities Press.
Shakespeare, W. *Henry IV, Pt. I. The Riverside Shakespeare.* Boston: Houghton Mifflin, 1974.

Part III

Death of the Analyst

11

Manifestations of Grief and Grievance: A Therapist's Response to an Analyst's Death

DAVID A. S. GARFIELD, M.D.

INTRODUCTION

"Some impressions last a lifetime": In *The Psychogenesis of Mental Disease,* Jung (1907) aptly captured the lasting imprint through which human events etch themselves into the mind. In my first year of residency training in psychiatry, I had been treating a young woman, an actress, then ten years into a psychotic illness, who frequently commented that she "bore the mark." A metaphorical schizophrenia, I half-concluded. In that first year of training, I decided to go into psychotherapy for myself, not knowing that my insistence that my therapist be the "old man" was, in fact, the framing of my constitutional illness. The "old man" had been one of the founders of the psychoanalytic institute, analyst to my most prized teachers and supervisors, and when I called him to see if he would treat me, I received a resounding "no!"

He was retired, he said, not seeing patients any more, no longer a training analyst because of his age. He had had two ruptured aortic aneurysms and he had survived. He had, in his earlier years, gone to Vienna to try to be analyzed by Freud but had ended up being analyzed by Federn. At that time, I had never heard of Federn. But, as a professional "child," I had found my hero. At that time, the early 1980s, the theaters were filled with *Star Wars* and *The Empire Strikes Back*. Here was my wise old teacher, a venerable and endangered species. There wasn't much time left. I begged for a consultation and he finally relented.

Immediately, he started in with his narcissism attack. "You must give up your illegitimate entitlements," he insisted. What did I know about narcissism? Entitlements, as I understood them, had to do with Medicaid. I promptly went off to the library and read Freud's (1914) paper, "On Narcissism: An Introduction." It was a start. Federn's (1953) book *Ego Psychology and the Psychoses* was hard to read but I tried anyway. On top of *The Diagnostic and Statistical Manual of Mental Disorders* (DSM-III) (American Psychiatric Association, 1980), psychopharmacology, progressive community politics, beginning to learn psychotherapy, a new Tai Chi Chuan teacher, and an attempt at a real romance, there was my therapy, there was the "old man."

Spiro Agnew had once said that in today's world, adolescence had been extended too far into the twenties. At age twenty-seven, there I was stuck not only with Erikson's (1950) "intimacy versus isolation" but in a feverish pursuit of heroes. I had immersed myself in Mahler's subphases (Mahler, Pine, and Bergman, 1975), Freud's (1933) psychosexual stages, Piaget's (1952) sequence for cognition, Kohut's (1966) "forms and transformations" of narcissism, Anna Freud's (1937) hierarchy of defense mechanisms, and Erikson's (1950) psychosocial hurdles. Patients were placed on the matrix and formulations were constructed. I was learning psychiatry. Was this whole business a developmentalist's love affair? I sought refuge in the interpersonal school and asylum with the existentialists.

"Old Man" Anecdotes

Perhaps most memorable was the winter morning when I showed up for my usual 11 A.M. appointment. It was a particularly cold Northeast winter and I was bundled up. His wife answered the door (he saw patients in the den) and quickly said, "Just one minute" and, to my surprise, returned with her purse and asked how much she owed me for the newspaper subscription. I replied that I was Dr. Garfield, here in my therapy hour. Before it could register with her, he came up behind her and also asked me how much they owed me for the newspaper subscription. For a moment, I panicked that I would not be recognized as an adult but rather that I would be locked into the identity of the newspaper boy and sent on my way. Would it come to an end like that? Trapped in transference? Was I once again at the doorstep of the "old man" with his not knowing who I *really* was? I could tell that he did not recognize me. Luckily, my words had registered with his wife and she intervened and told him that it was Dr. Garfield, here for his therapy hour. "Oh. Oh. Of course" he stammered and then he invited me into the den. A moment of horror, it seemed, later turned into reels of humor—to be mistaken by your therapist for the newspaper boy. It was funny—funny, like a "near-miss" when your scariest fantasy is materializing rapidly, only to be averted at the last minute and cast back into unreality.

Another snapshot from the album of this relationship which stands out is the "Freud contest." In the struggle to learn and *not* be pigeonholed, I once exclaimed: "What the hell did Freud know about people anyway? Some asshole stuck in Victorian Vienna in a high-price consulting room." I was not aware that this was a not too subtle displacement. After a few moments of perplexity, my challenge was met with: "He knew a whole hell of a lot more about people than you do!" I was stopped in my tracks, I was delighted and taken by the reply. He could be terribly engaging—something I was obviously seeking.

Another example of his forcefulness was when he once pounded his fist on the arm of his chair in response to my obfuscating: "You are the most resistant patient I have ever treated!" I was very flattered. He had, after all, treated my most cherished supervisors. It wasn't until years later that I learned that he had said that to many of his patients, complete with the fist banging. When I asked him if I should be seeing him more than once a week if this were going to be considered analysis, he replied that the important thing was whether I wanted to change, not how many times a week I saw him. He had seen many of his institute analysands once weekly when he was younger and still of the age to be a training analyst.

Analyze the transference? Not a chance—the transference was elicited into full force rapidly and it served to clear up my life rather quickly. The residency, Tai chi, politics, and romance could not have been going better. A transference cure, as I understood it.

Stricken

He was a tall man and I found out that he had run track in his youth. He had also played basketball. I had been on vacation in Peru, one of my first overseas adventures, and had had a terrific time. One of my younger supervisors told me the news of the "old man's" stroke on my first day back to work. He knew that I would be devastated, for he had been in treatment with the "old man" some years back. Few others, however, knew that I had been in treatment at all. It had only been a year.

I went to see him at the hospital where he had been taken—I felt desperate and had called his wife who said that she thought it would be good for him to have his patients see him (he had only a few), and I went at my usual appointment time. He was severely aphasic but he could recognize me and remembered my name. He was paralyzed on the right side. In his characteristic fashion, he asked me how I felt about his stroke. "Awful" was all I could muster. "Reality is distasteful" he asserted. I was dumbfounded. I couldn't believe that he was going to speak with me as though we were still in therapy. How did I feel? Reality is distasteful? Could he be serious? He was going to continue to be therapeutic in the midst of his own disaster. Next to his stroke itself, the part that affected me the most about the interaction was his verbal assertion that reality was distasteful. How could one even attempt to put it into words?

On Becoming Mute

It is precisely this experience of becoming mute in the face of loss which will be explicated in this essay. There was for me, with the stroke of this analyst, a loss of my voice. It was not somatic; I could still make linguistic utterances, logically enough cohered, but, in an essential way, I, too, became aphasic. But more, I retreated inside, rapidly and completely, like a wounded animal. I was going through the motions.

Where was the emotion? I wasn't someone who cried a lot anyway, so that was one outlet pretty much closed to me. I'm not sure that I ever learned to grieve. There had been no major interpersonal losses in my life before so I had been spared in that regard. There were, however, other ways in which I had not been spared—in physical, personal ways. At age six and seven, I had been operated on for detached retinas. Memory fragments of these times were quite available to me. I remember having to lie flat on my back; I remember a midnight plane trip from Chicago to Boston to a hospital; I remember being in a wheelchair in the hospital lobby; I remember that John F. Kennedy was running for President and that he was giving a speech in the hotel next to where my mom and I were staying. Most of all, I remember the doctor unwinding the bandages from my eyes and wondering if I would be able to see. I must have been extraordinarily anxious.

Perhaps it was this anxiety of not knowing the extent of the damage that pervaded my life after the "old man's" stroke. How deep did it go? After a few weeks, it was clear that he was getting worse, not better. I continued to visit him, although not at my old appointment times. I knew that I was supposed to feel bad; I knew that I was supposed to go into treatment with someone else; I knew that this was therapy and not someone who was a part of my "regular" life—it was different. But how, and in what ways? I needed time.

I asked him what I should do. He said: "Tell me your feelings." I wondered who was taking care of whom. He would slip in and out of being lucid. He was to be transferred to a chronic care hospital. At one point, I asked him if he was going to die. He had been deteriorating for several weeks by that time and had become even more aphasic. He could, at times, be quite lucid and struggled to get his words out. He didn't respond to my question. Were we to confront "distasteful" reality together? I was angry, and the question now strikes me as cruel, although I didn't know it at the time. Any other aggressive or tender fantasies I might have had were pretty much bound up in my shock and guilt and were, thus, unavailable to me. Interestingly enough, he seemed to struggle honestly with my question about his dying, even though he declined comment.

Termination

My supervisors felt that I was prolonging my own agony. Perhaps they felt helpless. An old analysand of the "old man," then a senior analyst herself, visited him regularly also. She and I had a kinship of sorts. There was an acknowledgment of the importance of this man in our lives. Later, she offered to take me into analysis with her to continue the "old man's" work with me. I said no; my work would go on, but in my own way. I called a different analyst whom another supervisor had suggested in my original search. This was a younger man, not in the grandfather category, and more likely to have enough years left to complete an analysis. Luckily, he let me know that he was in good physical condition and had no life-threatening illnesses that he knew of, and, as silly as it seems, I needed to hear that to even consider beginning anew.

I wanted the "old man's" blessing to start with someone else—after all, he kept interacting with me within a therapeutic style even though it was clear that the therapy could not continue. I asked him who he would recommend. He had deteriorated cognitively even more. "Semrad," he said, "would be my first choice for you." Dr. Elvin Semrad was a beloved Boston analyst who had died some five years earlier. "But Semrad is dead," I replied. He looked puzzled. "No, he isn't. Semrad's not dead. He would be my first choice for you." I remember becoming "softer" at that time, as, obviously, the disillusionment which reality inevitably brings can be overwhelming.

So there we were. I asked about the new analyst, upon whom I had decided pretty much anyway, and he seemed to think that this new guy was "okay." This was less than the enthusiastic "stamp" which I would have preferred but, at least, an honest discussion about the transition had taken place. I had declared that I would no longer be seeing him for treatment but that I would come to say "hello" from time to time, if that was all right with him. He said that he would like that and, I guess, that marked the termination of our therapy. Was this a compulsion to announce the obvious? I don't think so, because he was still alive and did have some capacity, even if markedly impaired, to relate. It was something that was important to me in the transition.

GRIEF AND GRIEVANCE—PHYSICAL AND INTERPERSONAL FORMS

How does one grieve? There must be many ways. Time, although widely regarded as being the best friend of grief, does not wait on it. For me, there were patients to see, studying to do, and there was a marriage in the making. I brought my wife to be to visit the "old man" after his stroke, and she could see how he suffered from the paralysis and subsequent debilitation. She could see how torn apart I was. Grieving and grievance. Who would hear my grievance? Later, the "old man" would have his leg amputated due to stasis and severe atherosclerosis. An experiential symbiosis posttermination?

He was losing a leg; I had lost my voice. For me, suffering, anger, and guilt worked their way in silence.

To what address does one send one's grievance with regard to serious personal loss? My unconscious claim was, in retrospect, quite selectively addressed. In short order, I proceeded to alienate the two most powerful men in my residency program. These were full professors who had direct authority over me. To all others, I was, for all appearances, the same hard-working good guy. The other challenge was laid down at the feet of my Tai Chi teacher. I had quickly moved through the training process of the martial arts, first learning the forms, then staff, then "push hands," and sword forms. I started going three times a week, instead of twice, to class. I increased the amount of time and force with which I was "pushing hands" with my teacher. In "pushing hands," one stands in front of the teacher and pushes both hands against both the teacher's hands. The teacher positions himself to offset the student's force. In this way, the student learns to summon, feel, and direct his physical energy and maintain his balance.

After a long plane ride for a vacation in California, I stood up from my seat, only to have excruciating buttock and low back pain, I had reherniated a lumbar disc. I had pushed too hard. I had, as it were, addressed additional complaints to my lower back. Ironically, I had intended to propose marriage while on my knees from atop a mountain. Instead, I proposed while on my back in bed while convalescing. It seemed spineless and pathetic. I can remember that a thought circulated through my mind at that time. "A chain is only as strong as its weakest link." A metaphorical griever, one might half-conclude. What did I know about the ego ideal and the crumbling of heroes? Life wasn't going my way any more.

Given the little history heretofore afforded the reader of this essay, one might have speculated that the most likely organ to be affected by psychic forces in my situation would have been the eyes. Instead, it seemed, I was intent to locate the burden not only in, but on, my back as well. As evidence of my need to embrace the phrase "get off my back," there was my intense refusal to identify with my older male teachers in my training program. I was told that I was doing well in the program except that I was flunking my psychotherapy supervision with my two older male supervisors (the ones noted above, who had direct authority over my standing in the program). I was told that I had seemed to develop some kind of "dyslexia" in that when I was told that a situation was "God," I seemed to be interpreting it as "Dog." Here, the specificity of grievance manifested itself quite clearly. I had unconsciously intended to let my gods know exactly what dogs I felt them to be for disappointing me. Frightened that I might get in big trouble, I let the program know that I would go for treatment twice a week to work this out.

Grief and Grievance—Mental Forms and Transformations

Sorrow and rage? They were not a part of my feeling experience. They expressed themselves in the ways noted above, and mostly it was the anger that manifested itself in those ways. There were other, more complex forms as well. On my drive to my new analyst's office, I worried that flashing police lights were intended for me. Had I not been going 40 in a 30 m.p.h. zone? Later, the police car passed by and I would realize that it had nothing to do with me. This kind of "idea of reference" happened frequently as I began my recovery from the trauma of the analyst's stroke and death. A touch of paranoia: Not only had I physically and interpersonally orchestrated that powerful forces "be on my back" but I was on my own back as well—there was this increase in intrapsychic self-observation. The strain of having to dance to a "new" man's tune (the time of the new analytic hours) would put me in jeopardy of being ticketed by the police. All of these "big guys" would, no doubt, be my undoing.

Another manifestation of the power of the grievance was the segregation and accentuation of cognition into perception. While presenting a case in a conference to one of my two "powerful" male supervisors (who had recently condemned me), a strong "loud" thought repeated itself five or six times over in my mind. It was the name "Evelyn," not that common a name. This was the name of the patient's wife in the case that I was presenting and I was concerned that my supervisor would take offense as I believed that *his* wife's name was Evelyn also. The conference itself went well. This "hearing" of a voice, especially for a psychiatry resident was disturbing. Was I getting psychotic? I soon discovered that the supervisor's wife's name was *not* Evelyn after all. In analysis, I remembered that my mother had originally been named "Evelyn" before her parents changed it. My grievance, it appeared, could not only yield bouts of increased self-observation and fear, but could also transform memory into thought into voice in a quite selective fashion. Searles (1965) has described this transformation of emotion into perception, and later I would write about the governance of psychosis by emotion (Garfield, 1987, 1988) as well as the role of the ego ideal in paranoia (Garfield, 1988). Left unbalanced by the loss of my hero, my facility for self-observation and critique was left unchecked and, as it were, in a condition of overdrive.

Grief and Grievance—Coping Strategies

The strategy of intellectual activity, puzzle-solving, and writing as a way of organizing myself in times of severe distress had had its antecedents in my latency. The cycle of ambition followed by injury and then recovery had all been laid down early. My detached retinas were precipitated by hard-driving physical pursuits. One, at age six, occurred while learning how to ice-skate and suffering a fall on my head. The other occurred the following year while chasing my beloved older sister in a gleeful game of tag, during which I ran headlong into a wall. The injury, bandaged eyes, and the fear were noted above, the impact of the injury was another story. The sense of defect, fear of rejection for being cross-eyed and "four-eyed," were dealt with by this intellectual activity and by a methodical attention to the nuances of my surroundings—how people, things, and games played themselves out. Aspirations replaced ambitions and an intense idealism emerged. It is, no doubt, a common form of recovery in a child and one which sets the intrapsychic stage for events such as the loss of an analyst to reopen earlier wounds.

There is a "going underground" which self psychology refers to as a response to empathic failure (Lachmann and Stolorow, 1980). Neurotic conflict is viewed not so much as an interplay between wish, prohibition, defense, and affect, but rather, as a product of developmental arrest at a given age, due to an "unattended to" self. No one ever asked me about my eye injuries, no one asked me about my glasses or how I felt about being called names. I didn't know how I felt and, after all, "you shouldn't let it get you down." I lost my voice. Perhaps that was the first time.

In an essay such as this which has been so concerned with "the father-complex," it would be remiss not to say something about my relationship with my own father as it, undoubtedly, impacted on this later experience. My father had also suffered from severe eye problems when I was a baby (six months old or so). He had detached retinas which were not repaired well and left him functionally blind in one eye. His anxieties about having a family and being able to financially support it were intense. He continued at his business and was able to develop it into a quite successful company. He was not a complainer and didn't speak at all about any hardships or anxieties he had. He redoubled his work efforts to ensure his survival and success and as a result did not spend a lot of casual time with his children. His health status, his way of coping with it, and his not spending a lot of time at home all combined to frame the kinds of responses to my first therapist's illness. It wasn't until I was in analysis the second time, on the couch, at least three times a week, that I discovered how intense a transference had developed to my first analyst, demonstrated by my referring to him as the "old man" as opposed to my real father. The fact that I have mentioned so little about the second analyst—we spent a good deal of time discussing the loss of the first—is probably a testament to the fact that I think the completed analysis "worked." I am indebted to my analyst for putting up with my rageful protests and continuing to persistently ask me about my pain, which helped me become much more able to bear it and put it in perspective.

Since the "old man" died, I have been in a process of recovery. It has gone in fits and spurts. I regret not having gone to the memorial service given for him by the analytic community. Why didn't I go? A valued woman supervisor, herself an analysand of the "old man," had noted: "I don't believe in public mourning. Grief is a private affair." I felt that I, too, should grieve by myself. The only problem was that I didn't know how. Funerals are essential to answer this need.

Unresolved Grief and Refinding One's Voice

Unresolved grief, is, according to Lazare (1976), multifaceted. He identified social and psychological causes including: social negation of the loss; socially "unspeakable" losses; social isolation; having to be "strong"; and uncertainty about social consequences of the loss. The psychological causes included: guilt; reawakening old losses; multiple loss; inadequate ego development; and loss as an extension of self. It seems most probable that several of these categories combine in any given case of unresolved grief. That was certainly true for me. What is missing in such descriptions is the phenomenological element.

Havens (1986) aptly titled his book on psychotherapy *Making Contact.* It concerns both the liberation and the development of the self through a psychotherapeutic relationship. Insofar as the therapist can "make contact" with the patient, the patient is enabled to give voice to his own true interests. Thus, it is not enough for the therapist to make contact with the patient but the patient needs to make contact with himself. Whether this is by means of the "self finding *itself* in the superego" (read: ego ideal) as Havens suggests, or by some other means, is unimportant. That the patient makes contact with himself and acts on the discoveries therein is what is crucial.

Grievance, in its many and myriad forms, is not a form of grief. It is not a lump in the throat, not a welling-up of tears, not even a delusion of disintegration. Rather, it is a form of despair. Clearly, it also has elements of rage, as evidenced by my cruel question to my first therapist as to whether he was going to die. Perhaps what is most disabling about grievance is not that it results in pain and suffering but that it can result in *being lost* and *not knowing it*. Grieving may not be able to begin until all grievances are heard and until one's voice has been found. It's ironic that one becomes mute in the midst of one's own protests.

I will shortly be entering the father–son relationship from the other side; I become the "old man." As I already have a daughter, I have already enjoyed being a father. Do I rework it all again? I don't think so. "Reorient" may be the better descriptor. Much of my second analysis was devoted to understanding how I was tied in by my "big guy" complex, and it, indeed, helped me to free myself from that and grow in significant ways. Plotting a course through the various paternal and parental identifications has been and, no doubt, will continue to be tricky and I frequently find myself sad in what should be a time of happy, if anxious, anticipation. Seven years after the death of my first analyst, I have only now begun to regain my voice. The sadness, I suspect, marks the beginning of my grief and the second analysis has made it tolerable. If life is, in some way, like a song to be sung, one may hope that the impressions that do last a lifetime need not necessarily still one's voice.

References

American Psychiatric Association (1981), *Diagnostic and Statistical Manual of Mental Disorders (Third Edition)* Washington, DC: American Psychiatric Press.

Erikson, E. (1950), *Childhood and Society*. New York: W. W. Norton.

Federn, P. (1953), *Ego Psychology and the Psychoses*. London: Hogarth Press.

Freud, A. (1937), *The Ego and the Mechanisms of Defense*. New York: International Universities Press, 1965.

Freud, S. (1914), On narcissism: An introduction. *Standard Edition* 14:67–102. London: Hogarth Press, 1957.

——— (1933), New Introductory Lectures. *Standard Edition*, 22. London: Hogarth Press, 1964.

Garfield, D. (1987), Affect translation in the psychotherapy of psychosis: Semrad's approach revisited. *Psychother.: Theory, Pract., Train., & Res.*, 24:381–386.

——— (1988), Paranoia and the ego-ideal. *J. Amer. Acad. Psychoanal.*, 16:29–46.

Havens, L. L. (1986), *Making Contact*. Cambridge, MA: Harvard University Press.

Jung, C. G. (1907), The psychogenesis of mental disease. In: *The Collected Works of C. G. Jung*, Vol. 3. Princeton, NJ: Princeton University Press, 1976.

Kohut, H. (1966), Forms and transformations of narcissism. *J. Amer. Psychoanal. Assn.*, 14:234–272.

Lachman, F., & Stolorow, R. (1980), *Psychoanalysis of Developmental Arrests*. New York: International Universities Press.

Lazare, A. (1976), Unresolved grief. In: *Outpatient Psychiatry*, ed. A. Lazare. Baltimore: Williams & Wilkins.

Mahler, M., Pine, F., & Bergman, A. (1975), *The Psychological Birth of the Human Infant*. New York: Basic Books.

Piaget, J. (1952), *The Origins of Intelligence in Children*. New York: W. W. Norton.

Searles, H. (1965), *Collected Papers on Schizophrenia and Related Subjects*. New York: International Universities Press.

12

The Death of the Analyst in the Post-termination Phase of Analysis: Impact and Resolution

THOMAS WOLMAN, M.D.

> A small boy speaking to his father says, "What's that Daddy?" The answer: "a cow." "Why is it a cow, Daddy?" Answer: "Because his Mummy and Daddy were cows." "Why were they cows, Daddy?" These three simple questions asked one after another take one directly into realms of complexity which include problems still unsolved. . . ."
>
> [Bion, 1977, p. 8].

Introduction: The "Mask" Dream

I last saw my analyst, Dr. G., in a dream I had shortly before writing this chapter. It went as follows: I start to cry or whimper when Dr. G. appears. I have been waiting for him on the doorstep. He looks somewhat old, and a little decrepit. He is wearing a greatcoat, and most significantly, a kerchief over the bottom half of his face. Given the subject matter of this chapter, I was bound to find this dream of great interest. It is the only one of my dreams that shows me grieving openly. I inferred that the whole ordeal of coming to terms with Dr. G.'s death, six months after the end of my analysis, constituted its "day residue." The timing of its appearance after considerable associative work made it easy to interpret. In this respect, it resembled certain dreams from the terminal phase of analysis that practically interpret themselves.

I took particular note of Dr. G.'s remarkable appearance in the dream. The kerchief, for example, along with hat, boots, and "greatcoat," reminded me of the "uniform" worn by the western heroes of my childhood. Through a slight displacement, the kerchief became the mask of a specific western hero—the Lone Ranger. All the Lone Ranger stories portray him as a mythical deus ex machina: at the moment of crisis, a masked man gallops into town and puts everything to rights just in the nick of time. The rescue accomplished, off he goes, riding out into the sunset to the strains of the William Tell Overture.

It occurred to me that this story expresses a romantic fantasy about the death of my analyst: when I was in trouble he appeared in the nick of time to help me, and then he died. In the Lone Ranger fantasy, his death was symbolized by the phrase, "riding out into the sunset." I often said to myself that "he died with his boots on," alluding to both the suddenness of his death and his intense involvement with life. On his wall there was a Teddy Roosevelt quotation (1899)—another western-style hero—which could well serve as his epitaph: "Far better it is to dare mighty things, to win glorious triumphs, even though checkered by failure, than to take rank with those poor spirits who neither enjoy much nor suffer much, because they live in the gray twilight that knows not victory nor defeat" (p. 686). These words recalled Freud's motto (1915) borrowed from the Hanseatic league: "Navigare necesse est, vivere non necesse" (It is necessary to sail the seas, it is not necessary to live) (p. 291).

But in addition to a glorious death, the Lone Ranger fantasy proclaimed his triumphant return. With every new episode the hero miraculously reappeared, just as he did so strikingly in this dream. Some of the symbols of death in the dream—the greatcoat, the death mask—were equally symbols of immortality. If death is inevitably followed by resurrection, then I had only to "wait for him on the doorstep." In cyclical time, the timing of Dr. G.'s death in relation to my analysis would count for little. Nevertheless, his reappearing in the "nick of time" implied the opposite. The dream itself appeared "in the nick of time" to help me with this chapter.

The phrase "somewhat old and a little decrepit" evokes an image of the ravages of time. An old, disheveled man appearing on my doorstep made me think of a "street person." Perhaps the "whimpering" belonged to the pathos of this image. The word *step* made me think of "one step from the grave." A man lying on the ground is only one step from being underground. Advanced age is just one step from death. "Decrepit" is just one step from decomposed. "Disheveled" is just one step from "naked and uncovered" like a corpse. It now seemed as if my aim was not to bury Dr. G. in style, but merely to dispose of his body.

Such an ignoble death could only apply to a "masked outlaw," as suggested by the kerchief worn over the bottom half of the face. A "masked outlaw" gets away with a crime because his identity is hidden. Death too is a kind of "getaway" that frees us from earthly accountability. Hence I might have imagined Dr. G. getting away with the crime of leaving me, because death put him beyond reach. Conversely, I might have imagined myself as the "masked outlaw" whose secrets remain safe after the death of the only witness—the analyst.

For myself, the contrast between hero and antihero suggested a wider contrast between romantic and morbid attitudes toward Dr. G.'s death, symbolized by the "mask" and the "corpse." The "mask" seemed to play up the mystery of death or possibly to dress it up as something it was not. The whole series of phallic symbols comprising the hero's garb may have served to "mask" castration fear. The aim of the romanticizing trend was, I thought, to weave a rich texture of associations around the dreaded event. The "corpse," on the other hand, seemed to portray death at its most gruesome, "naked" if you will, with all its disguises and "covers" ripped asunder. Here then was death in all its "poverty" of associations. In a sense, the "mask" as symbol of death stood opposed to the "corpse" as antisymbol. The former attempted to find meaning in Dr. G.'s death, while the latter saw his death as an affront to meaning itself.

Both of these trends found expression in the image of the kerchief displaced to the upper part of the face, where it becomes a shroud or blindfold. This implies a literal "loss of face" with its attendant narcissistic mortification. The loss of the eyes might refer to my own ignorance and mystification in the face of Dr. G.'s death. At the initial stage, I may have imagined his death as a kind of terra incognita, and my efforts to penetrate its mysteries as a journey into dark Hades itself. To combat my blindness and to avoid getting hopelessly lost, I would have had to lay down a thread like Ariadne, or a path of pebbles like Hansel in the story of Hansel and Gretel. Only by going back over my psychic traces, my dreams, for example, could I retrace my steps and find my way again.

By now it should be clear that I view the "mask" dream as a condensed summary of my effort to reconstruct the psychical changes initiated by the death of my analyst. The two motifs of the "mask" and the "corpse" came to represent two distinct phases in a lengthy process. But they must also be viewed as two figures in the evolution of a personal myth. As I wrote this chapter, I was only too well aware that my entire exposition rested on a web of interconnected fantasies. Naturally, I was assuming that these fantasies stand in some truthful relationship with the process they seek to encompass. At the very least, they respect the actuality of death in graphic images rather than in mere ideas. As a counterweight to this approach, I have interpolated some theoretical commentary along the way. Nevertheless, I encourage the reader to make his or her own interpretations and to use the material to invoke similar or contrary experiences. I trust that this format offers enough detail to make this goal possible, without unduly compromising privacy.

First Questions

The invitation to write this chapter raised a first question in my mind: did I in fact have anything to say on this subject? I drew a blank. This "drawing of a blank" gave me pause. Normally, I thought of drawing a blank when I didn't have any answers. But what if the reverse were true? Could I be drawing a blank because I didn't have any questions? Maybe there were some questions that I didn't want to ask, and others that I didn't want to hear. In any case, it seemed clear that I was far from reaching any conclusions on this matter.

In this new light, I began to question the apparent reason for my lack of material; that I was currently immersed in another subject, a study of Camus' *The Stranger* (1942). How would it be, I asked myself, if the two subjects were not so far apart as I thought, or even that they were, in fact, one subject. This assumption allowed me to draw a different conclusion from something I already knew, namely that I was deeply identified with Mersault, the protagonist of *The Stranger*. In the first chapter of that novel, Mersault attends his mother's funeral. Like him, I too was vaguely aware of the absence of grief vis-à-vis Dr. G. And like him I was vaguely aware that "others" might be inclined to judge me as unfeeling.

I first had to consider whether this lack of feeling represented a simple inability to mourn, a kind of "alexithymia" analogous to that of Mersault. I knew of the tendency to equate the complex processes of mourning with the simple expression of grief. Grief alone is no guarantee of grief work, I thought, nor is the absence of grief pathognomonic of the inability to mourn. However, despite these considerations, I could not dismiss out of hand the possibility of an island of "alexithymia" locked within my own psyche.

These thoughts set me to thinking about a reference to a "missing man" in one of my dreams. In answer to the question, "who is missing?", I could now answer, "myself." I was somehow acting as if mourning was going on without me. Or could it be that only part of me was missing—the part that remained only as a blank state? Then it occurred to me that the missing part was the part that "missed," the part that missed Dr. G. This left open the possibility that Dr. G. could be the "missing man"—the man who was missed.

Maybe I was in mourning after all. The first reaction to loss is likely to be one of "numbness." Bereaved persons will sometimes switch to "autopilot," going about their business as if nothing tragic had occurred. This type of denial may permit the postponement of grief while the urgent demands of reality are attended to. Naturally, there are some individuals who manage to evade mourning altogether by indefinitely prolonging the mask of normality.

Up to now, I must have been bolstering my denial with a series of alibis. The first was the argument of "anticipatory mourning," which asserts that I had finished mourning during successful termination of my analysis before Dr. G.'s death. In support of this argument, I could draw upon the real grief I had felt in anticipation of our parting. In this light, Dr. G.'s death would be something of an *anticlimax,* although that very word implies a "let down" that is not acknowledged. In sharp contradiction to this alibi, the second held that I could not mourn him at all because "I never really knew him"—a phrase that actually appeared in one of my dreams. There is at least some plausibility in the idea that the analyst is not known in the same way a parent or a spouse is known.

The alibis raised questions about some well-accepted theoretical assumptions, which I was using to buttress my rationalizations. I knew that Freud (Breuer and Freud, 1895) had a tendency to equate the work of mourning with "working through," both of which he saw as variations of "psychical working over." Similarly, he expanded mourning way beyond that of bereavement proper, for example, in a discussion of the aesthetic sense (1916). In his wake, many analysts (Firestein, 1978) have tended to blur the distinction between grief work and analytic work, particularly in discussions of the terminal phase of analysis.

The new intensity of my questioning brought to mind the role of the "private eye" in mystery novels. In one of my dreams, I applied the epithet, "mystery man" to myself. At the time I had been reading the case of Little Hans (Freud, 1909), whose "infantile sexual researches" took up a great deal of Freud's attention. I noted with interest that, in addition to sexuality, Hans was interested in the mystery of death. Thus the counterpart of his question, "where do babies come from?" might have run "where do people go when they die?" The private eye, however, avoids such deep questions, preferring to concentrate on knowable questions such as "where were you on such and such a date?"

But I am getting a bit ahead of myself. At this stage, I didn't even know the nature of the crime, much less the identity of the perpetrator. Of course, I might have assumed the crime to have been murder, given the obvious allusion to "murder mystery." And I had to admit that circumstantial evidence to support this view was not lacking. The very timing of Dr. G.'s death invited the inference: post hoc, ergo propter hoc. Because he died after the analysis, therefore he died because of the analysis. I even had a dream which elaborated this thought into a fantasy of a slow-acting poison, which might not take full effect for six months.

Nevertheless, I wanted to avoid jumping to conclusions. So I resolved to put an x into the equation, and to proceed as if I really did not know anything about the crime. This decision was to prove fruitful, not only in terms of a real solution, but also in allowing a preliminary answer to unfold at each separate stage of the process. Retrospectively, I would judge the initial crime to be a form of self-deception, a misrecognition of the process upon which I was now embarked.

The Scene of the Crime

In keeping with the "private eye" fantasy, I then set myself the task of reconstructing the circumstances of Dr. G.'s death, starting with the most concrete and material facts.

I first asked myself when and where I had last seen Dr. G. alive. I assumed it was his office, since I often found myself visualizing and revisualizing that setting. In these ruminations I seemed to place particular emphasis on the waiting room, where I always sat before meeting him. During the time I was in analysis, the waiting room always exuded an air of quiet and tranquility, like a calm before the storm. In the office itself, the same role was played by the reassuring presence of the objects and furniture in the suite, the couch, the pillows, the chairs, the pictures, and the coffee mugs.

As a child, I had focused on the details of the operating suite where I was to undergo tonsilectomy in exactly the same way. I still remember the anteroom where the surgeon reassured me with his calm voice and green suit (I was expecting white). In the operating room itself, I recall the narrow table with its hard mattress, and overhead, the blindingly bright lights.

In other words, it was like seeing Dr. G. for the last time in the "waiting room," where everything was still familiar, reassuring, and tranquil. So far as I was concerned, he might still be alive. Or at the very least, it was a relief that he had not died in my presence. I was in effect "placing" the event of his death within the office environment. In this regard I was acting as if the traumatic event was not his death per se, but rather its occurrence outside the time and space of the analysis. This seemed very odd, considering the relief I felt that he died outside the office, and the knowledge that the trauma would have been all the greater had he died during an actual session with me.

I speculated that perhaps the office setting functioned as a "landmark" with which to locate Dr. G.'s death in space, as well as in time. Naturally, my analytic hours took place at fixed times and places. With a glance at my watch, I could easily determine when I had last seen Dr. G., and when I would see him again. Perhaps my "fixation" on the office was an attempt to "fix" the time of death in a similar fashion. I probably felt disoriented during the temporal dislocations between the end of the analysis and the time of Dr. G.'s death, the onset of the "physical event," and the time of death, and the time of death and the moment I heard tell of it.

I could give an exact answer to the question of when and where I first heard of Dr. G.'s death. In this case as well, the external details of the scene "fixed" themselves upon my mind. But any illusions of stability melted away as soon as I heard the sad news. It came in the shape of a question: "Have you heard about Dr. G.?" My first response was one of mild depersonalization, as if I was looking down on the scene from outside my body. The question seemed to imply that Dr. G. died completely outside the sphere of my own knowledge. Instead of telling me of his death directly, it put me in the position of having to guess, and the only evidence it offered was "hearsay."

The funeral rites reinforced these feelings. Aware as I was of the time, place, and overall substantiality of the proceedings, I still could not help feeling that something tangible, or was it intangible, was missing. For one thing, the ritual seemed hurried, perfunctory, and lacking in richness. And all the eulogies made scant reference to Dr. G., "the Analyst." The comments of the mourners sounded to me like hackneyed clichés—mere "hearsay." Indeed, Dr. G.'s poor showing—his pallid "specter"—contrasted sharply with the vigor and robust good health of one of his contemporaries.

In every one of these settings I seemed to be reacting to Dr. G.'s sudden disappearance by hunting for some physical sign of him. Like a lost child, I was running from room to room searching for a familiar face. By focusing on the external details, I was trying to reconstruct his traces from the surroundings. This situation reminded me of comparable "disappearances" at various phases of my life: the sudden death of my best friend at age six, and the abrupt removal, often in the dead of night, of patients' bodies during my internship.

Later I understood these behaviors as reactions to the shock of sudden death. Freud (1920) recognized the factor of unpreparedness in the initial response to any severe trauma. For myself, the signs of shock included the spatiotemporal dislocation and the bewilderment at something happening outside my knowledge. At the time, I attempted to deal with this feeling by "perseverating" on the last scene before the trauma, by searching my mind for some landmark or grid with which I could restore order, and by mentally inspecting the details of the physical environment. In short, I was acting as if the delicate veil of meanings that insulate us from "reality" had been ripped asunder. It was Lewin (1948) who first pointed out the unconscious association between "reality" and the female genital.

Because of the traumatic impact of the disappearing body, I might reconstruct the crime at this juncture as premature or improper burial. But "premature" brought to mind the antithetical thought that perhaps one of us had arrived too late. In the context of the office, the crime was simply a missed analytic appointment. If Dr. G. had died right before our analytic session, I would have been left standing at his door, wondering if one of us had gotten the time wrong. This scenario, besides emphasizing yet again the importance of "timing," reiterates the shock of death occurring outside my knowledge.

The Recovery of the Body

To obtain first-hand knowledge about something as intangible as death, I had to reappropriate Dr. G.'s body on the imaginative plane. Perhaps if I could examine the body, I thought to myself, I might learn the answers to the medical questions of when, where, and how he died.

Dr. G.'s body first reappeared in a resuscitation fantasy. In this fantasy, I am head of the CPR team that is working on Dr. G.'s body after cardiac arrest. I beat him vigorously on the chest as he lies naked and moribund. By placing myself on the scene, I make myself accessible, in fantasy, to all the medical information at hand. By beating him, I am, in effect, conducting a therapeutic trial to observe his reactions. Moreover, by identifying with his body, I can become privy to all his interior pains and sensations. And by repeating the scenario over and over in my mind, I can pick up tidbits of information missed on the first go-around.

A second fantasy involving Dr. G.'s body had me conducting a postmortem examination, presumably to determine the cause of death. The search for in vivo knowledge had become a search for in vitro knowledge in this fantasy. In my mind, the postmortem was closely linked with the anatomy laboratory of my early medical student days. At that time, the only way I could learn anatomy was to return to the lab at night to go over the structures in concretio, in the body itself.

One of my dreams of the period joins these two fantasies in a "case conference." An old man with end-stage Parkinson's disease is being examined by doctors and medical students in white coats. The patient is treated as a "cadaver" without ceremony or the amenities: his body is touched, palpated, probed, and his ear is pulled. The team searches for physical signs such as involuntary movements. At one point in the dream, the head of the patient is seen in profile, suggesting an X-ray with different views, or a clinical laboratory "profile."

Another dream brought these fantasies into connection with a third medical scene—that of anesthesia induction. This dream showed me blowing air into Dr. G.'s mouth through a short pipe, in yet another version of the resuscitation fantasy. However, the "short pipe" reminded me of a film about the first use of ether as an anesthetic. Ether had been the agent used during my tonsilectomy at age eleven. The overwhelming smell of the gas was related to the reek of formaldahyde in the anatomy lab. A second pipe dream placed the nozzle in the anus instead of the mouth, implying the stench of fecal gas, not to mention that of the decomposition of a corpse.

My sensory memories of anesthesia came back to me now with great vividness and force. In addition to the strong smell, there was the harshness of the lights, the hardness of the narrow table, the hum of the fans, and the tightness of my hands holding the thumbs of the male nurse. This was clearly a case of "input overload." Another dream compared this scene to my "first surgery" as a medical student. In the new scene,

I was calmly collaborating with the surgeon in performing the operation on the anesthetized patient. Most remarkably, the postmortem/dissection fantasy had been directly inserted into the manifest content of that dream.

In all my attempts to obtain first-hand knowledge about Dr. G.'s body, I took special pains to ensure its preservation. In the resuscitation fantasy I was fighting for the preservation of life at all costs. For without a "live" body, how was I to discover the medical facts? I was even prepared to substitute my own "live" body to keep this avenue open. And in the postmortem fantasy I was protecting the in vitro avenue by carefully preserving the anatomical structures in my dissection. Similarly, the formaldahyde "fixes" the structure of the body. The surgery dream was a hybrid of both methods of preservation, since the body is alive, the anatomical structures are respected, and any damage can be repaired.

The themes of preservation, reconstruction, and repair comprise a first attempt at reconstructing the relationship to the lost object. Through a kind of denial in fantasy, all the reactions to shock are magically reversed: the word *recovery* itself implies a reversal of both the disappearance and the fatal illness. In vivo/in vitro knowledge is substituted for the absence of any first-hand knowledge. Concrete answers to the question of what happens when people die take the place of perplexity (i.e., the dead are frozen at the moment of cardiac arrest; or they slip into anesthesia). Overwhelming change is "fixed" at the moment before the trauma. A familiar trauma, that of anesthesia induction, replaces an unknown trauma through the associative links of sleep, cadavers, rotting smell, and immobility.

I believe the effort at "recovery" functioned in a manner analogous to the burial rite. In fantasy, I was in effect preoccupied with preparing the body—washing, covering, facial reconstruction, embalming—for a "viewing," if not a "vigil." It is especially important to reestablish the visual image of the lost object, at this stage. Visualization quiets fears of the unseen, and also prepares us to recognize the dead person as no longer alive. The resulting posture of observation helps to preserve a concrete "remnant" of the observing ego.

However, the restitution failed to bind the latent aggression lurking behind all the medical scenes. During my tonsilectomy, the sudden, overwhelming, and violent incursion of gas into the interior of my body felt like a violation of physical boundaries. During my "first surgery"—the one on which I assisted—the surgeon had inadvertantly punched a big hole in the patient's pulmonary artery. I had fainted during my "first postmortem," when I perceived the lack of ceremony in ripping open the body. This reminded me of my old anatomy lab, which came to look like a butcher shop. Even my first CPR, at which a certain amount of rough handling is justifiable, resulted in broken ribs and extensive bruising.

The discovery of the crime of butchery revealed to me the intensity of my rage, and the manic efforts to deny it. I was finding it increasingly harder to separate the antithetical aims of reconstruction and destruction. On reflection, it occurred to me that my scientific interest might dovetail quite well with "cannibalism." Both aims concentrate their attention on the "flesh" of the dead man, combining destructive and libidinal wishes.

Cul de Sac: The Macabre Attitude

The exclusive focus on the physical reality of the body signifies a thoroughly materialist attitude toward Dr. G.'s death. The kernel of truth in this weltanschaung may be summed up in the phrase "dust to dust." Freud (1900) learned this lesson from his mother, who used to rub his two hands together until flakes of dirt appeared. He was fond of quoting—or misquoting—Shakespeare's line, "we owe Nature a death" (1915). At funerals, the debt to nature is expressed in the literal throwing of dirt onto the coffin.

But a fixation of the attitude into a total fascination and preoccupation with the corpse is defined as macabre. According to Huizinga (1949), an authority on medieval society, the derivation of the term is as follows:

> At the close of the Middle Ages the whole vision of death may be summed up in the word macabre, in its modern meaning. Of course, this meaning is the outcome of a long process. But the sentiment it embodies, of something gruesome and dismal, is precisely the conception of death which arose during the last centuries of the Middle Ages [p. 143].

The macabre attitude attaches itself to all of the concrete, sensory aspects of the corpse: its mutism, blindness, immobility/paralysis, pallor, rotting smell, and rigor mortis. In so doing, it deemphasizes the spiritual dimension of the dead. The usual saying, "the body is gone, but the spirit shall remain" is strangely reversed to become "the spirit has fled, but the body remains." For myself, this meant that my preoccupation with Dr. G.'s corpse had made me oblivious to the less tangible mark he left on my life. As Huizinga puts it:

> The desire to invent a visible image of all that appertained to death entailed the neglecting of all those aspects of it which were not suited to direct representation. Thus the cruder conceptions of death, and these only impressed themselves continually on the minds. The macabre vision does not represent the emotions of tenderness or of consolation. The elegiac note is wanting altogether. At bottom the macabre sentiment is self seeking and earthly [p. 150].

My most gruesome fantasy about Dr. G.'s death followed the plot of an old Alfred Hitchcock television program that went as follows: A man becomes completely paralyzed while in hospital, is presumed dead, and is taken down to the morgue for burial. Completely helpless, he is unable to cry out, or to give any sign that he is alive. Then, just in the nick of time, an alert nurse spots tears streaming down his cheeks. The feeling of morbid terror in the fantasy stemmed from the man's clear consciousness despite appearances to the contrary. In just the same way, I had felt hyperesthetic during my anesthesia induction, when I should have felt an-esthetic.

The fantasy of "burial alive" brought to mind a whole series of macabre variations including grave robbery, tomb desecretion, and disinterment. Freud (1915) alludes to the related act of jumping into the grave in the following words:

> The complement to the cultural and conventional attitude towards death is provided by our complete collapse when death has struck down someone we love—a parent or a partner in marriage, a brother or sister, a child or a close friend. Our hopes, our desires and our pleasures lie in the grave with him, we will not be consoled, we will not fill the lost one's place. We behave as if we were a kind of Asra, who die when those they love die [p. 290].

All of these found their way into a dream I had shortly before moving to a new home: I had apparently entered our old house at midmorning, presumably to get some stuff from the basement. But when I opened the door, I saw the new owners asleep on a mattress laid out on the living room floor. They were naked and the room was dark, as if all the blinds were drawn. As soon as I saw them, I made my excuses and left.

The manifest content of this dream presents a transgression—I am trespassing. The house which was no longer my own is represented as a kind of tomb: It is reduced to a dark, windowless "shell." Moreover, the new "owners" are laid out, naked—like corpses—on the floor. And even though it is midmorning, they are "asleep."

The transgression of breaking and entering the tomb suggests a lack of proper separation between the living and the dead. Transposed onto the context of the dissecting room, this fantasy might read "burrowing into the anatomical cul de sac." Hiding inside the dead man's body would certainly be the epitome of the macabre attitude.

It also represents the epitome of despondency. This phase

has all the earmarks of a transient depression: morbid fantasies full of "doom and gloom," hints of suicide (jumping into the grave), absence of consolation, feeling of transgression, inner emptiness (the empty house), and bodily preoccupations (cul de sac). From these symptoms, I could infer typical depressive themes. In the first place, the denial of the restitutional phase had broken down into a pervasive image of catastrophe. The "moving" dream depicted my inner world as a house stripped of all furniture, ornament, and mementos, a mere "shell" or "skeleton." The observing posture of the previous phase had now degenerated into narcissistic self-absorption. Nothing remained of the earlier scientific interest save the reference to an anatomical structure.

The images of joining the corpse in the grave, of living inside the body, or conversely of the body lying inside my inner "tomb," all betray a profound identification with the dead. These same images also convey my feeling of having reached a "dead end" in the work of mourning.

Communicating with the Dead

But given my immersion in the "concrete," I would be quite unlikely to understand "cul de sac" as a metaphor of my state of mind. For me, the "corpse" had become the ultimate point of reference for thinking about Dr. G.'s death. It had become my literal cul de sac; I was hemmed in on all sides by the walls of his "rotting flesh." I therefore came to think of the "corpse" as a graphic antimetaphor of my inability to speak of anything beyond the given, a state of affairs amounting to an arrest of my capacity to symbolize. At base, I could commune with the dead man but I could not communicate with him.

It was only in retrospect, after I had worked through the depression and recovered my symbolic sense, that I could reconstruct my previous state of mind. I had noticed the same sequence of loss and recovery on several occasions in my life. Most recently, I recalled a phase of my analysis in which I lost the ability to process Dr. G.'s interpretations, especially those that contained metaphorical expressions like, "if the shoe fits, wear it." Often it took years before I could appreciate the multiple meanings of such phrases. My first confrontation with poetry set the tone for such experiences. I remember the moment when I first grasped the symbolic dimension in Robert Frost's poem "Stopping By Woods On a Snowy Evening" (1963). But what struck me most of all, in retrospect, was the *subject* of the poem's "hidden meaning": Death.

I began to recover my symbolic sense by way of the primitive body imagery that occupied my thoughts. The dream of breaking and entering a tomb pictured the cul de sac as a locked room in a house. In the scene of the crime, I had been thinking of suites of interconnected rooms: the office and the operating rooms. I made a distinction between the anterooms and the inner sanctums. Could I have been constructing a crude map of Dr. G.'s body? The rooms would symbolize the various "compartments." The objects in the rooms would represent extensions of his body, especially the couch and pillows. The paintings on the wall might reveal his face. One of my dreams presented an author talking ex cathedra: from the chair—in this case the empty analytic chair.

The Body as Metaphor

The recovery of the body as metaphor revealed to me successive stages in my ability to conceptualize pain. The anesthetized body stood for my initial "numbness," just as the body frozen at the moment of cardiac arrest stood for my initial lack of emotion. Later I could imagine physical pain by translating the cardiac "seizure" into a "beating." But the "beating" did not as yet signify anger or the feeling of futility conveyed by such a phrase as "beating a dead horse." The copious tears on the face served as a bridge between the physical pain and the emotional vicissitudes of mourning such as numbing, pining, gnawing, and the like.

The first indication that the body could remind me of Dr.

G.'s absence was in a series of dreams that brought him back in the guise of others. I remember saying in one of them, "I have the fantasy that you are not Dr. G."—a phrase that might apply equally well to his corpse. Soon after, I had a dream about Claire Winnicott (1978) that alluded directly to a striking dream she had after her husband's death. In that dream, he had returned, and the two of them were engaged in a wonderful conversation. But at a certain point his face turned serious, and he said: "you know I've really come to tell you that I have died."

In time, the recurring reappearance of the dead man served the purpose of reality testing, since his presence was always followed by a painful pang that reminded me of his absence. One dream pictured this process as a "thorn in my side" that contained a "slow release poison." Thus the pang of reminder was a thorn in my side—a memento mori if you will—and the slow release poison was the pain I was forced to endure until well after his actual death. The "tomb" dream pictured the work of mourning as a difficult move to another house, a job that seemed interminable, requiring countless trips back and forth between the two houses.

The body also served to remind me how hard it is to sustain "meaning" in the absence of material backing. In all the medical scenes, I was helpless to proceed unless the body was right there in front of me. Dwelling on or in the body drove home the lesson that the soul requires the support of the body, that the internal requires the support of the external, and that analysis requires the support of the analyst. *In this light, the various medical scenes could be read as the equation of medical failure with analytic failure.* In the case of the resuscitation fantasy, a line of association took me back to the memory of another resuscitation scene during my internship.

The patient was an acquaintance of my parents, of German-Jewish background, who had recently converted to Christian Science. At first he had been reluctant to accept any medical treatment. But after having been successfully resuscitated, he no longer protested, as if he no longer disputed the superiority of medical science. If I were to substitute analysis for faith healing, then the fantasy concerned my disillusionment with analysis. I would be saying that only medical science can bring people back from death; I was a fool for thinking that analysis can cure someone from a fatal "psychosomatic" illness. *So it was my belief in analysis that I was desperately trying to revive in the resuscitation fantasy.* Similarly, the postmortem fantasy, with its allusions to Freud's dream of the dissection of his own pelvis (1900), pictured a "moribund" analysis.

If I was angry and disillusioned with Dr. G., the "person," then I was equally angry and disillusioned with Dr. G., the "analyst." It was impossible in practice for me to "compartmentalize" my feelings of bereavement in this way, despite my feeble attempt to "compartmentalize" his body. For myself, and for anyone in analysis, the two Dr. G.s were one and the same. Hence losing the ability to analyze only reflected the fact that Dr. G. was an analyst through and through. The suspension of the activity I most associated with him was analogous to observing a period of silence for the dead. It would have felt insincere to go on as before when analysis seemed as dead as the analyst.

Naming the Dead

Along with a lessening of my preoccupation with Dr. G.'s body went a greater awareness of the associations surrounding his name. In fact, I had always had some questions about that name. For a long time I did not know his first name, since it was hidden behind a mysterious first initial, and everyone called him by his middle name. There was a time in my life when I too was called by my middle name. When I discovered Dr. G.'s real first name, I realized that both our names concealed a hidden German origin—his by the suppression of his first name, mine by the replacement of my German middle name by an anglicized substitute.

My associations to the concealed name revealed numerous links with my "Grandfather complex." First, I could cite the fact that when I became a father, Dr. G. became a grandfather. In a dream in which Dr. G. appears in the guise of another analyst, that analyst's name was the same as a friend of my father who had died before his time, leaving behind a cluster of grieving women. My middle name belonged to my maternal grandfather, who also died before his time, leaving behind a number of grieving women. I knew, of course, that Dr. G. had left a widow, a daughter, and at least one granddaughter.

The theme of grandfathers brought me to the subject of my analytic forefathers. I always remembered how Dr. G. paid careful attention to the way people pronounced his own last name, which was German, and how he paid equal attention to the way I pronounced the names of first-generation European analysts. I thought of this generation as a "lost generation," even though they had been saved from the Holocaust by their American colleagues. In my mind, they were still identified with the Jews of the Holocaust, because of the fact that Dr. G. had helped liberate one of the death camps. Also "lost generation" seemed to apply to the European analysts who stayed behind, and felt abandoned by their brethren who emigrated to America.

References to Europe and Germany reminded me of the German language, the language of Freud. I strongly associated Freud's tongue with the original Hebrew of the Bible. This line of associations led to the theme of dead languages in general. It dawned on me that I had developed a preference for Latin phrases in the writing of this paper. Deus ex machina, ex post facto, in concretio, post hoc ergo propter hoc, in vivo, in vitro, memento mori, are a few examples. Both German, via the German psychiatrists, and Latin and Greek, via ancient physicians, led me to "medical jargon."

In the "case conference" dream, the doctors were trying to classify the patient in the correct diagnostic category. In their zeal to apply the right labels, they lost touch with the live patient in the room. I have already mentioned the lack of respect with which they palpated, probed, and prodded the patient. Their use of language was in keeping with this attitude. The dead Latin words became so many little "boxes" to bury the patient alive. Thus the "names" were treated as things in themselves, just as previously the corpse had been so treated.

Consequently, the name of the dead man pointed beyond the loss of Dr. G. as an individual. It evoked en entire lost history, a lost culture (German–Jewish culture), a lost heritage or legacy, and a forgotten crime. The crime was clearly the annihilation, not just of a people, but of a whole tradition. Hence, the metaphor of the body and the metaphor of the name both implied the loss of psychoanalysis.

The Mute Speaks

The "mutism" of the corpse appeared in two of my dreams I call "telephone relationship" and "note of condolence." These two dreams and the copious associations that followed delivered me from my period of silence. Like the corpse itself, my mutism changed from a thing in itself to a metaphor for noncommunication.

In the "telephone relationship" dream I was talking to a friend over the telephone. An uncomfortable pause in the conversation made me realize that we had little to say to each other. In this relationship, the telephone substituted for actual "getting together." This thought seemed to fit with the theme of bad relationships in general. Specifically, I was reminded of "bad marriages." In the "condolence note" dream, someone asked me if I knew about a certain couple's divorce. Other couples I knew stayed on in "barren marriages," still others were guilty of adultery.

These musings drew my attention to associations dealing with the role of women in the "battle of the sexes." "Cherchez la femme" could be the slogan of most of them. In the divorce mentioned in the dream, I judged the woman to be at fault. And with "old couples" I tended to be begrudging toward the wife because she had outlived her husband. I felt this way about the death of a distinguished woman analyst. Apparently, she and Dr. G. constituted a couple in my mind because

I had once seen them together in a photograph. In the "condolence note" dream, my "failure to send the expected note of condolence" made sense as an expression of resentment toward the surviving woman.

Perhaps I was assuming that death is the outcome of a bad marriage. If such were the case, the death of one of the partners would legitimize the impulse to be unfaithful. Freud (1905) captured this sentiment in one of his favorite jokes: "If one of us dies, I shall move to Paris." On the day I heard about Dr. G.'s death, I felt a little like the woman who is the last to know of her husband's well-publicized affair. All these years and I never even knew him. One of my dreams appeared to echo this thought in the phrase, "I don't even know them."

Identifying with the surviving woman was only one of the ways in which I was equating a bad marriage with my "post-mortem" analytic relationship. During my analysis, I had often made the comparison between a good marriage and a good working alliance. That such a "marriage" might even survive the death of one of the partners was implied in the allusion to the extreme longevity of the partners in many barren marriages. But after the analyst's death, it was I who had "adulterous" impulses. For example, in one dream I felt as if a great burden had been removed from my shoulders, and "I had the field to myself." I was acting as if Dr. G.'s death was a breach of contract which rendered our relationship null and void. In the telephone dream, my infidelity to analysis was expressed through the figure of a colleague who became bitter and disillusioned about analysis.

The "pause in the conversation" stood for the significant pauses in my relationship with Dr. G.: the period between his illness and death, the period between analytic termination and death, and the three-year hiatus period in my analysis. The dream was therefore assuming that Dr. G.'s death was merely another such pause. Playing upon Dr. G.'s use of the phrase "pregnant pause," it was comparing the "pause" not to a death, but to the period of confinement before birth. If taken to its logical extreme, this might imply that death cancels the entire time period of the relationship—the pause—returning the survivor to the time before conception, which was in this case the preanalytic era.

Our noncommunication was also represented as an exchange of letters. The background of the "telephone relationship" dream had included an exchange of birth announcements and an angry exchange of letters with the analytic institute, undertaken by my disaffected colleague. My analytic progress had been the subject of another exchange of letters between a supervisor and the analytic institute. And on a more positive note, there was my promise to write a letter to Dr. G. reviewing my posttermination analytic progress. On one occasion, the rueful thought had struck me that now such a letter would end up at the dead letter office. In that respect, it was like a "note" I wrote but never sent to one of my analytic supervisors some time after Dr. G.'s death. Was this the meaning of the reproach that I was "failing to send the expected note of condolence"?

The phrase "dead letter" seemed so full of meaning I decided to look it up in the dictionary. I was surprised to learn that I was only half aware of its meaning. Like most people, I was using it in the sense of "undeliverable," rather than in the full sense of "undeliverable and unreturnable." This slip was especially significant in light of my assumption that the letter could not be returned to the sender. A true dead letter is totally inaccessible. It is comparable in this regard to a letter written in a "dead language."

Both the "telephone relationship" dream and the "condolence note" dream represented Dr. G.'s death as a breakdown in communication. In the former dream's concrete language, "a pause in the conversation" indicated a "strain in the conversation." I could just hear Dr. G. himself remark with his customary irony: "It is a little bit difficult to hold a conversation with a dead man."

Solution/Resolution

That last comment sounded like a good rationalization for my own complicity in the crime. A brief review of the material showed that it was hardly the first to appear. In "the scene of the crime" I took pains to prove "that I wasn't there"; in the "recovery of the body" I was beating the body so as to save it; in the "condolence note" dream, I failed to send the note because "I didn't really know him."

Even my efforts to divert blame away from myself always boomeranged. My original accusation of adultery led to my discovering adulterous impulses of my own. And my errant colleague who walked out on the "old men" was only expressing my own faithlessness. If I followed the policy of "cherchez la femme" far enough, I would catch up with myself, since I was identified with the surviving woman. In short, it seemed as though I was reversing the usual relationship of "criminal" to "victim," of "deceased" to "survivor." Perhaps Dr. G. was struggling to get through to me, rather than I to him. The letter I failed to send corresponded to an unopened posthumous letter from Dr. G., to be read in the event of his death.

These considerations accorded with the fact that all the "crimes" were more or less crimes against the dead. Furthermore, they all seemed to converge upon the one highly condensed phrase, "complete lack of ceremony." This phrase tied together all the crimes against the body through the intermediaries of premature or hasty burial, failure to cover the body, and brutalizing it with "a complete lack of ceremony." Everything turned upon my reluctance to observe the formalities: failing to send the expected note of condolence, failing to record Dr. B.'s history, failing to write his "epitaph." In other words, "ceremony" included all the rites and obligations owed to the dead.

A related point of convergence was the idea of excluding Dr. G.'s name from circulation. Consider that the "dead letter" I failed to send or to receive had a place for his name in the salutation and the address. As mentioned, one of my dreams gave him a new name—actually new initials—and had me declare, "I have the fantasy you are not Dr. G." Besides concealing the name, the initials tended to make his name unintelligible, a device alluded to in the associations to "dead languages." This trend culminated in the crimes against the body, which treat him as a nameless corpse, tagged only with a number, and slated for an unmarked grave. Normally, the name—epithet/epitaph—reserves a place in the symbolic network that outlives its bearer. Hence, the removal of Dr. G.'s name breaks the filiation that links his name with a past tradition and a future legacy. It effectively obliterates the traces of his passage.

With this rather harsh insight, I realized that the "solution" was finally at hand. The time had come, it seemed to me, to pause and survey the path I had cleared. This meant retracing my steps, just as I had done in reaching these conclusions. But in so doing I realized that "returning to the beginning" was an additional point of convergence, and one that I had hitherto neglected. All the scattered references to time and timing should have put me on the scent. Of these, the most common were time reversals of various kinds: birth instead of death, youth instead of age, before instead of after. In one version of the resuscitation fantasy, I was reviving Dr. G. as a medical intern, thus ensuring the survival of my future analyst.

I asked myself if the very process of reconstruction itself was not a constantly recurring "return to the beginning." I often used to think of it as a retracing of my steps. Each step in that process, it seemed to me, always returned to the beginning in a different way. Each of the early stages offered their own interpretation of that beginning—as something missing, a missing body, an anatomical cul de sac. The interpretations of the latter stages retrospectively reinterpreted the earlier stages. Could it be, I wondered, that my "final solution" applied not to the end point but to the beginning?

If so, then I must have started out from a position of symbolic rupture where I lacked the means to make sense of Dr. G.'s death. Given this assumption, my reconstructive effort was simultaneously an attempt to reconstruct this initial state and to reconstruct/repair the symbolic rupture from which it sprung. This effort finally succeeded by rebuilding a symbolic network that included a place for my analyst's name.

The unopened posthumous letter underscored the connection between Dr. G.'s name and his "word." How often I used to turn that letter over and over in my mind. One time I found myself feeling sad rather than "rueful" that Dr. G. would never receive the letter. But then I could hear him saying to me, rather passionately, "Look, it doesn't matter if I get the letter. What matters is that you get it." And then I thought that the basic message was the same as in my analysis: "It always takes two to tango—why don't you see how you may have contributed to the problem?"

So I had really reconstructed Dr. G.'s posthumous interpretation, and by doing so I had reestablished the analytic relationship. The solution to the crime led to its own resolution, because reconstructing an interpretation is the first step in heeding it. In turn, reconstructing the letter meant putting it back in circulation, putting Dr. G.'s "name" back in circulation. Now the "formalities" could be taken for granted, for the rehabilitation of the letter also implied the restoration of the "written" part of the mourning ritual—the will, obituary, memorial, and condolence note. The letter was Dr. G.'s legacy to me, which I could now reclaim, along with the heritage of which it was a part.

Of course, the achievement of symbolic continuity is marked with the sign of the memento mori. This Latin phrase is in the imperative voice, and means literally "remember that you must die." In the wake of Dr. G.'s death, I began to be aware of my own mortality, a milestone in my transition to midlife (Jaques, 1965). By paying more attention to my body's signals, I realized that I had been overeating as a way of putting on flesh to counteract the cathectic appearance of the dead or dying. Stopping the overeating was like a modified "fast," which recognized the reality of Dr. G.'s death, heightened my awareness of bodily cues, and reestablished an "abstinence" conducive for the joint work of mourning and analysis.

Last Things

With the passage of time, I managed to draw together the loose ends, and to formulate some view of the process as a whole. I tackled this final task by reconsidering the dreams that form the backbone of this chapter. The "mask" dream and the "condolence note" dream appeared to embody the two nodal points of a biphasic process. The overall course of my mourning experience was not dissimilar to the Kleinian schema of loss: manic defense–depressive position–reparation, and I felt the observation called for some theoretical commentary. After further reflection, I was led to some tentative conclusions on the meaning of the phrase "resolution of the transference."

The initial traumatic shock is represented in the "mask" dream as the appearance of Dr. G.'s naked corpse on my doorstep. The "poverty of associations" surrounding this image conveys my initial "alexithymia." The references to "naked" reality, the typical identification of the body with the phallus, and the multiplication of masculine symbols, all point to the equation of "symbolic rupture" and castration. Thus the appearance of the body in the dream reverses the sudden disappearance of the body, already likened to the sight of the female genital.

By making Dr. G. reappear, the "mask" dream reconstitutes a visual image of the lost object. The dream's associations are replete with different nuances of the word *image*. Each of these meanings carries a different psychic function: The "illusion" of the Lone Ranger fantasy characterizes this restitutional effort as a specialized transitional state, in limbo between life and death. Similarly, the death mask and other "ikons" act as photographs or other "linking objects" (Volkan, 1972). The "face" implies the narcissistic repair of "saving face," and "facial reconstructive surgery." The "eye" promotes recognition. Seeing the "corpse" tests the reality of death. Finally, the inner preservation of the total "imago" of the lost object supports object constancy.

By contrast, the depressive phase is presented in the "mask" dream as an image in the process of dissolution—the "rotting corpse." Hence the "face" becomes the faceless angel of death. The "ikons" are broken into a thousand fragments. The "eye" can no longer see in this dark and gloomy place.

The locale has changed from outside to inside. External trauma has been transformed into inner wound. Disillusionment has taken place quite literally.

My illusion of omniscience suffered the most. In a curious variant of the Lone Ranger fantasy, Dr. G. does not in fact die, but instead changes his identity and "goes underground." Thus he becomes another "mystery man." Musing on this reverie, I discovered that if you substitute Dr. G. for "mystery man" in the question, "Who is the mystery man?" you get "Who is Dr. G.?" This question—a restatement of the phrase "I didn't really know him"—implies that I ceased to know him only after he died. In life, I never would have overemphasized his analytic "anonymity." Over the course of a long analysis, I had made some good guesses about Dr. G.'s history and personality that he acknowledged to be correct. Thus I was pointing to a knowledge gap opened up by the reality of his death. My conjecture that he "went underground" is in fact only a confession of ignorance, since it merely asserts the obvious fact that he died and was buried ("went underground").

It is only at this point—the nadir of mourning—that the analytic ideal/ideal analyst can be given up as lost. By the time of the "condolence note" dream, I had renounced the attempt to resurrect the lost ideal, and was instead preoccupied with symbolic substitutes in the form of "names," "sayings," "titles," "letters." No longer at a loss for words, I could now characterize the original symbolic rupture as a cataclysm, with the various meanings of breakdown in communication, purloined letter, debased ceremony, and knowledge gap. When Dr. G.'s words began to speak to me, and I to them, I knew that I had repaired the analytic relationship in the absence of the analyst.

The Kleinians have written extensively about these matters. They claim that all adult mourning includes a transient depression, which harks back to the so-called "depressive position" of early childhood (Segal, 1964). But whether in childhood, or in its adult incarnation, the "depressive position" requires the working through of guilt, ambivalence, powerful destructive fantasies, and manic defenses. I believe I approached something like the "depressive position," when I could no longer separate the analyzing analyst from the "flesh and blood" analyst. I have little doubt that my angry fantasies further devastated my internal world, perhaps damaging my "psychical machinery," and requiring extensive efforts at "reparation."

Where I think the Kleinians err is in their overemphasis on unconscious fantasy, and their relative neglect of psychical trauma. They tend to explain reparation solely as a fantasy of repairing the destroyed object. I view imaginary repair as a primitive forerunner of the crucial symbolic restitution, although this too is implied in Hannah Segal's (1964) discussion of naming the anonymous dead so they will stay buried. They also lean toward a negative evaluation of manic denial, stressing only its evasive purpose. There is no doubt that a certain degree of denial allows depressive anxiety to be experienced in small doses over a long period, rather than in overwhelming amounts, all at once. I believe this is what Freud (1917) is getting at when he describes the work of mourning as the "hypercathexis of each and every partial image of the lost object."

This aspect of the work of mourning is not really compatible with the maintenance of the analytic attitude. Imagining the object in all its concrete materiality is very different from associating freely. Free association is hampered even further by a weak symbolizing capacity. During the depressive phase of mourning, the observing ego virtually disappears. Besides, it may be necessary to briefly renounce this benign split in the ego, in the service of mastering ambivalence.

When a patient sustains a severe loss during an analysis, the analysis may have to take a back seat to the work of mourning. Similarly, the death of the analyst posttermination may require the suspension of self-analytic work. My own case offers the alternative possibility of a "blank phase" followed by the simultaneous restitution of mourning and the analytic attitude. In either of the last two cases, the death of the analyst underscores the importance of the postermination phase of analysis.

The terminal and postterminal phases of psychoanalysis are generally characterized by a work of mourning for the analyst. The resolution of the transference requires the patient to give up the analyst as object and to replace him with his formal function designated by his name/title "analyst." To the extent that reality reinforces the fantasy of seeing the analyst again, this detachment is held up or inhibited, and the analyst is never fully mourned. This is where the death of the analyst in the posttermination phase can act as a catalyst for the final detachment from him as an object, and the consolidation of the self-analytic function.

I wondered whether mourning is the primary method of resolving the transference. Successful mourning effects a transfer—a transference—from the lost object on to a new object. Similarly, a beneficial analysis frequently results in a freeing up of energies for new attachments and commitments. My experience of mourning produced the same result as analytic termination: I could continue with the work, in the absence of the analyst. Did this mean that the very "personality" of the analyst was just another "mask," the last of love's illusions?

Pondering these matters, I recalled a quotation from Freud (1913) that might serve as a fitting conclusion to this chapter:

> Man, as we know, makes use of his imaginative activity in order to satisfy the wishes that reality does not satisfy. So his imagination rebelled against the recognition of the truth embodied in the myth of the Moerae and constructed instead the myth derived from it, in which the Goddess of Death was replaced by the Goddess of Love and by what was equivalent to her in human shape. The third of the sisters was no longer Death; she was the fairest, best, most desirable and most lovable of women [p. 299].

References

Bion, W. (1977), Emotional turbulence. In: *Borderline Personality Disorders,* ed. P. Hartocollis. New York: International Universities Press, pp. 3–13.

Breuer, J., & Freud, S. (1895), Studies on Hysteria. *Standard Edition,* 2. London: Hogarth Press, 1922.

Camus, A. (1942), *The Stranger.* New York: Vintage Books, 1954.

Firestein, S. K. (1978), *Termination in Psychoanalysis.* New York: International Universities Press.

Freud, S. (1900), The Interpretation of Dreams. *Standard Edition,* 5. London: Hogarth Press, 1953.

——— (1905), Jokes and Their Relation to the Unconscious. *Standard Edition,* 8. London: Hogarth Press, 1960.

——— (1909), Analysis of a phobia in a five-year-old boy. *Standard Edition,* 10:5–149. London: Hogarth Press, 1955.

——— (1913), The theme of the three caskets. *Standard Edition,* 12:291–301. London: Hogarth Press, 1958.

——— (1915), Thoughts for the times on war and death. *Standard Edition,* 14:273–300. London: Hogarth Press, 1958.

——— (1916), On transience. *Standard Edition,* 14:305–307. London: Hogarth Press, 1957.

——— (1917), Mourning and melancholia. *Standard Edition,* 14:243–258. London: Hogarth Press, 1957.

——— (1920), Beyond the pleasure principle. *Standard Edition,* 18:3–64. London: Hogarth Press, 1955.

Frost, R. (1963), Stopping by woods on a snowy evening. In: *Selected Poems of Robert Frost.* New York: Holt, Rinehart & Winston.

Huizinga, J. (1949), *The Waning of the Middle Ages.* Garden City, NY: Doubleday/Anchor Books, 1954.

Jaques, E. (1965), Death and the mid-life crisis. *Internat. J. Psycho-Anal.,* 46:502–514.

Lewin, B. (1948), The nature of reality, the meaning of nothing, with an addendum on concentration. *Psychoanal. Quart.,* 17:524–526.

Roosevelt, T. (1899), Speech before the Hamilton Club. Chicago, IL. Quoted in Bartlett, J. (1980), *Familiar Quotations.* New York: Little Brown.

Segal, H. (1964), *Introduction to the Work of Melanie Klein.* New York: Basic Books.

Volkan, V. (1972), The linking objects of pathological mourners. *Arch. Gen. Psychiat.,* 27:215–221.

Winnicott, C. (1978), D.W.W.: A reflection. In: *Between Reality and Fantasy,* ed. S. A. Grolnick & L. Barkin. New York & London: Jason Aronson.

13

Death of the Psychoanalyst as a Form of Termination of Psychoanalysis

ABRAHAM FREEDMAN, M.D.

INTRODUCTION

Aside from Freud's epic work, "Analysis Terminable and Interminable" (1937), discussion of the psychology, problems, and technique of termination of treatment are scarce in the early psychoanalytic literature. In fact the topic of termination was not included in the curricula of most psychoanalytic institutes. In 1969 and 1975 there were panels on the subject at meetings of the American Psychoanalytic Association. Questions raised by the 1975 panel prompted its reporter, S. K. Firestein, to conduct research by means of interviews with patients who had terminated, the candidates who had treated them, and their supervisors. This resulted in a book, *Termination in Psychoanalysis* (1978). The panels, book and several papers on the topic of termination (Wallerstein, 1965; Ticho, 1972; Firestein, 1974) discuss the indications for termination and the phenomena of the termination process. They describe psychoanalytic goals from the standpoint of the analyst and analysand. As these goals are achieved the termination phase of the analysis appears and requires acknowledgment. The ensuing termination process includes further resolution of the transference, especially those aspects of transference stemming from preoedipal object relations. Separation anxiety in some degree becomes a more immediate problem. If it has been previously handled, unresolved remnants become subject to further analysis. In Mahlerian terms, the termination phase of analysis presents an opportunity to complete the separation–individuation phase of development. In addition, material which was previously kept out of the analysis, or was well defended, comes to the surface and the termination phase presents a final opportunity to resolve conflicts.

The cited authors have described many forms of termination, including those initiated by the analysand and those initiated by the analyst. However, none of these publications has discussed a form of termination that cannot be avoided, namely that which is caused by the death of the analyst. Although such a termination is not preceded by the attainment of analytic goals, if the coming termination is acknowledged there might still be an opportunity to complete some of the tasks of the termination phase, namely the analytic resolution of the separation and the uncovering of previously repressed conflicts.[1]

[1]Some analyses are terminated by the death of the analysand but that is not the subject of this book. Still, thoughts of the death of either the analyst or analysand appear in many analyses. An example from my own analysis: My analyst was George Smeltz who had retired from his professorship at Pittsburgh Medical School and moved to Atlantic City where he was aiding the Institute of the Philadelphia Association for Psychoanalysis by continuing to conduct training analyses. In order to make it easier for the candidates he took a studio room at the Warwick Hotel in the center of Philadelphia for a few days every week so that we did not have to drive to Atlantic City for all of our sessions. For the first session of the week, we would inquire at the desk and proceed to his room. We ordinarily went to the same room for the other sessions of the week without inquiring. On such a day, I went to what I thought was his room and found the door wide open and the day bed stripped, with the mattress rolled back exposing the bedsprings. My immediate association was to my internship days when, after attending a very sick patient for many hours, I was relieved by another doctor and took a short nap, but upon returning to the room, found the bed stripped with the mattress rolled back. The patient had died. Distressed, I phoned the front desk and was told that there was heating pipe trouble in Dr. Smeltz's room and was given his new room number. In my hour I associated to thoughts of his death and his age (over 70). A few days later I was talking to Dr. Morris Galinsky (older than I but much younger than Dr. Smeltz) who had been a previous analysand of Dr. Smeltz, and told him of the incident and my fear that Dr. Smeltz would die before I finished my analysis. Morris said, "You're afraid that *he* will die before you finish your analysis. I was always afraid that *I* would die before I finished my analysis!"

In the past few years I have known several psychoanalysts who have died while they were still in active practice. Three of them will be considered in this chapter (Dr. A., Dr. B., and Dr. C.) but most of the data derive from the case of Dr. A. Dr. A. was a personal friend who spoke to me about his illness both before and after he knew it would be fatal. His widow has given me some personal notes he had made about his dreams, with associations, before his last illness. She also contacted some of his patients who had spoken to her after his death and asked them if they were willing to be interviewed about their experience. In order to preserve confidentiality I did not know who they were until they called me. I asked colleagues to contact other patients who had told them that they had been with an analyst who died and have them call me if they wished to be interviewed. Some analysts who were candidates in supervision with an analyst who died have also spoken to me.

Our topic involves the personal feelings of the writer and the people who have reported to him, and the possibility of identification of the deceased analysts cannot be absolutely avoided. Pertinent parts of the manuscript have therefore been shown to those concerned and they have had the right of censorship or recommending changes. We trust that in the interests of helping patients who are caught in a tragic situation, the readers will continue to respect the deceased and the courageous people who have shared their personal experiences with us. The purpose of this research is to devise a more effective way of planning termination when the analyst has a fatal illness and to care for the patient following the death of his therapist.

The Data

Dr. A.'s illness first became known to me at the end of a summer when he was my partner in a doubles tennis game. He had missed many shots that were usually easy for him and asked to stop after the second set. One of our opponents was an internist and Dr. A. told him that he was not feeling well. They went to Dr. A.'s home where he was examined and the internist found a palpable mass in the abdomen. Dr. A. was hospitalized for studies, a cancer of the colon was diagnosed, and surgery was scheduled. Dr. A. told me that he had been worried about something being wrong with him. He was usually constipated but had had diarrhea and abdominal cramps for the past few months. He had avoided medical attention until the day of the tennis game when cramps and weakness made him ask for help. This avoidance was due to his knowledge of the probable cause of his symptoms. In the hospital before surgery he said that whether or not it had spread he wanted to get "the thing" cut out of him. He spoke of it like an internal enemy that he wanted to fight against. Metastasis to the liver was found at surgery but the cancerous part of the colon was removed and chemotherapy was begun.

Dr. A. was eager to return to work as soon as possible and was back in his office in about three weeks. He felt fairly well and told me he had decided he must tell his patients about his illness and the uncertainty of the prognosis. He was still glad that the tumor had been cut out because it was something he could fight against. In retrospect it is clear that he needed something tangible to fight against at that time. He would let his patients decide whether they wanted to continue in treatment with him or when they wanted to stop. He was a training analyst and would do the same with his supervisees. He was still optimistic about his prognosis but in any case wanted to live a normal life as long as possible. In the course of the next few months he gave a paper and most people in the audience did not know that he was sick. He no longer played tennis. Interviews with his former patients disclose how well he followed his plan for termination of their treatments.

Dr. M. was a young woman psychiatric resident who had begun treatment with him about six months before his illness. As arranged, she had returned from summer vacation after Dr. A. was scheduled to return from his vacation and was to call him for her first appointment. She was eager to resume treatment because of contacts with her family during the vacation that had made her aware of some problems she had to work on. She phoned for her first appointment when she returned and got through to his answering machine. When Dr. A. returned the call he told her that he had been trying to get in touch with her because he had to postpone his return to work. He had to go to a hospital, would be out of his office about four weeks, and would notify her when she would have her next appointment. She assumed he was to have surgery because he knew when he would go to the hospital and the approximate time of his return.

She was called for her appointment around the end of September. When she came into the office she asked how he was feeling and was surprised to hear the reply, "slowly gaining strength." This made her realize for the first time that his illness was serious. She continued in treatment and felt that she was being helped. She often wondered how he was feeling but did not ask him again. At that time she still had an inclination to be reticent and was not accustomed to verbalizing all her thoughts. He used to intersperse her treatment with explanations of psychoanalytic concepts as they arose in connection with her material and were useful in understanding what she had said. In retrospect she thinks that he was trying to teach her everything possible as if time were short.

The next interruption came in March of the following year when she was told that he would be out for about two weeks for further treatment. She now recognized that his illness was indeed serious and he had not recovered, but she did not speculate on what the illness was. She did not ask him and he did not tell her. When he returned and she asked him how he was feeling he told her that he had been to Boston for an attempt to inject medication directly into his liver. It had failed because he had an anomolous liver artery. She assumed that he had liver disease, probably cancer, but she did not ask him and he did not tell her any more about it. She was beginning to feel sad for him but did not verbalize this in any of her sessions. In retrospect she noticed that he was increasingly didactic. He told her that she must pay attention to her dreams and try to associate to them. She thought that he might have been trying to prepare her for self analysis after he was gone.

One day in May she appeared at the office and found his door locked. She was distraught, telephoned him, and got the usual message on the answering machine. She returned to work and in her distress discussed her problem with a psychotherapy supervisor who offered to try to find out for her what the situation was. She refused the offer because she wanted to take care of the problem by herself. The next time she called Dr. A.'s office, a woman answered who was surprised that Dr. M. had not been told about Dr. A.'s absence. It was intended that all patients would be informed that Dr. A. was sick and would not be in the office, but somehow Dr. M. had been missed. Dr. A. himself then got on the phone and said that he would call her again in about a week for an appointment, but he never called again. She did not know whether she should go to another therapist. She again discussed her dilemma with her sympathetic supervisor and this had a therapeutic effect.

The following June she met the same supervisor in a hallway of the hospital and he told her that he was sorry about Dr. A. She went to the library for a newspaper and read the obituary. She felt very sad. She went to see another therapist for six sessions but discontinued for two reasons: Although she felt his remarks to her were true, he tended to speak in a snide or sarcastic manner which rubbed her the wrong way. (My personal knowledge of this therapist is that he is an erudite, highly regarded training analyst, but he does have a smug, arrogant attitude which Dr. M. picked up on. The reader can draw his own conclusions about the quality of his sensitivity to Dr. M. in her predicament.) He forgot her fourth session and she remained in his waiting room for a half hour. In view of what had recently happened, this was a disastrous event and she could not stay in treatment with him.

The reaction of the patient to the analyst's death had important antecedents. She was fond of her father's grandparents who lived nearby when she was a child. They had been important in raising her father. When she was age fifteen, her great-grandfather had died after a two-year illness (cerebrovascular disease). Her great-grandmother grieved deeply and Dr. M. would visit and comfort her. When she was in college, this woman became ill with terminal cancer and Dr. M. worried and mourned for her.

Dr. M.'s family was of a cultural group in which concealment of feelings and reticence were common. Thus, when she knew her doctor was sick she could not talk about it, but she thinks that she could have talked about it if only he had opened the subject. Before he was sick, when she had difficulty talking in her sessions, he often structured the hour with questions which were very helpful. After she knew he was sick, she would have liked him to have opened discussions about terminating treatment or helping her get another therapist, but this was never done. It would have been helpful if another professional had been asked to counsel her about continuing treatment with somebody else. In the final stages of her doctor's illness she often had thoughts of getting another therapist but was afraid to hurt him by talking about it.

Mr. L. was age fifty-five when he first consulted Dr. A. He had been having some personal difficulties in business and an industrial psychologist recommended that he see a psychiatrist and referred him to Dr. A. He liked Dr. A. as a person but was surprised at the end of the first visit when medication was prescribed. The first dose made him feel odd and at the next visit he told Dr. A. that he did not want to take medication. He was afraid that the doctor might not appreciate being told what to do but Dr. A. was not offended and the treatment continued. He saw Dr. A. once weekly, felt that the treatment was helping him, and his wife was also seen for a few visits. After being in treatment for about four months he received a telephone call canceling the next appointment because "an emergency has come up." He was concerned because he liked Dr. A. but made no further inquiries.

About a month later he was called to resume appointments. He noticed that the doctor had lost weight and although he was not sure whether he was privileged to ask for personal information, he asked what the emergency had been. Dr. A. replied that he had a change in his bowel habit and a blockage had been found in the descending colon. Mr. L. was surprised that he had been answered so specifically in that he had been told the anatomical location of the difficulty. He asked about the expectation for the future and the doctor told him that it was hopeful.

Dr. A. continued to see him weekly and his outward attitude and behavior did not change. He seemed physically vigorous. For example, at the end of a session, he would stop taking notes, strike a line across the page, and get out of his chair energetically and politely to open the door as he had always done. He did not seem preoccupied and seemed interested in the patient's problems, not his own. This patient felt that Dr. A. had sicker patients than he was because occasionally the analyst would take a phone call and what Mr. L. heard indicated that the person on the other end of the line had serious difficulties. He was telling me this to show that the way he felt about the doctor's illness might not be the same as patients who were more needy.

A few months before Dr. A. died, Mr. L. noticed that he was looking very drawn and had lost considerable weight. There was such a visible loss of weight in his cheeks that his teeth were more prominent. He verbalized these observations and Dr. A. replied, "It's the disease." He was surprised because he had never heard cancer spoken of as "the disease." Similarly he had been surprised when Dr. A. spoke of his (Mr. L.'s) condition as "your illness." He had not considered himself to have a mental illness.

One day he received a phone call that his appointment had been canceled. About two weeks later he was shocked to read Dr. A.'s obituary in the paper. He felt sad because he had personally liked him and thought he was a nice person. His wife also felt sad about it. He did not have a great sense of loss or despair because he felt he was not that much in need of Dr. A. Over the following year he occasionally felt he would like to talk over a situation with Dr. A., but he never felt the need to see someone else. He and his wife sometimes had the same feeling together that they wished there was Dr. A. to talk to. He thought that a sicker patient might have been more devastated by Dr. A.'s death.

About a year later he needed a top security clearance in his business and was being interviewed by the FBI. When he was asked about psychiatric treatment he told the truth, and when asked for the name of the psychiatrist, said that he was dead. They asked his permission to read the doctor's file. He did not want them to see the file because he did not know what was in it. "Suppose it said I'm some kind of a kook without any explanation?" He would have readily permitted the investigator to talk to the doctor but he did not want him to read unexplained notes. This stance was acceptable and there was no further pressure to get the notes. The incident gave him some concern about what should be done with the records of a deceased psychiatrist. I agreed with him that there should be a movement to get psychiatrists and psychoanalysts to dispose of patient files in their wills. Perhaps there should be a short waiting period when the patients could be informed that the notes could be obtained or sent to a doctor of their choice or, if unclaimed, destroyed. Mr. L. thought that there might be a problem in giving psychiatric notes to a patient because there might be things in the file that would disturb him. (It should be noted that today patients have access to their medical records, if they wish.)

Mr. L. had no idea that the end of his doctor's life was imminent. He felt that the doctor should have prepared him and should have been ready to suggest another doctor if needed. He himself did not suffer much by this omission but he would have suffered more if he had been more in need of continued treatment or had been at a point in his treatment when it would have been harmful to stop. In fact he had already asked about ending the treatment a few months before Dr. A.'s death and was told that they would know when it was time to stop but that he should not stop yet.

I discussed with him the general mechanism of denial and cited other examples to show that even when a person has cognitive awareness of his impending death he might still deny it in words and deeds. I referred to the case of a former department chairman who had lung cancer with metastasis. When I visited him in the hospital during his final relapse he discussed with me his plans for the department the following year as if he expected to be there. He had already indicated at other times that he knew his disease would soon be fatal. It is also possible that Dr. A. was not aware of how near the end was and might have been planning to discuss the termination of treatment with him. However, when Mr. L. had remarked how sick Dr. A. looked, he was told, "it's the disease," and his thoughts and feelings about his observation were not further explored. Mr. L. thought that this was the point when he might have been given the opportunity to prepare for termination of the treatment or for future treatment with somebody else. If he had known that Dr. A. was dying (as he suspected unconsciously at that time) he might have been able to talk about it with him. However, it is also possible that he would not have wished to disturb Dr. A. and might have dropped the subject. Mr. L. remarked that you can't expect even psychoanalysts to be superhuman, especially when they are dying.

Mr. L. then returned to the topic of confidentiality after a doctor had died. When Dr. A.'s widow communicated with him, she sent the letter to his business address, and it was opened before he received it. He had not wanted anyone in his office to know about his psychiatric treatment and he would have preferred that it had been sent to his home address.

Dr. K. is a colleague who had been in treatment with Dr. A. at the time of his illness and death, and his willingness to share his observations gives us an unusual opportunity. Dr. K. had a neurological disease and had become paraplegic but was still working from a wheelchair. About ten years earlier, he developed a depressive reaction to his illness and sought treatment with Dr. H. who was a neighbor as well as a colleague and used to see him at Dr. K.'s home. Dr. H. moved to the suburbs and it was geographically difficult for him to continue to treat Dr. K. Mrs. K. also needed help in coping with the situation so it was arranged that she would continue to see Dr. H., and Dr. A., who was also a neighbor, would treat Dr. K. He saw him for weekly psychotherapeutic appointments at Dr. K.'s home for which Dr. K. paid a fee. As a result of the treatment of himself by Dr. A. and his wife's treatment with Dr. H., Dr. K.'s depression had begun to improve.

At the end of a summer vacation period, Dr. A. told him, probably at their first resumed session, that he had been diagnosed as having cancer of the colon and was scheduled for surgery. He seemed optimistic about the outcome, probably too optimistic it seemed to Dr. K. He believed that Dr. A. did not know at that time he had metastasis to the liver and thought the tumor had been found in time. After a break in treatment of a few weeks, while Dr. A. had his surgery and convalescence, the treatment was resumed. Dr. K. noted a marked change in Dr. A. who told him that a metastatic lesion had been found in the liver.

Dr. A. was very worried about himself. Gradually in the course of the sessions he began to share his thoughts and feelings with Dr. K. The treatment had never been carried out in complete analytic abstinence and there had always been the atmosphere of two colleagues discussing a problem. Previously the problems on the agenda had always been those of Dr. K. but now Dr. A. would talk about the state of his health and treatment. He also began to talk about his family and children. Gradually there was a reversal in the roles of the two men. Although Dr. K. was still paying for the treatment he often found himself in the position of having to make supporting remarks to Dr. A. He claimed that he did not resent this. The role came naturally for him because chronic illness had been a special interest even before his own incapacity, and he had worked for years as the consulting psychiatrist with cancer patients. He also admitted that this role with Dr. A. helped him with his own emotional problems because it eased him out of the position of the helpless, passive invalid.

Dr. A. told him that he had told all his patients about the illness and the bad prognosis after surgery. They had the option of whether they wished to continue treatment and all of them elected to remain with him. Dr. K. did not know whether Dr. A.'s therapeutic stance had been modified with them as it had been with himself.

I asked Dr. K. if he had any ideas of why Dr. A. had decided to keep his practice as long as he was physically able to be in his office. I shared the information that Dr. A. had told me soon after the surgery that even if he had known about the metastasis he still would have wanted the surgery. He personalized the cancer as a foreign invader that he wanted to have cut out of his body. To have it stay and be treated only by chemotherapy would allow it victory. He wanted to destroy it wherever it appeared. Being in the office was a defiance of his enemy, the cancer. It was part of his character that he needed always to win and not be defeated without a struggle. Dr. K. thought that staying in the office and continuing his work was Dr. A.'s way of holding onto life. He had experienced it himself. The maintenance of interest in the outside world is a part of living. It tends to counterbalance the tendency to regress which is a dangerous part of a disabling or serious illness. In his own case, Dr. K.'s condition did not allow for many kinds of interests. It was physically difficult for him to read although he had tried many kinds of book supports. He did not find recorded tapes entirely satisfactory. It was only by continuing his work in the medical school and his psychiatric office, despite the difficulties of transportation, that he was able to retain his interest in the outside world and maintain a quality of life that was optimal for him. Therefore he did not think that the wish to keep working in his office as long as possible necessarily indicated only denial by Dr. A. It could have been his way of holding onto life and giving more meaning to what was left. Dr. K. did not know what effect the decision to keep working had on Dr. A.'s patients but he thought that it had helped Dr. A.

The saddest time of his experience was on Dr. A.'s last visit. He arrived at the appointed time but did not know why he was there and did not recognize Dr. K. He was confused and wanted to go home but did not know where it was or how to get there. He asked to use the telephone but did not know what to do when it was shown to him. At that time, Dr. K. was still able to use a telephone unassisted. He called Dr. A.'s home and someone came for him. Dr. A. died within two weeks. Dr. K. was sad after this last visit as he was when Dr. A. died, but his loss had begun many months earlier when he had first learned of the illness. There was no separation anxiety, only sadness over the loss. As with a family member with a fatal disease, the loss was tempered by a feeling of relief that the inevitable had happened and the suffering was over. Dr. K. believed that his reaction could have been similar to that of other patients of Dr. A.

Dr. T. was a psychoanalytic candidate who had begun supervision with Dr. A. over two years before his illness. He recalled that the supervisory situation was not entirely satisfactory because Dr. A. seemed cold and humorless. He had the impression that the office was dark. He knew that other candidates had found supervision with Dr. A. very satisfactory. Perhaps he was uncomfortable during that supervision because he had a difficult patient. However, he was unable to discuss some countertransference problems with Dr. A. and both the case and supervision were not going well.

In September of the year of Dr. A.'s illness there was a break in supervisory appointments for several weeks and other cancellations but he was not told the reason. He learned through gossip in the institute that Dr. A. had cancer and he thought it was cancer of the colon. He did not know that there was a liver metastasis. During the following spring there were more cancellations and he noticed that Dr. A. looked sick. Although the illness was not discussed directly it was acknowledged when he would ask Dr. A. how he was feeling and was told "not so good." Dr. A. did remark to him that he was concerned about his practice. As patients were leaving treatment he was not filling their time because people knew that he was sick and were not referring patients to him. Dr. T. did not know whether Dr. A.'s patients were leaving because they had finished treatment or were dropping out because of his illness. In any case he did not report any experiences similar to those of Dr. K. with whom Dr. A. had shared more personal feelings as his illness had progressed. About one month before Dr. A.'s death, Dr. T. received an official letter from his institute which advised him to seek another training analyst to continue his supervision.

His experiences in supervision with Dr. A. stirred up some conflicts which prompted him to return to his former analyst and he underwent an additional one-and-one-half years of analysis. The result was excellent. He resolved some problems that had not been completed in his first analysis and felt that this would not have been done if it were not for his experience with Dr. A.

We have been provided with some valuable data in the form of Dr. A.'s dreams. Hand-written notes of his dreams and associations were found by his widow on the table beside the analytic couch and she bravely made them available to me because she recognized their importance for this research. They are much too personal and revealing to be quoted in detail but an abstract of their contents will add much to our understanding of Dr. A.'s reaction to his illness and how it affected his handling of his patients.

The first dream is dated over eighteen months before the initial symptoms of his illness. It starts with, "I had a cancer on my back and there was a woman doctor. . . ." The association was to a patient that Dr. K. had told him about. She was very brave in the face of having cancer. He admired her and also Dr. K.'s courage in the face of his disease. The notes then described feelings of despair that Dr. A. had been having and the same feelings were associated to a series of dreams which occurred over the next six months. He was feeling old and losing his strength. He had diabetes which was affecting his potency. He felt dissatisfied with his marriage but felt helpless to do anything about it. He was depressed. He was angry at himself for being helpless. He was angry at strong women like his wife and felt unable to cope with them. He envied men who were able to leave women when they were unhappy with them. All this was occurring during the year before he actually knew he had cancer!

Dr. B. was a training analyst in his seventies who seemed to be in excellent health when he died suddenly one morning as he was getting ready to go to his office. Of course, the event of sudden death does not allow for a termination phase of the treatment and is not in the mainstream of this chapter. However, it will still be useful to observe the effect on patients and the care of the patients after the analyst's sudden death.

Mrs. S. was a young woman who had been in weekly psychotherapy with Dr. B. for two years before he died. She had a compulsive–obsessive neurosis and had been dissatisfied with therapists before she went to Dr. B. She liked him. He did not say much but she felt that he listened and cared about her. As the treatment progressed, she (a Catholic) felt that Dr. B. was like the Father, Son, and the Holy Ghost. She could tell by his expression or a nod of his head whether or not he approved of what she was saying, and in general she felt accepted by this wonderful person.

She used the interview with me to talk about herself. She was the second of four children and always felt that her siblings were smarter than she. Her mother was a schoolteacher who raised them strictly and demanded accomplishment. She always felt she could never satisfy her mother. For example, if her mother were ill and she took coffee to her in bed, mother complained that it was not hot enough. From age five she had felt a religious calling and this feeling came and went as she grew up. After high school she entered a convent but came to dislike it after about five years because of the politics. It seemed that her superiors valued earthly accomplishment more than her religious feelings. She was a teaching nun for about two years but gave it up for fear that she was not a good teacher. She is still religious and goes to church weekly but does not go to confession.

She feels that some of what the Catholic Church regards as sins are not really sins in the eyes of God. She believes in God and respects all religions. She personally accepts atheists if they are good people. The latter thought was probably derived from her experience with Dr. B. who was not of her religion. She always thought of Dr. B. by his first name (a biblical name) and spoke of him that way to me but she never called him that when she saw him.

After leaving the convent she married but the marriage was not consummated because of the severe pain she had when intercourse was attempted. She could not get over the feeling that sex was dirty. She and her husband tried to have sex in other ways but the marriage failed and they were divorced after two years. She first sought treatment when the divorce was pending.

She has been employed by a large corporation in a mid-level position for over fifteen years. She always thought she was not doing her job well enough although she had received commendations and promotions. In order to accommodate her work, her psychotherapeutic appointment was at 7:30 A.M.

One morning she arrived for her appointment and found the door locked. This was unusual because Dr. B. was very constant and always there before she was. She waited in the hall over a half hour and left. She phoned the office several times that day and the next day, reached his telephone service, but they had no information. She went to his office at the usual time the following week, found the door locked, and assumed that he was sick. She sent him a humorous “get well” card which showed an old man in bed drinking from a bottle with the caption “Keep your spirits up.”

A few days later she was home from work because she had to take her sick mother to the hospital when the phone rang. It was the doctor’s son who told her that his father had died. He had said that there had been a mixup about notifying people. She did not believe that he was dead because she had been looking in the obituaries and had not seen it. He gave her some names she could call for further treatment, but she decided not to go at that time. She felt that nobody could treat her as well as Dr. B. and she wanted to see how she would do without treatment. Dr. B.’s son was also a therapist and she eventually went to see him, mostly out of curiosity. She stayed with him on and off for several years. They frequently had fights but she would come back after breaking treatment. After he moved his office and it was geographically inconvenient, she went to see a psychiatrist with both analytic and pharmacological training because she thought that she might need medication. She did not get medication but stayed with him because she liked him and his style was more like Dr. B.'s. It was he who asked her to talk to me.

Her chief feeling about the death was that Dr. B. had deserted her. This was related to the death of her father by suicide during the time she was married. He said that he was coming to visit her but committed suicide by gunshot in his own cellar while she was waiting for him in her apartment. She worried whether Dr. B. had been alone when he died. I reassured her that he was not alone and told her some details of his death. She appreciated the fact that the death was sudden and he did not have the time to talk to her about it. She had felt guilty about her father's death because he was alone when he died and that reminded her of the fact that she should have spent more time with him when he was alive. Some of this feeling was displaced onto Dr. B.

Surprisingly, she did not resent the fact that she had not been informed earlier. She said that people do the best they can and she does not blame them for unintentional errors, especially under such disastrous circumstances. However, she had become angry with God over the deaths of her father and Dr. B. She felt that her father had wanted to die and had waited as long as he could but Dr. B. did not want to die and it was unfair. However, she still believed in God and still went to church. Several months after Dr. B. died, her mother died from a perforated stomach after several months in intensive care. She did not express as much regret over that death as over the deaths of Dr. B. and her father.

In my own experience and in discussion with analysts who have treated other patients whose analysts have died suddenly the effect upon the patient depends on the transference situation at the time that it occurred. For example, a patient who had a strongly positive idealizing transference had great difficulty in accepting a second therapist because of the fixity of the constellation of feelings about the deceased analyst. The narcissistic enhancement of feeling that one is special to the idealized object can only be sustained if the lost object is not relinquished. Not only the new therapist but also other important objects are not allowed to replace the lost idealized object in order to defend against recurrence of the narcissistic injury.

Dr. C. was a highly respected training analyst who became ill with cancer and metastasis. None of his analysands who were asked to speak to me about their experiences agreed to be interviewed. They were too upset by what had happened and either they did not want to talk about it or would talk about it only if and when they resumed psychoanalysis with another analyst. None of them wanted to handle it on the superficial level of a research interview. Some of his supervisees did speak to me and they all had similar experiences which I assume were also shared by his analysands. Additional soft data consist of generalized comments, perhaps gossip, within the institute.

Dr. C.'s illness was a carefully guarded secret. People would come to his office for scheduled appointments and find the door locked. No information was available. Sometimes they would be called and told to return at a certain time. Even then, sometimes there would be nobody there. They would try desperately to get information from colleagues. Even the nature of the illness was not known by all. Some assumed it was heart trouble or vascular disease. The truth of the situation gradually became general knowledge amongst patients and supervisees. As far as I could ascertain from the meager data, nobody was prepared for termination of treatment or informed when Dr. C. had died until the obituary in the newspapers and formal announcement of his death by the institute.

One candidate reported that during the last few months of his supervisory sessions Dr. C. would not be able to remain seated in a chair and would walk about the room. When the candidate asked how he was feeling, Dr. C. replied that he had some back problems. He said nothing else about the state of his health. One day the candidate arrived and found the door locked. He waited about forty-five minutes and left. He phoned the institute but nobody had any information for him. He continued to inquire for a few days until he was told that Dr. C. was ill and would get in touch with him later. A few months later he received a note from Dr. C. saying that the supervisory sessions were temporarily suspended and he would be informed about the time of his next appointment. He was not called back and Dr. C. died about a month later. He assumed that Dr. C. must have been in the last stages of his fatal illness when he had received that note and commented that even training analysts are not immune to the defense of massive denial. He had had in supervision for three years a particularly difficult patient whom the institute had asked him to treat after another candidate had failed with the analysis. Dr. C. had assured him that despite the difficulties of the case he would be given credit for it because he was doing good analytic work. However, Dr. C. had left no written notes or instructions for the institute, and after his death the candidate did not receive credit for his supervised treatment of the case. The failure of Dr. C. to keep the institute informed about the candidate's work as if he expected to be able to inform them later supports the candidate's hypothesis about the defense of denial.

Discussion of the Data

We can study several different problems from the above data: one, the problem of termination of treatment when the psychoanalyst knows that he has a fatal illness; two, the dilemma of patients who are faced with the loss of their therapist; and three, assistance needed by patients after the death of their therapist. We shall first discuss these problems from the viewpoint of termination of treatment.

Although the authors cited in the introduction to this paper do not discuss termination in case of a severe illness of the psychoanalyst, Firestein's book gives examples of termination necessitated by the geographical move of the analyst or analysand, and this situation is closest to what we are considering. Usually a psychoanalytic termination phase begins when it appears that the analytic goals are being attained, but termination precipitated by geographical move often occurs without consideration of the goals of the analysis. In cases when the termination is forced by the analyst for his own goals, the effect on the patient can be disastrous. Many years ago I had referred a medical student with severe character problems to a senior candidate for a reduced fee analysis. About three years later, the analysand came to see me in a very angry mood. His analyst had finished his training and had moved to another state after giving only one month's notice. The patient assumed, probably correctly, that his doctor had kept the impending move a secret because he had feared losing his practice with its financial rewards if the move became known too early. There was no chance to analyze issues of separation. The resolution of the transference was left undone and the move precipitated rage that was partly transference and in part based upon a real injury. In addition, the chance was lost to uncover important conflicts which often become available only in the termination phase.

The handling of the termination phase is an important part of every analysis; a thesis of this chapter is that a psychoanalyst who knows that he cannot continue the analysis until goals are reached must inform the analysand at the appropriate time so that the phenomena of the termination phase can occur. (Another variety of obligatory termination occurs in psychoanalytically oriented psychotherapy conducted by senior psychiatric residents in clinics. They usually do not continue their cases after they complete their residencies. In supervision, I teach that clinic patients of residents who are graduating in June should be informed as early as January or February so that termination phenomena are made possible.)

With fatal illness of the psychoanalyst, as in the case of Dr. A., the analysis will come to a close, not to achieve the life goals of the analysand as in the above examples, but by necessity. Although it is not happening by intention of the analyst, neither does it have anything to do with the needs of the patient. It is therefore incumbent upon the analyst to introduce the problem so it can be dealt with in the analysis. In his discussions with me about his illness Dr. A. fully intended to do this. The question is why he did not carry out this intention and why he acted differently with different people. A main target of inquiry, as with any problem of psychoanalytic technique, is the countertransference and the state of the analyst's psyche.

Here we are aided by the availability of the dreams and associations of Dr. A. which give us a picture of his state of mind *before* he had cancer diagnosed. His feelings could only have been intensified by the knowledge that his dire fantasies were becoming real. Dr. A. was determined to be brave. He had disliked himself for passivity both in his marriage and in his professional relationships with other men. He was depressed and felt aging and feeble. In a dream association he admired the struggle of Dr. K. who continued to be active while sorely afflicted, and the patient of Dr. K., a woman who struggled against her cancer. When he actually began to develop symptoms of an intestinal disorder, he delayed seeking medical advice out of fear of what would be found. Thus he might have lost the chance for a cure before metastasis occurred. Later he was angry at himself for this further evidence of passivity and weakness. Therefore, when it was discovered that he had a cancer of the colon, he was happy to have it extirpated. The vague dissatisfactions with parts of himself could now be personalized in the tumor and he was glad to have it cut out of him. He told me that even if he knew he had metastasis before the surgery, he would still have opted for the operation. Surgical attack on the tumor was more satisfying than attacking it only with chemotherapy. He did not want to surrender, and keeping working in the office was part of his desperate holding action in the face of a more powerful enemy. Although he had remarked to Dr. T. that he was not getting referrals because of his illness, I do not think that his regret was over loss of income but more an evidence of wounded pride because he had made no effort to keep his illness secret from his colleagues. It was also partly separation anxiety (see below). I agree heartily with Dr. K. who believed that in the face of catastrophic illness it is an affirmation of life and gives meaning to life if one continues one's usual work. This is not only the defense of denial but it is also in the nature of a resolve to go down fighting, to hold objects, and to continue to give meaning to life.

Another example of an afflicted psychiatrist that shows the interplay between holding onto life and denial is that of the former psychiatric chairman mentioned above, who had lung cancer with metastasis after pneumonectomy. Chemotherapy had been moderately successful at first and then ineffectual. I visited him in the hospital and he so much as said goodbye because he knew he was dying. Ten minutes later in the conversation, he was telling me of his plans for the department the following year and talking as if he expected to be there. He unconsciously accepted death and unconsciously denied it. After the first few months of his illness, Dr. A. never spoke to me as if he expected the illness to be anything but fatal. However, in the last stages of his illness he did tell Dr. M. that she would be called for a future appointment. There could have been elements of denial in that.

Dr. A. had intended to tell all his patients of his condition when he returned to work after the surgery. He carried this out only with Dr. K., but there was more of a collegial relationship between them than with Dr. A.'s other patients, and eventually the supportive role was reversed and Dr. K. the patient became the therapist. Dr. A.'s final attempt to keep his appointment with Dr. K. came only about two weeks before his death. The second patient with whom Dr. A. seemed to be most frank was Mr. L. who was told anatomical details of the illness even though he was not a physician. However, Mr. L. was a businessman, was not very sick, and can be seen as a realist whose attitudes influenced Dr. A. to be more realistic with him. Of all the people I interviewed, Dr. M. was the least informed by Dr. A. about his illness. As a professional woman was she the object of some antifeminist bias which was shown in his dream associations? She had a history of being traumatized by the death of loved relatives. Did that make it more difficult for him to take up the subject of his impending demise with her? He did not try to hide facts from her in that he answered factually her questions when he returned from the unsuccessful chemotherapeutic attempts in Boston, but he did not give her an opportunity to talk about it. That was also his chief difficulty with Mr. L. I thought Mr. L. was a surprisingly acute observer of the psychotherapeutic process for a layman; he noted that Dr. A. did not encourage him to associate further to his remarks about Dr. A.'s sick facies and loss of weight and he thought that this would have been more appropriate and therapeutic. In fact when Mr. L. suggested termination at one time in his treatment, Dr. A. replied that it was not yet time but that they would know it when the time came. Still, when Dr. A. knew that the time was fast approaching when he could not work and that his powers were rapidly failing he did not reintroduce the topic of termination of the treatment.

Dr. M. thought that she was being informed indirectly of her impending separation from Dr. A. by the fact that he was increasingly didactic with her and encouraged her to do self analysis. Her retrospective idea was that he was saying: "I'm going to leave, learn to take care of yourself." I believe that Dr. A.'s inner need to keep active, not to surrender to the enemy, and to struggle heroically overcame his resolve as an analyst to allow his patients to separate. The conscious behavior in accepting support from his patient Dr. K. might have represented the unconscious need to hold onto his other patients also.

Separation anxiety is one of the fears of dying. All the cited authors who wrote about termination mention separation anxiety on the part of the analyst as a possible countertransference interference with the process of termination when the time for it is indicated by the progress of the analysis. It is reasonable to assume when the termination is due to the analyst's approaching death and loss of all objects that separation anxiety would be higher than in the normal course of an analysis and the analyst would be less inclined to encourage the process of termination.

We have not said much about the fact that Dr. A. dreamt that he had cancer before the illness was evident. There are some who see in this phenomenon an unconscious awareness of the bodily affliction that has not yet appeared in the form of conscious symptoms. However, it is known that people have dreams about cancer without ever developing the disease. I leave further inferences to those who study the psychogenesis of cancer and they are welcome to use this one case in their data. I believe that the dream of having cancer was part of the feeling of bodily dissolution that accompanied his depression. Thus the cancer was more easily able to be the symbol of all his dissatisfactions with himself and became the main defect which he could physically fight against. The dream of having cancer might have furthered this condensation and entered into the narcissistic problem which interfered with his psychoanalytical work.

If it now seems evident that countertransference can interfere with the process of termination, the next question is what to do about it. We have seen that Dr. A. managed to get some supportive treatment from his patient Dr. K. He did not do it consciously, and might even have denied that was his intention, but it still happened. As Edith Jacobsen is said to have remarked (reference unknown, probably in passing at a meeting), countertransference is not a sin, the only sin is failing to recognize it and to analyze it. Countertransference that interferes with the psychoanalytic process is an indication for analysis. What I am suggesting is that if Dr. A. had sought help from another analyst, instead of getting supportive help surreptitiously from an analyst–patient, he might have resolved his countertransference sufficiently to help his remaining patients into a termination phase of their treatment as he had originally intended. Experience as a psychiatric consultant on an oncological teaching service taught me that clarification of mental states and conflicts can be helpful to patients who are fatally ill. It is quite possible in the case of Dr. A., who left the notes of self analyses of his dreams, that he tried to do this for himself, but at any rate he was not successful in helping his patients terminate, express their feelings, or analyze the conflicts stirred by his illness.

The experiences of patients and supervisees who could not get information when their analyst was sick, dying, or dead indicate a need for preparation for these unhappy situations. Not only was Dr. M. not sufficiently informed about Dr. A.'s illness to work on termination but she also was distraught when she could not find out what had happened to him. When she did reach him she was given the impression that she would be able to see him again. She suspected that he was dying and looked for his name in the obituary columns but missed it, and was finally told by a psychotherapy supervisor. She sought help from another analyst but was further traumatized by the way he handled her situation.

Dr. B. had not been ill before his sudden death and there was no way he could have prepared his patients for it. When I heard what his patients told me I thought that analysts should have information readily available for a family member or colleague and a preplanned procedure for saving their patients as much grief as possible in the event of an unexpected disaster. The case of Mrs. S. and another patient of his I had seen show that the effect of the analyst's sudden death on the patient is largely determined by the transference situation at the time death occurred. Mrs. S.'s association was to the death of her father. Her immediate concern was whether Dr. B. had died alone as had her father. She felt deserted but readily forgave him because of her guilt over her desertion of father. She saw herself as a generally forgiving person, probably in guilt-induced reaction formation to her anger over desertion. She was an obsessional character and tried to work out her problems with a therapist—Dr. B.'s son. She was not satisfied with him but remained until a geographical change gave her a chance to leave. In typically ambivalent, obsessional fashion she tended to fight, leave, and return but not easily give up the object.

A female psychiatric resident who was being analyzed by

Dr. B. and had an idealizing transference at the time of his death had a recurrence of narcissistic problems when she lost him. She felt that he had loved her and made her worthwhile. Her strongly positive transference and the fear that nobody could love her as he had caused difficulty when she sought treatment with another analyst.

In the case of Dr. C. there was evidently no attempt to help his patients handle his fatal illness or death. It is noteworthy that of the three analysts, his patients were the most unwilling to talk about his loss. My assumption is that the lack of information so interfered with the resolution of the conflicts stirred by his illness and death that years later the people involved were not ready to recall their experiences.

The candidate in supervision was probably correct when he thought that Dr. C. had an overwhelming defense of denial. He had made no preparations to terminate his cases or even to record his judgment as a supervisor so that the educational committee would have known better what to do about the candidate. His lack of action fortifies my belief that terminally ill analysts should get some analytic help.

Recommendations and Summary

If the termination phase is to be considered an essential part of psychoanalytic technique we must introduce it if any outside event, including human frailty, threatens the continuation of the analytic process. I believe that a psychoanalyst, or anyone involved in the process of psychotherapy, must do the best for the patient in any untoward situation. In the event that he is seriously ill or knows that he has a fatal disease, sufficient information must be given to the patient so that the patient's thoughts will turn to the expected end of the treatment. If the information is given and the patient does not express anything about it, the analyst should probe for the defenses as in any analytic situation when the patient is avoiding the obvious. It is particularly important to be watchful for anything that is a clue to the patient's opinion about the state of affairs. For example, when Mr. L. commented on Dr. A.'s marked loss of weight, Dr. A. replied "It's the disease." He missed the opportunity to help Mr. L. develop ideas connected with his observation. Only after Mr. L. had expressed his observations, fantasies, and conflict derivatives, and they became analytic material, should the reality comment have been made and then further attention could be paid to the effect of the disclosure.

It is a requirement of analytic technique that the analyst continue an analysis after he knows that he has a fatal disease in order to help the patient with the termination process, or immediately retire and refer the patient to another analyst so the patient has a chance to analyze the effect of the tragedy upon him. Patients who think their analyst is sick or will die might have a fear of hurting him if they talk about it. Conflict over hurting the analyst is not an uncommon cause of resistance but we all know that the analyst's fear of being injured should not be allowed to make him collaborate in this resistance. Here, the analyst's personal anxiety about illness or death can interfere in his analyzing the resistance. He must recognize this possibility in himself and if he cannot handle it alone, he must seek help from another analyst. In fact, it is probably desirable that any analyst who is under medical care for a severe illness and is still seeing patients should include another analyst in his list of caring medical specialists.

One might argue that such an attitude would be difficult in a person who has reason to be more concerned with himself than with his patients. Are we expecting too much? After all analysts are only human. But that is exactly why I believe that if one decides to continue analytic practice under these conditions it is all the more necessary to get help. Even the decision to continue to see patients, and for how long, could properly be an early subject in the analysis of the sick analyst. Some might argue that imparting information about oneself to the patient is not analytic but there are many situations when one gives necessary information and then waits to observe the effect in the analysis. A common one previously mentioned is change of the analyst's location. And how about canceling appointments because of meetings or vacations, or absences necessitated by some outside occurrence out of the analyst's control? The decision whether or not to give the patient information about one's self should be determined by whether the facts change the analytic situation. The analysis of the patient's fantasies does not answer requirements of reality under all conditions. Ordinarily an analysis is a controlled situation with a set of constants in which one strives as far as possible to keep the patient as the only variable. Although this is a goal which is not humanly possible to attain, an analysis cannot succeed if one does not conduct the analysis with this goal in mind. Anything which makes the state of the analyst the most important variable at that time must be considered to be an interference in the analysis and must be dealt with. If reality threatens to end the analysis, the patient must be informed in order to produce associations and continue to analyze in the termination phase.

I am suggesting that knowledge of one's approaching death is a specific example of the above. If it causes an unconscious need for gratification from the patient—countertransference—this has to be analyzed as in the case of any other countertransference, by self analysis if possible or alternatively a return to analysis.

We have seen in the case of Dr. A. how he was unable to carry out his intention to inform patients of his condition and let them decide when to stop the treatment. His intention probably could not be carried out because of the analyst's personal conflicts. Even if his intention had been carried out it was not the solution for the problem because it did not include the analytic management of the patient's ideas and emotions about the event. Note that this occurred in Dr. A., a psychoanalyst who was always interested in continuing self analysis as evidenced by the discovery of dreams and self analysis preceding his illness. It shows how much a person might be unable to carry out an intention to do analytic work in the face of impending death. I see no other solution than a return to personal analysis in such a situation. I do not necessarily mean formal analysis, five times weekly on the couch, but getting help from a colleague, using analytic principles to clarify one's conflicts and what one is doing with patients.[2]

The advice to seek psychoanalytic consultation to clarify countertransference problems is similar to that given by Martinez (1989) in her study of forced terminations. When a change in the analyst's life, such as a geographical move, necessitates termination of an analysis, she advises that the analyst seek a psychoanalytic consultant for help in understanding unconscious ideation which accompanies the necessary departures from orthodox psychoanalytic technique. In 1955, Anna Freud pointed out to a class of psychoanalytic candidates that the psychoanalytic rules are protective for the analysand and analyst (but may be misused to protect the analyst against recognition of his feelings). From this we can see that ordinarily, in following psychoanalytic rules the analyst is able to avoid acting out unrecognized countertransference feelings. When the rules have to be abrogated, as in the case of forced termination, the analyst is left without their protection and an outside consultant could help prevent misadventure.

In his conversations with me, I might have had an opportunity to help Dr. A. in this way but, regretfully, until I undertook this study I had not thought through the problem thoroughly. The purposes of this book and especially this chapter are to use our past experiences to discover how to do better with the problem of illness and death of the analyst in the future.

In addition to helping patients get into a termination phase, there is the problem of helping patients who have lost their analyst either expectedly or unexpectedly. Here too, I had not seriously considered the problem before undertaking

[2]Dr. Bryce Templeton commented at a presentation of this paper that it was probable that a therapist faced with fatal illness might not be able to make the decision to seek personal analysis. If his condition interferes with the treatment of his patients, he would be in the category of an "impaired physician." His colleagues who are aware of the situation have a responsibility to see that he gets help.

this study. Now I believe that every analyst should make provision for an event that is generally predictable but specifically not predictable. I am now taking these steps myself.

In a place easily found in the event of an emergency there should be information about how to help one's patients. The best place to put these instructions is probably in the appointment book or daily log. A member of the family should be told to inform all patients in the book who have had appointments for the past six months or who are scheduled for present and future appointments. The name of a colleague or colleagues available for consultation should be stated. These instructions should be made known to the family members who might be needed to take the actions and to the colleagues who would be called upon to help the patients. Patients should be told that their analysts' notes will be made available to a professional person of their choice. If there is no response or no choice within a specified time (one month?) the files will be destroyed. I agree with Mr. L. who did not think that files should be given directly to the patient, although there might be a legal problem in refusing if patients ask for them. It might be helpful if those analysts who take this advice would show this chapter and their instructions to family and selected colleagues after the instructions are prepared.

Some analysts would argue that such a procedure would betray the confidentiality of the treatment. They might consider that this would be more traumatic than the experiences that patients have described. However, with everyone I interviewed, nobody had a fear of breach of confidentiality except for Mr. L. who only did not want information sent to his business office. It is important to inform the patient privately. Everybody I spoke to would have greatly appreciated immediate information instead of the uncertain worries their analyst's death inflicted upon them. I recall that when Dr. Robert Waelder died suddenly, the people who tried to notify his patients were handicapped by the fact that he was so concerned over confidentiality that patients in his appointment books were identified only by initials. It was the general feeling that the patients would have preferred prompt notification to conservation of absolute confidentiality.

Although I did not consider these problems in detail, the sudden death of Dr. B., who seemed to be in good health, had made me think about my age in relation to continuing analytic work. At about age seventy I had made the decision to accept no case without telling the prospective patient my age, answering inquiries about the state of my health, and inviting a discussion of this aspect of the treatment situation during the evaluation period. It is a serious question whether any analyst at an age when he statistically might not complete the treatment should start a new analysis, but he should certainly not do it without informing the analysand and encouraging him to express himself about the disclosure. The same can be said for intentions to change locations or retire.

A simple known fact that must be accepted, as analysts must accept all truths, underlies this chapter: Nobody lives forever.[4]

To put it in more analytic terms, omnipotence is a fantasy especially when it is eternal. We must not allow ourselves to agree with the words of Woody Allen who said in a film, "I do not want to achieve immortality by my works. I intend to achieve immortality by never dying."

Summary

This chapter has investigated the effects on patients of the fatal illness and death of psychoanalysts by interviewing patients and supervisees, by personal knowledge of some surrounding events, and by written dream material and associations left by a deceased analyst. It presents the point of view that the termination phase is a necessary part of the analytic process and should be introduced by the analyst if it

[4]In an earlier draft of this paper, I wrote "except" instead of "accept" in this sentence. I did not notice the slip until the publications editor called it to my attention. The parapraxis testifies to the strength of denial of our own mortality even when we are writing about it.

is forced by events before analytic goals have been reached. The state of mind of the analyst facing his own fatal illness can cause countertransference problems for which he should seek analytic assistance. Upon the death of an analyst there should be a means of notifying patients promptly and helping them as much as possible. All living analysts, even in a state of good health, should recognize their lack of omnipotence and have a procedure for helping their patients in case of an unexpected severe illness or sudden death. Psychoanalysts should consider whether patients should be informed of the analyst's age and state of health during the evaluation process. Armed with this knowledge, patients would start the analysis with an idea regarding the probability of the analyst being able to complete the treatment.

References

Firestein, S. (1974), Termination of psychoanalysis of adults: A review of the literature. *J. Amer. Psychoanal. Assn.*, 22:873–894.

——— (1978), *Termination in Psychoanalysis*. New York: International Universities Press.

Freud, A. (1955), Lecture to candidates of Institute of Philadelphia Association for Psychoanalysis.

Freud, S. (1937), Analysis terminable and interminable. *Standard Edition*, 23:211–253. London: Hogarth Press, 1964.

Martinez, D. (1989), Pains and gains: A study of forced terminations. *J. Amer. Psychoanal. Assn.*, 37:89–116.

Panel (1969), Problems of termination in the analysis of adults, S. K. Firestein, reporter. *J. Amer. Psychoanal. Assn.*, 17:222–237.

——— (1975), Termination: Problems and techniques, W. S. Robbins, reporter. *J. Amer. Psychoanal. Assn.*, 23:166–176.

Ticho, E. (1972), Termination of psychoanalysis: Treatment goals, life goals. *Psychoanal. Quart.*, 41:315–322.

Wallerstein, R. S. (1965), The goals of psychoanalysis: A survey of psychoanalytic viewpoints. *J. Amer. Psychoanal. Assn.*, 13:748–770.

14

Death of the Analyst: Termination, Interruption, What?

STEPHEN K. FIRESTEIN, M.D.

In the brief contribution that follows I shall try to summarize observations drawn from information provided by a number of generous colleagues. The patients about whom they reported had consulted them for continued treatment following the death of a former analyst or psychotherapist. Of this group eight patients had been treated with regular psychoanalysis, and five with psychotherapy.

For reasons of discretion little specific case history can be offered. The data have been pooled. It is a small series, to be sure, yet the circumstances are very dramatic, and certain observations repetitiously impressive. Practical suggestions to avoid some of the artifacts that aggravate what is always a catastrophe will be included.

It is always a catastrophe when an analyst or therapist dies. This is true even if an analysand is working in a termination phase, because what has occurred registers as no mutual emancipation following achievement of treatment goals, but as a desertion and abandonment.

Were There Signs in the Analytic Situation of Impending Disaster?

In almost all reported situations there were: in some instances patients were alerted by the hospitalization of the analyst for diagnosis and treatment. In others there were clear signs of physical deterioration. Unexpected circulatory collapse was rare.

While this suggests there was time in which to do useful things for the welfare of patients, this occurred but rarely. Analysts tended to deny the seriousness of their condition, or rationalized delay in informing their patients. The rare exception was the analyst or therapist who informed patients of his or her intention to retire from practice because of illness, and offered comprehensive assistance in arranging consultation and referral for further care.

Once the patient has inferred that the analyst is seriously ill, or if the news has been directly communicated, the treatment has ended. Even if analyst and analysand continue to meet, the treatment of the patient has concluded. This is true because roles are instantly reversed; the patient feels that he or she must in many ways serve as therapist for the analyst. The setting for the work has lost its usefulness for the patient who no longer can feel free to verbalize whatever comes to mind.

What Was the Impact of Such Behaviors?

Based on this series, the consequences were varied. In some, the analyst's denial was shared by the patient. Some felt that something untoward was pending and experienced urges to leave treatment, urges about which they felt guilty. As later observations often noted, patients felt rage or resentment at the infantilizing character of not being informed in a timely way; or even wondered whether the omission of forewarning reflected the analyst's judgment that the analysand was too fragile to be able to tolerate the news. Other patients felt inhibited in their freedom to express aggressive or critical sentiments, fearing that such expressions might aggravate the analyst's medical problem.

The analyst's ability thereafter to collaborate in the analytic work was circumscribed. This was perhaps clearest in several examples of patients' dreams reported with clear references to the analyst's deteriorating health. Work with those dreams avoided pathways of association leading directly to the analyst.

In another instance an analyst terminated an analysis abruptly, explaining that the work had ceased for some time to be "truly analytic." Two months later that analyst died, leaving the former analysand to wonder whether serious illness had been concealed, and his trust in his former analyst's effective diligence betrayed.

How Did the Patient Learn the Analyst Had Died?

The range here was very great. The best way was to be telephoned with the news of serious illness and incapacity by a family member or colleague. Intermediate was to arrive for a scheduled appointment to be informed by a family member. The worst was to arrive for an appointment to discover the office door locked, and have to do some investigative work to elicit the straight story from someone. Plainly, the latter maximizes the traumatic character of the circumstances.

When the analyst has interrupted the appointment schedule without warning, and successive bulletins conveyed to patients contain circumlocutions and other ambiguities, the impression may be made that the analyst or his family is more concerned with the preservation of the analyst's practice than with the ongoing needs of his patients. This undermines trust and may aggravate the difficulties of moving ahead to a substitute analyst or therapist in place of the incapacitated one.

What Help Was Offered to the Abandoned Patients?

In less than half these clinical situations did colleagues respond with offers of assistance to arrange further care. In the other instances the abandonment of patients was complete and endured indefinitely. Those patients who found their way to subsequent treatment did so through their own initiative, usually because of functional status regression, a return of earlier symptoms, or some sense that there were aspects of the interruption that required to be tidied up as is only possible in the setting of an analysis.

How Long Were the Intervals Between the Death of the Analyst or Therapist and the Continuation of Treatment?

Where referral to a consultant for placement was initiated by the retiring analyst, the interval was very brief. Where the abandoned patients were left to their own devices, the intervals varied from several months to a couple of years. (This statement applies only to this group of patients, as no information is available concerning those lost to follow-up.)

What Features of the Resumed Treatment Were Directly Linked to the Death of the Former Analyst or Therapist?

Expectably, the resumed treatment included periods of mourning for the deceased analyst. This mourning was experienced idiosyncratically, as is always true: where there was strong attachment to the previous analyst, the grief was more intense. Where feelings of resentment and anger at failure to have been informed about serious illness; at failure of thoughtful notification of the fact of death; at failure to have been offered assistance in arranging further care were most intense, the mourning responses were closer to depressive syndromes.

There was generally a degree of distrust of the durability and dependability of the new treatment situation. Was the new analyst in good health, likely to survive for the duration of the work? In some instances patients needed time to convince themselves of the stability of the analyst before being able to permit direct expressions of aggressive or critical sentiments in the transference. There might be fears of becoming attached and risking loss and pain again. There could be exceptional worries about separations from the analyst; or about anything interpretable as a possible sign that the analyst was "slipping." Some patients revealed feelings of guilt that the particular difficulties of working with them might have hastened the former analyst's demise.

Are There Special Difficulties Encountered by the Analyst Who Renders Further Care?

This depends specifically upon the relationship between the current and the deceased analyst. Where this was a relationship of close friends, the follow-up analyst experienced discomfort at the requirement to listen patiently while the analysand reviled the departed colleague. Where the relationship was not close, or where the deceased analyst was gratuitously cruel to the patient, the follow-up analyst did not experience such a problem.

What Suggestions Arise Out of This Brief Inquiry for Practical Improvements?

The dimensions of the catastrophe of the death of an analyst or therapist suggested to me as a serviceable model a surgical operation during which the surgeon collapses. Whatever is done for the surgeon, no one for a second can forget the plight of the patient, and colleagues immediately step in to substitute and meet the patient's need for care.

Analysis, to be sure, is not surgery, and yet there are parallels between the analysand immersed in the transference–neurotic experience and entrusting his care to the analyst, and the surgical subject who has entrusted his vital processes to the surgeon–anesthesiologist team. Each expects his trust to be repaid by the operator staying diligently on the job until the task is suitably completed.

The situation of the deserted patient is worst where the incapacitated analyst has no family. Where there is family present, the situation may or may not be better, depending upon the capacity of the family member to be sufficiently in control of his or her own turmoil to be appropriately available for patients. In such crisis circumstances it is admittedly difficult to keep the needs of patients—strangers to the family members—in continuous focus.

It should be redundant to say that the care of the patients must remain the primary, or coprimary, concern. This requirement is implicit in the compact that any patient makes with a physician. Families of incapacitated analysts and therapists may be overwhelmed with their own needs. The sickening analyst may be engulfed by his own denials and unable to offer timely warnings; or may as part of his illness be experiencing an organic mental syndrome with impaired judgment.

The clinical vignettes shared with me underscore how in the crisis of the analyst's death there are immediate, unmet patient needs; and that the management of this period has critical impact on the patient's capacity to trust not only the current analyst but *any* subsequent analyst.

These considerations prompt the following suggestion: that as part of usual practice management an analyst or therapist develop an understanding with two trusted friends that they will intervene if the analyst (1) shows signs of impairment in his work life; (2) experiences sudden total incapacitation, or dies. Probably nonfamily members who are professional colleagues can be depended upon to step in at such critical moments.

Further, the information shared with me suggests that patients be referred to consultants who are able to place them for further care with analysts or therapists who were *not* personal friends of the former analyst, facilitating in this manner the exploration of negative affects without intrusion by the new analyst's feelings toward his departed friend. This point can hardly be overemphasized, if we are to provide traumatized patients with an optimally useful therapeutic setting.

I hope that this brief communication will stimulate others to try to address this little discussed problem and arrive at suggestions superior to those offered here.

INDEX